SCM STUDIES IN
AND LITUF

Comfortable Words

*Polity and Piety
and the Book of Common Prayer*

Edited by

Stephen Platten and Christopher Woods

scm press

© The Editors and Contributors

Published in 2012 by SCM Press
Editorial office
3rd Floor, Invicta House
108–114 Golden Lane,
London, EC1Y 0TG, UK

SCM Press is an imprint of Hymns Ancient & Modern Ltd
(a registered charity)
13A Hellesdon Park Road
Norwich NR6 5DR, UK

www.hymnsam.co.uk

British Library Cataloguing in Publication data

A catalogue record for this book is available
from the British Library

978-0-334-04670-7
Kindle 978-0-334-04671-4

Typeset by Regent Typesetting, London
Printed and bound by
Lightning Source UK

Contents

Preface

Hensley Henson, when Bishop of Durham, was asked by a priest in his diocese if he would come to preach at Evensong for a particularly innocuous anniversary. Henson replied, in a recognizably irascible tone, to say that fortunately he had a previously booked engagement on that Sunday evening, and anyway, 'I don't think anniversaries are a very worthy cause, do you?' Now nostalgia has become almost a disease, if not an industry, at the same time that our national historical consciousness is receding or at the very least underplayed.

That is probably a good reason for showing a certain reticence in embracing every anniversary with alacrity. There are some, however, that it would be irresponsible to forget. The 350th anniversary of the Book of Common Prayer is one such case. As Chair of the Church of England's Liturgical Commission, I was clear that this milestone should be acknowledged and honoured not only with a great service of thanksgiving, but also with a proper scholarly observance of the occasion, allowing new research and reflection to be focused on this book that has had such wide influence not only in England but across the world.

To this end, we offer this collection of essays. Six of them were first offered as contributions to a symposium at the British Academy in March 2012. The essays have been revised and are accompanied in this volume by another four so that a comprehensive reflection may be made on the Book of Common Prayer of 1662, its use over the past three and a half centuries, and its impact upon both the Church and wider culture. We are enormously grateful to the British Academy and to its Chief Executive, Professor Robin Jackson. We owe still greater thanks to Professor Diarmaid MacCulloch, who first mooted the possibility that the symposium might take place there. I would also here like to thank my co-editor, Christopher Woods, for all his work on this book and for his encouragement and assistance as Secretary to the Liturgical Commission. We hope that these essays may both prosper further scholarship and also greater appreciation of a truly remarkable book.

Stephen Platten
Wakefield
Easter 2012

Foreword

DIARMAID MACCULLOCH

Let me sound a characteristically diffident Anglican note in saluting this fine collection of essays. The commemoration of 350 years since Parliament authorized the final version of the Prayer Book in 1662 cannot compete as a tidy number with the quatercentenary celebrations during 2011 for another milestone of Stuart English prose composition, the King James Bible. Moreover, there will be many who will regard this simply as a tribal occasion for a particular Christian denomination, and so they will choose, like the Priest and the Levite in the Gospel for the Thirteenth Sunday after Trinity, to pass by on the other side.

That would be a mistake. The modern Church of England might look like and often behave like a 'denomination', but from the sixteenth century to at least 1800, it was not: it was the national Church, enjoying the allegiance of the great majority of the population in both England and Wales. Its liturgy was not a denominational artefact; it was the literary text most thoroughly known by most people in this country, and one should include the Bible among its lesser rivals. This was because the English and the Welsh were active participants in the BCP, as they made their liturgical replies to the person leading worship in the thousands of churches throughout the realm: they were actors week by week in a drama whose cast included and united most of the nation, and that therefore was a much more significant play, and more culturally central, than anything by Shakespeare.

The year 1662 is a decisive date in the history of the BCP, as it was then that a century of argument about its form and content was settled, and indeed that form remained unchallenged until 1927–28, when proposals to alter it engendered a nationwide controversy played out in Parliament, which, to the astonishment and fury of the Church's bishops, rejected the innovations. The year 1662 was also significant because the freezing of the BCP at that moment prompted the departure of 2,000 clergy from the parishes, refusing to sign up to the new book, and forming what became Old Dissent, whereas before the mid-

ix

century civil wars, most of them would have served in the Church of England with reasonable good grace. This was a major reformulation of national life, ensuring that thereafter the Established Church was never so overwhelmingly hegemonic in England as were Scandinavian Lutheranism or Mediterranean Catholicism in their respective cultural spheres. English and Welsh Protestantism remained divided between church and chapel, with the vital consequence that religious and then political pluralism became embedded in national identity. All this was the fault of the Prayer Book's return in 1662.

Even so, if the BCP had remained what it was to begin with, a vehicle for national worship in a marginal and second-rank kingdom in Europe, then its significance would have remained limited. But instead, the English created two successive world empires beyond the archipelago they inhabit, the second of which is still with us in the ghostly form of the Commonwealth. Where Anglicans went, so did their Prayer Book. A heroic work of chronological listings published by Archdeacon David Griffiths in 2002 rounded up about 4,800 editions of the Prayer Book or of liturgies stemming from its Scottish and American derivatives; around 1,200 of these are in 199 other languages, ranging from the Acholi of Uganda to Zulu. Griffiths demonstrated that the peak year for production of versions of the Prayer Book was at the height of the second British Empire's vigour and self-confidence, 1850, and despite predictable subsequent decline, around 1,000 editions still appeared in the twentieth century.

What a babble of voices those translations represented across the globe. Archbishop Cranmer's work in presiding over the creation of the first English BCP in 1549 had been designed to replace the Latin liturgy of the Western Church, because he and his fellow Protestants felt that Latin excluded uneducated laity from the proper praise of God. Yet Cranmer had absolutely no objection to Latin as such; it was the international language of his era, and in the right circumstances, it might be just as much a vehicle for godly Protestant worship as it had been an ally of popery. Such was the prospect in Ireland, the other realm of the Tudor monarchs. In 1560, Cranmer's former publisher and posthumous relative by marriage, the Dutch printer Reyner Wolfe, brought out the first proper Latin version of the BCP, specifically for use in the Gaelic-speaking parts of Ireland, which were then far more extensive than the embattled Anglophone zone around Dublin called the Pale. The fact that the English church authorities thought this Latin translation to be worth the effort is a tribute to the scale and sophistication of Irish Gaelic culture at the time. By contrast no one had listened in 1549 to the plea of Cornish rebels protesting against the introduction of the first English Prayer Book, that some of them spoke no English: that was probably hardly true even then, and the government of Edward VI had no hesitation in massacring them for their linguistic obduracy. Early translations into major modern European languages followed, for diplomatic purposes, to demonstrate to potential Roman Catholic royal brides or their anxious advisers that the English Protestant liturgy was a respectable route to God: a French translation in 1616 and one in Spanish in 1623 were both connected to proposed Catholic royal marriages. An Italian version had already been commissioned in 1607 by the scholarly diplomat Sir Henry Wotton as English ambassador in Venice, in an optimistic bid to cash in on a bitter stand-off between the Serene Republic and the Pope, by converting the Venetians to the Church of England. Portuguese came later, in 1695, and that translation was significantly sponsored by the East India Company, as the British Empire was beginning to make inroads on the decaying Iberian overseas possessions in Asia and elsewhere. In 1821, the Wesleyan Methodists were still close enough to their Anglican roots to feel it worthwhile to translate the Prayer Book into Portuguese pidgin-Creole for their work in what is now Sri Lanka. The Polish BCP had to wait until 1836, in an effort at Anglican mission among Jews in Eastern Europe even more quixotic than Sir Henry Wotton's wooing of Venice. This translation was suppressed by the Russian authorities, predictably without any signs of regret in the Polish Roman Catholic Church; interesting questions arise as to how different history would have been if the *shtetls* had come to resound to Stanford in B flat. And who would have expected the King of the Sandwich Islands personally to have undertaken the translation of the Prayer Book into Hawaiian?

The first essays in translating parts of the Latin liturgy into English were done during the 1530s by a variety of enthusiasts for Reformation, in the teeth of murderous disapproval from Henry VIII, a fierce conservative in liturgical matters, despite his own break with the Bishop of Rome. His watchful and scholarly chaplain, Thomas Cranmer, did not share the King's prejudices. On Cranmer's first encounter with Protestantism in mainland Europe, on embassy in Lutheran Nuremberg, he took a keen interest in the innovative liturgy he saw there, but also in Margarete, niece of the pastor presiding at worship in the church of St Lorenz; he married the lady just before Henry VIII chose him as Archbishop of Canterbury, and she eventually joined him in his archiepiscopal palaces. That gesture by itself showed that Cranmer had embraced the Reformation in more than one sense; medieval priests might commonly take mistresses, but Protestant clergy were quick to show their contempt for compulsory clerical celibacy by making respectable and public marriages. When Cranmer came to compose a new version of the marriage service, which has stood the test of centuries remarkably well, this first married Archbishop of Canterbury said for the first time in Christian liturgical history that one of the reasons for getting married was that it was good for you, and also quite fun: 'for the mutual society, help, and comfort, that the one ought to have of the other'.

While Henry's religious moods and diplomatic priorities continued to sway between old mumpsimus and new sumpsimus, Cranmer squirrelled away in his luxuriously large library at Croydon Palace the many liturgical experiments both of English evangelicals and the emerging Reformations of the mainland. He began his own efforts to meld them with the main tradition of medieval Western liturgy popular in the English Church, which took its cue from practices devised for Salisbury Cathedral in previous centuries – the Sarum Use. Various initiatives in Henry's lifetime produced nothing more than a vernacular processional rite (a litany) pestering God to back the King in his last major war against the French, but matters changed rapidly from 1547, once Henry's young son Edward was on the throne and his advisors were determined on a real religious revolution. By 1549, Cranmer's first English vernacular liturgy was in place, authorized by Parliament to be universally observed on Whitsunday, an appropriate festival, since it celebrated the occasion on which the apostles had been heard to speak in many languages. No one, not just the Cornish rebels, much liked this book at the time; it was a compromise with one eye on the formidable phalanx of traditionalists among Cranmer's episcopal colleagues, and few among his evangelical soul-mates appreciated its nuanced presentation of Protestant theology under traditional forms. Once some of the less co-operative English bishops were safely locked up for various demonstrations of opposition to the accelerating religious changes, Cranmer got something more like what he actually wanted, a liturgy whose sole use came into force in autumn 1552. There was less than a year for it to bed down (and in Ireland, virtually no time) before Edward VI was dead and Catholic Mary on the throne, but in 1559 the BCP was brought back virtually unaltered by a Protestant government much less disposed to compromise with Catholics than Edward's government had been ten years earlier.

It was this production of Cranmer's unbuttoned Protestant Indian Summer that remained in place until the wars of the 1640s, and then in 1662, after the unexpected return of both monarchy and episcopally governed Church in Charles II's Restoration, the Book took on its final form. By then, its significance and symbolism had greatly changed since Cranmer's time. In 1552, it embodied Protestant religious revolution, but less than nine decades later, it provoked Protestant religious revolution in its turn in Scotland, and by domino effect, then in England too. Because of that, the historical logic of its recall and revision in 1662 signalled an end to revolution in the kingdom. That tangled story embodied a great argument about what English Protestantism was. The C of E has become 'Anglican', a word that only came into common use in the nineteenth century, and originally the property of a faction within the Church that also self-consciously saw itself as 'Catholic'. Cranmer would also of course have called the Church of England 'Catholic', but in the sense that John Calvin of Geneva or Heinrich Bullinger of Zürich would likewise have called their churches Catholic: they were all parts of the Universal Church that had rejected the medieval corruptions of the Church of Rome, in order to regain an authentic Catholicity. Many Anglicans, however, have come to see Anglicanism as a 'middle way' between Rome and Protestantism, a position that would have bewildered Cranmer: how can one have a 'middle way' between Antichrist and truth? How might this have happened, he would have asked?

The answer lies in the Prayer Book that he himself had created. Probably Cranmer would have revised and simplified it further, had his time as Primate of All England been prolonged for another ten or twenty years; certainly that was what people who had known him said he had intended. Instead, his effort of 1552 was fossilized in its revival in 1559, and it remained the most elaborate liturgy of any Reformed Protestant Church in Europe, its observance of the traditional festival shape of the Church's year more conservative than any other. Even the Lutherans of mainland Europe did not go on observing Lent with the punctiliousness demanded both by the English Prayer Book and by English legislation enforcing fasting during those 40 days. Reformed Scotland went so far as to abolish Christmas; by contrast, Cranmer gave the day a special little prayer or Collect which he specified should be used in services every day till New Year's Eve. And his four-score Collects for particular days of the Church's year are one of the glories of his liturgical work, sometimes composed brand new, but more often a sparkling brooch of tiny verbal gems culled from the worship of the Universal Church as far back as the fifth century and crafted together in his own sonorous English. Even those who are not natural fans of set liturgy (or of brief prayers) can grudgingly concede the worth of Cranmer's Collects.

The liturgical peculiarity of the English Church coincided with its other unique feature: its great cathedral churches survived as institutions with virtually all their medieval infrastructure. It is a puzzle: no other Protestant Church in Europe was like this. Chantries and all the apparatus of purgatory were abolished, certainly, but an Elizabethan cathedral still had its surrounding close like a miniature town, populated not just by a dean and chapter as might survive in attenuated legal form in Lutheran Germany or Scandinavia, but also by minor canons, choristers, organists, vergers: a formidable machine for worship. The worship could only be that of Cranmer's BCP, but cathedrals performed it with benefit of choir and organ, even some vestments – a totally different approach from the way the Prayer Book was used in England's thousands of parish churches, with their services largely said, and the only music the psalms sung metrically in the fashion of Geneva. In Cranmer's last months of power, cathedral organs were being demolished and the choirs set to singing metrical psalms, but when Queen Elizabeth ascended the throne, she ignored that trajectory, and her own Chapel Royal set a standard of musical elaboration and beauty which the Church of England has never forgotten. Westminster Abbey, across the road from the Palace of Whitehall, was frequently infuriated when Elizabeth's Chapel Royal hijacked its best singers, but the dean and chapter might have been consoled if they had known that these royal kidnappings were safeguarding the future of the English choral tradition.

There was more to this unexpected turn in the English Reformation than good music. The cathedrals and the Chapel Royal fostered an attitude to the sacred that strayed far from the normal Protestant emphasis on communal praise by the people and the Word of God interpreted by the minister from the pulpit. English cathedrals preserved a sense that regular prayer and the contemplation of the divine through beauty constituted an equally valid road to divinity. In counterpoint to Cranmer's evangelicalism, they erected a fabric of sacramental – yes, catholic – devotion. This made the Church of England theologically Janus-faced, and in the time of Queen Elizabeth's Stuart successors, the tension tore the nation apart. That was how Thomas Cranmer's attempt to turn Reformation truths into set liturgy ended up being seen by many of the English as a symbol of popery, an insult to God's pure service. Worse still, in 1637 the English Court tried imposing a version of the BCP on the proudly Reformed Church of Scotland, and even more seriously than that, theirs was a version revised away from the English Book and 'backwards' towards 1549. It was hardly an advertisement for the beauty of holiness when the Bishop of Brechin led worship from the new service book in Brechin Cathedral glaring at his mutinous congregation over a pair of loaded pistols, just in case they tried to drag him out of his prayer-desk. Such was the trigger of the Scottish revolt against the government of Charles I which led to the Wars of the Three Kingdoms. And when the episcopally governed Church of England was set up again in 1660, it did very little to conciliate the party that had so objected to the Prayer Book: one or two small concessions, and otherwise a book that sorted out a few angularities in Cranmer's old text, added some useful afterthoughts to deal with new pastoral situations, such as the existence of a much enlarged Royal Navy, and then delicately tiptoed slightly further from the Reformed European mainstream. Anglicanism was born.

The Prayer Book is by no means simply a historical document; it lives as Shakespeare lives, and often therefore in translation or adaptation. Its presence or its memory is the main thing that unites that not especially united family of churches that now calls itself the Anglican Communion. Parts of the book are unquestionably as much past history as the Thirty-Nine Articles of Religion, which are still the theoretical doctrinal norm of the Church of England, yet which have their eyes unhelpfully fixed on the concerns of the mid-sixteenth century. For instance, the service for 'Thanksgiving of women after child-birth, commonly called ... Churching' was still in regular use in my father's rural parish in the 1960s, but its overtones of purification from ritual uncleanness could hardly survive the revolution in gender relations that then occurred, and the epitaph for Churching can be found in the adroit title of Margaret Houlbrooke's charming recent study of its twentieth-century history: *Rite Out of Time*.[1] Indeed, during the 1960s and 1970s, it seemed that most of the church hierarchy were content to let the whole book die, as they became preoccupied with revisions and extensions of liturgy, some of which were admittedly long overdue. It was the heroically grumpy efforts of the Prayer Book Society that then shamed Anglicans into arresting the decline. In one respect the BCP flourishes as never before: in the popularity of Choral Evensong, gloriously performed with an aesthetic care which Archbishop Cranmer would have deplored, in great churches like cathedrals for which he had no perceptible affection. Nor would he have approved of what makes Evensong so attractive to so many who now crowd cathedrals

---

1 Margaret Houlbrooke, 2011, *Rite Out of Time: A Study of the Churching of Women and its Survival in the Twentieth Century*, Donington: Shaun Tyas/Paul Watkins Publishing, 2011.

and choral foundations as extras in its musical drama. For those who view a well-signposted theological motorway, straight as an arrow, as an unconvincing route to divinity, or who are repelled by the bleak certainties and bullying self-righteousness of much organized religion, Choral Evensong according to the Prayer Book affords understated hospitality, of that gentle, accepting sort described by one who loved the 1559 BCP, lived his life by it, and wrote much verse about how to use it:

> Love bade me welcome: yet my soul drew back,
> > Guilty of dust and sin.
> But quick-ey'd Love, observing me grow slack
> > From my first entrance in,
> Drew nearer to me, sweetly questioning,
> > If I lack'd any thing ...
> ... You must sit down, says Love, and taste my meat:
> > So I did sit and eat.

George Herbert, 'Love (III)', from The Temple (1633)

Bibliography

David N. Griffiths (ed.), 2002, *The Bibliography of the Book of Common Prayer, 1549–1999*, London: The British Library, and New Castle, DE: Oak Knoll Press.

Contributors

Paul Avis was until 2011 the General Secretary for the Church of England's Council for Christian Unity, after which he became Theological Consultant at the Anglican Communion Office. He is also a Professor at the University of Exeter and Canon Theologian of Exeter Cathedral. He has authored and edited several major volumes in the fields of Ecumenism, Anglican Ecclesiology and Systematic Theology.

Paul Bradshaw has been Professor of Liturgy at the University of Notre Dame since 1985 and a Priest Vicar of Westminster Abbey since 1995. He has been both a member and a consultant on the Church of England Liturgical Commission for many years. He has written or edited over 20 books and contributed more than a hundred articles or essays. His volume, *The Search for the Origins of Christian Worship*, has become a standard textbook. It has gone through two editions, and has been translated into French, Italian, Japanese and Russian.

Hannah Cleugh was ordained in the Diocese of Oxford in 2009, where she currently serves as Curate of The Baldons, Berinsfield and Drayton St Leonard. She completed her doctoral thesis at the University of Oxford on the English Reformation.

Brian Cummings is Professor of English at the University of Sussex and was a founding Director of the Centre for Early Modern Studies from 2004 to 2008. He has written widely on medieval and Reformation literature and has edited *The Book of Common Prayer: The Texts of 1549, 1559, and 1662*, published by Oxford University Press.

William Jacob was previously Warden of Lincoln Theological College. Since 1996, he has been Archdeacon of Charing Cross in the Diocese of London and Rector of St Giles-in-the-Fields. He is also a visiting research fellow in King's College London. He has written widely on religious history in England and Wales in the eighteenth and nineteenth centuries. His publications include *Lay People and Religion in the Early Eighteenth Century*, *The Clerical Profession in the Long Eighteenth Century, 1680–1840* and *The Making of the Anglican Church Worldwide*.

Gordon Jeanes is an Anglican priest and has written on many aspects of worship. He was formerly Geoffrey Cuming Fellow in Liturgy in the University of Durham and Lecturer in Church History in the University of Wales, Cardiff. His publications include *Signs of God's Promise: Thomas Cranmer's Sacramental Theology and the Book of Common Prayer* and 'Cranmer and Common Prayer' in the *Oxford Guide to the Book of Common Prayer*.

Diarmaid MacCulloch is Professor of the History of the Church at the University of Oxford, a Fellow of St Cross College, Oxford, and a Fellow of the British Academy. He is an award-winning scholar, author and broadcaster. His book, *Reformation: Europe's House Divided 1490–1700*, won the 2004 US National Book Critics Circle Award and 2004 British Academy Book Prize. In 1996, he won the James Tait Black Memorial Prize for *Thomas Cranmer: A Life*. *A History of Christianity: The First Three Thousand Years*, won the 2010 Cundill Prize, and the related six-part television series was shown on BBC 2 and BBC 4. He was knighted in 2012 for his services to scholarship.

Peter McCullough is Professor of English at the University of Oxford and Sohmer Fellow and Tutor in English Literature at Lincoln College, Oxford. He is also Lay Canon (History) at St Paul's Cathedral, London. Peter is a leading expert and widely published writer on the religious history of early modern England. He is also General Editor of *The Oxford Edition of the Sermons of John Donne* and is currently writing a new biography of Lancelot Andrewes for Oxford University Press.

Stephen Platten is the Bishop of Wakefield and Chairman of the Church of England's Liturgical Commission. He previously served as the Archbishop of Canterbury's Secretary for Ecumenical Affairs and as Dean of Norwich. He is a member of the House of Lords. He has edited and written numerous volumes, including *Rebuilding Jerusalem: The Church's Hold on Hearts and Minds*, *Anglicanism and the Western Christian Tradition* and *Reinhold Niebuhr and Contemporary Politics: God and Power*, which he co-edited with the Lord Harries of Pentregarth.

Bryan Spinks is Bishop F. Percy Goddard Professor of Liturgical Studies and Pastoral Theology, and chair of the programme in liturgical studies at Yale Divinity School. He was ordained in the Church of England in 1975 and was Chaplain at Churchill College, Cambridge, for 17 years. He was formerly a Consultant to the Church of England Liturgical Commission. He has published widely in liturgical theology, including *Liturgy in the Age of Reason: Worship and Sacraments in England and Scotland, 1662–c.1800* and *The Worship Mall: Liturgical Initiatives and Responses in a Postmodern Global World.*

Christopher Woods is Secretary of the Church of England Liturgical Commission and National Worship Adviser as well as being a Tutor at Westcott House Theological College, Cambridge. He was ordained in the Church of Ireland, where he was Assistant Secretary of the Liturgical Advisory Committee as well as being assistant curate of a large suburban parish in Belfast. He then moved to Cambridge, where for four years he was Chaplain and Director of Studies in Theology at Christ's College in the University. He has contributed to the annual best-selling volume *Reflections for Daily Prayer* and also *Words for Worship: Classic Anglican Prayers.*

All Such Good Works

The Book of Common Prayer and the
Fashioning of English Society

STEPHEN PLATTEN

And we most humbly beseech thee, O heavenly Father, so to assist us with thy grace, that we may continue in that holy fellowship, and do all such good works as thou hast prepared for us to walk in; through Jesus Christ our Lord, to whom, with thee and the Holy Ghost, be all honour and glory, world without end. *Amen.*

So concludes the second of the two post-communion prayers in the 1662 'Order for the Administration of the Lord's Supper, or Holy Communion'. That prayer, generally referred to as the 'Prayer of Thanksgiving' is a finely balanced piece of theological prose. There is no doubt as to the desired effectiveness of the rite: 'we ... [should] ... do all such good works as thou hast prepared for us to walk in'. It is an *improving* rite and the intention is that piety and devotion should have an immediate impact upon our behaviour, and it is *our* behaviour; it is not a purely individual matter. Worship is a corporate act and so it is *we*, 'who should continue in that holy fellowship, and do all such good works as thou hast prepared for *us* to walk in'. So one of the most powerful effects of Cranmer's translation of the liturgy into the vernacular was to overcome the danger of the Communion rite becoming largely an individual act of piety relating each person to their Creator and Redeemer.[1]

---

1 Cf. here David Loades, 'The Revision of the Prayer Book in 1552', in *Word and Worship: Essays Presented to Margaret Johnson*, ed. David Loades, Oxford: Davenant Press, 2005, p. 78. See also C. S. Lewis, *English Literature in the Sixteenth Century Excluding Drama*, Oxford: Clarendon Press, 1954, especially pp. 215–21. And also Rowan Williams' Christmas Day Sermon 2011. At one

Another element in the balance of this passage and of the rite as a whole is the rooting of all in grace. This was not simply an outflow of the Lutheran emphasis on 'justification by faith alone' with its subsequent rejection of salvation by works. It also stood in continuity with Western catholic mainstream teaching on grace. Through this understanding, the liturgy remains the *opus Dei*. It is primarily God's act into which we are incorporated through grace. Both the Christian community (the Church) and individual members of the faithful are fashioned by God through worship. The significance of this prevenient grace is easily lost. Even in contemporary liturgical revision, this lesson has not always been learned. So, for example, the contemporary form of the Collect for Advent begins:

Almighty God, give us grace to cast away the works of darkness and put on the armour of light, now in the time of this mortal life ...

This is a significant shift from Cranmer's version, followed in 1662, which reads:

Almighty God, give us grace that we may cast away the works of darkness, and put upon us the armour of light, now in the time of this mortal life ...

In the original version, the initiative remains firmly in the hands of God. God's grace makes it possible for us to cast away the works of darkness and *God* 'puts upon us' the armour of light. We are created by God and further fashioned through our participation in the liturgy, which is itself the *opus Dei*. This remains a crucial realization, especially as one explores how the liturgy is transformative,[2] and it also lies at the heart of the impact of the Book of Common Prayer upon Church and society, in its varied revisions between 1549 and 1662.

Cranmer begins with the formative and transformative aims of the Prayer Book in his Preface to the 1549 edition which later is incorporated into the 1662 Book, with minor revisions, as 'Concerning the

---

point, the Archbishop notes of the impact of the Book of Common Prayer: 'It has shaped the minds and hearts of millions; and it has done so partly because it has never been a book for individuals alone. It is common prayer, prayer that is shared.' www.archbishopofcanterbury.org/articles.php/2292/archbishops-christmassermon.

2 On this, see, for example, Christopher Irvine, *The Art of God: The Making of Christians and the Meaning of Worship*, London: SPCK, 2005.

Service of the Church'. Cranmer praises the tradition of 'common prayers' in the Church, and notes how they have been corrupted. He continues with reference to common prayer:

> The first original and ground whereof, if a man would search out by the ancient fathers, he shall find that the same was not ordained, but of a good purpose, and for a great advancement of godliness: For they so ordered the matter, that all the whole Bible (or the greatest part thereof) should be read over once in the year, intending thereby, that the Clergy, and specially such as were Ministers of the congregation, should (by often reading and meditation of God's word) be stirred up to godliness themselves, and be more able also to exhort others by wholesome doctrine, and to confute them that were adversaries to the truth. And further, that the people (by daily hearing of holy scripture read in the Church) should continually profit more and more in the knowledge of God, and be the more inflamed with the love of his true religion.[3]

Holy Scripture is at the heart of this Preface, but it is clear that the whole enterprise of this new Book of Common Prayer is to bring liturgy and worship to the people both in the vernacular and in a manner that is accessible to all. Godliness of the people is its aim and ultimately such godliness is achievable by God and God alone. Later on, Cranmer notes:

> So that here you have an order for prayer (as touching the reading of holy scripture) much agreeable to the mind and purpose of the old fathers, and a great deal more profitable and commodious, than that which of late was used.

Later still, we read:

> It is also more commodious, both for the shortness thereof, and for the plainness of the order, and for the rules that be few and easy. Furthermore by this order, the curates shall need none other books for their public service, but this book and the Bible: by the means whereof, the people shall not be at so great charge for books, as in time past they have been.

---

3 I have transliterated this into modern English for ease of reading.

All that we have noted so far is further endorsed in the exhortations within the Communion rite. In the 1662 Book, the first exhortation gives notice that the priest is to administer the sacrament and that those who wish to partake of the sacrament should duly prepare themselves, examining their lives and if he or she:

> requireth further comfort ... he may receive the benefit of absolution, together with ghostly counsel and advice, to the quieting of his conscience, and avoiding of all scruple and doubtfulness.

The second exhortation once again reminds the prospective communicant of God's initiative in worship. Again the worshipper is called to reflection:

> These things if ye earnestly consider, ye will by God's grace return to a better mind.

Then finally, in the third exhortation, the spiritual nourishment received from the sacrament is affirmed:

> For as the benefit is great, if with a true penitent heart and lively faith we receive that holy Sacrament ...

Although the linguistic expression may now feel both archaic and even arcane, the profound understanding of the nature of worship is unquestionable. Cranmer, and those who followed him in the revisions of 1559, 1604 and 1662, understood that worship lay at the heart of human flourishing and fulfilment. Worship was not only for the priestly caste (the 'curates') nor indeed purely as devotional work for the individual. It was neither a pastime for the sophisticated alone nor an interesting addition to life for those who desired it. Instead worship and ritual lay at the heart of a healthy society. This was the perception of Thomas Cranmer and his liturgical successors. It is an understanding that has been pushed too easily to the margins of the life of the Church, the individual and the community.

Ritual, then, is a key element within the corporate life of nations, and notably religious rites. In a reflection on the crucial significance of worship, Michael Stancliffe traces this essential aspect of our humanity back to primitive societies. He notes: '... primitive man has a much simpler, more direct, basic and elemental motive in performing his rites than keeping or getting on the right side of God'.[4] He continues:

---

4 Michael Stancliffe, 'The Substance of Worship', unpublished essay, deliv-

In other words, his aim – indeed his overriding pre-occupation – is to make contact, as frequently and continuously as possible, with that unchanging reality upon which his and all life depends and so to ensure that, despite all the flux of change or decay, life in his visible world is constantly renewed and enhanced. This he does by performing certain rituals; he practices religion; he worships.[5]

Worship, then, relates to an innate human need that nourishes and edifies a healthy community. It is partly expressed within us as individuals, but it is essential to the health of any community. Stancliffe later writes:

So it is for the renewal and re-inforcement of their society, not of their individual selves, that primitive men perform their rituals. Their worship has a public not a private reference. Indeed a primitive society is largely held together by the performance of its corporate religious rituals.[6]

If this is true of primitive civilizations, it is equally true of developed societies. Stancliffe's concern elsewhere in his essay is that we are in danger of losing this key facet of our corporate existence. More recently anthropologists have indicated how avowedly atheistic societies have found the need to generate 'rites' at birth and more notably for the onset of adolescence and the gateway into maturity. Confirmation, or in the Jewish tradition, the bar mitzvah are replaced by a rite marking the onset of adulthood.[7] So Stancliffe suggests that in different ways rituals are sought to replace worship, but that such rituals ignore the essential nature of that link with the unchanging reality upon which all depends. This is at the root of the impact of the Book of Common Prayer upon English society (and through the Anglican Communion upon other societies throughout the world) over the past 450 years.[8]

---

ered to the Annual Ministry Conference of the Diocese of Portsmouth, 5 January 1985, p. 5.

5 Stancliffe, 'Substance of Worship', p. 5.

6 Stancliffe, 'Substance of Worship', pp. 8–9, and cf. John Macmurray, *Persons in Relation*, London: Faber and Faber, 1961, ch. VII, 'The Celebration of Communion'.

7 So here cf. James Thrower, *Marxism–Leninism as the Civil Religion of Soviet Society: God's Commissar*, Lewiston, Queenston and Lampeter: Edwin Mellen, 1992.

8 Cf. here Rowan Williams, in Kenneth Stevenson and Bryan Spinks (eds), *The Identity of Anglican Worship*, London: Mowbray, 1991. p. 8: '... it is the Com-

If this is so, then what has this impact been and by which means has it been effected?

Already we have set out some of the aims both of Cranmer and of the 1662 revisers in putting together the Book of Common Prayer. In the stimulating introduction to his recent edition of the 1549, 1559 and 1662 texts of the Book of Common Prayer, Brian Cummings captures the impact of the Book upon English society. He notes:

> It came into being as a physical embodiment of a revolution in religious practice and in the politics of religion which we know as the Reformation, although even that term is a ragged shorthand for the domino of personal communal and national transformations which it provoked.[9]

It was thus:

> An engine of change, imposed on congregations and causing riots through its perverse assumption of doctrinal oddity and destruction of the old ways of experiencing the divine; yet also at the same time a vehicle for new forms of religious devotion and a brilliant literary achievement in its own right.[10]

As Cummings indicates, and has been demonstrated by a number of revisionist Reformation historians, the English Reformation (or 'Reformations'[11]) was not a popular movement issuing from a revolution among the common people, but rather a revolution imposed from above for both political and religious reasons.[12]

---

munion Order of 1549, 1552 and 1662 that most clearly set out the "public" and social dimensions of belonging to the Body of Christ, since it is precisely at the Lord's Table that the congregation is called to answer for the life of the community.' 'Imagining the Kingdom: Some Questions for Anglican Worship Today.'

9 Brian Cummings (ed.), *The Book of Common Prayer: The Texts of 1549, 1559 and 1662*, Oxford: Oxford University Press, 2011, p. xiii.

10 Cummings, *Book of Common Prayer*, p. xiii.

11 Christopher Haigh, *English Reformations: Religion, Politics, and Society under the Tudors*, Oxford: Clarendon Press, 1993.

12 Note here particularly Eamon Duffy, *The Stripping of the Altars: Traditional Religion in England, 1400–1580*, New Haven and London: Yale University Press, 1992. But see also Diarmaid MacCulloch, *Tudor Church Militant: Edward VI and the Protestant Reformation*, Allen Lane: The Penguin Press, 1999.

Cummings refers to Cranmer as 'a determined but temperamentally unzealous Reformer'.[13] Not only was Cranmer an unzealous Reformer, he was also eclectic in gathering from his various sources, which is partially what helped the English Reformation to appear idiorhythmic in contrast to that in other parts of northern Europe. So Peter Martyr, Jan Laski and Martin Bucer all were welcomed to England. Bucer became Professor in Cambridge and Peter Martyr (Pietro Vermigli Martire) Professor in Oxford. Yet the Preface to the 1549 Book, already quoted, was based on the preface to the reformed breviary prepared by the Spanish Roman Catholic bishop, Cardinal Francisco Quiñones. This breviary had been prepared at the behest of Pope Clement VII and was published in 1535.[14] So Cranmer's sources were rich and various. In addition to this was the part played by the legislature. In developing the 1549 Book, one of the most extraordinary episodes was the debate in Parliament, which began on 19 December 1548. It was unique, even in an English Parliament, to debate the theology of the Eucharist and the meaning of the Latin words *Hoc est corpus meum*, 'This is my body'.[15] All this contributed to this formative and transformative book.

The publication of both the 1549 and 1552 Books was not the beginning of one constant religious and political order whereby English society would be fashioned. The Prayer Books experienced two exiles. The first was during the brief restoration of Roman jurisdiction under Mary Tudor, from 1553 to 1558. The second exile between 1645 and 1662 marked an opposite swing of the pendulum during the seventeenth-century Puritan Revolution. Interestingly enough, however, by 1641 the Book had already 'settled into the national consciousness', and Cummings reminds us that 'the abolition of the Book of Common Prayer in 1645 was equally as political an act as its imposition had been in 1549'.[16] The same would be true, once again, after the Restoration of the monarchy in 1660. At the Savoy Conference of 1661, John Cosin, the Bishop of Durham, was the key figure. He was a Laudian and would have taken the revised prayer book in that direction, but there were competing voices. Edward Reynolds, the Bishop of Norwich, and author of the much acclaimed General Thanksgiving, was effectively a Presbyterian and so the final result of the Savoy Conference and the book that issued from it emerged in the form of another 'political settlement'. It fell to the traditionalist Bishop of Lincoln, Robert Sanderson,

---

13 Cummings, *Book of Common Prayer*, p. xx.
14 Cummings, *Book of Common Prayer*, p. 689.
15 Cummings, *Book of Common Prayer*, p. xxv.
16 Cummings, *Book of Common Prayer*, p. xli.

a noted moral theologian, to write the new Preface. His introduction marks out the settlement very clearly:

> It hath been the wisdom of the Church of *England*, ever since the first compiling of her publick liturgy, to keep the mean between the two extremes, of too much stiffness in refusing, and of too much easiness in the admitting any variation from it.

So the Preface begins. It ends on a suitably similar mollifying note:

> Yet we have good hope, that what is here presented and hath been by the Convocations of both Provinces with great diligence examined and approved, will also be well accepted and approved by all sober, peaceable, and truly conscientious Sons of the Church of *England*.

Mollifying as these words now read, and compromising as many would see the 1662 Book of Common Prayer to have been, that was not the end of the story in 1662. The Book was accompanied by an Act of Uniformity. If the Prayer Book was to be both a formative and a per-formative instrument in the fashioning of English politics and piety, then it was clear that there must be enforcement. Thus followed what was later described as the 'Great Ejection'. Large numbers of ministers of a Presbyterian theological position were effectively exiled from the 'Church by law established'. Any reflection upon the formative nature of the Book of Common Prayer must take into account those who were excluded – Puritans and Roman Catholics – as well as the majority who were intended to be included.

In her seminal book on the impact of the Book of Common Prayer in Elizabethan and early Stuart England, Judith Maltby focuses on just these themes in the period before the Restoration and the publication of the 1662 Book. Early on she reflects:

> The role of liturgy as propaganda has been in large part overlooked – yet there was probably no other single aspect of the Reformation in England which touched more directly and fundamentally the reli-gious consciousness, or lack of it, of ordinary clergy and laity, than did the reforms of rituals and liturgy.[17]

---

17 Judith Maltby, *Prayer Book and People in Elizabethan and Early Stuart England*, Cambridge: Cambridge University Press, 1998, p. 4.

Then just a little later:

> liturgy is an expression of a community's beliefs, as well as a shaper of them. The relationship is a dynamic and interdependent one; and one in which it is not always possible to distinguish between cause and effect.[18]

Part of this propaganda included an intricate interweaving of the role of the monarch, who in this new reformed Church is the 'Supreme Governor'; this is an integral part of the new polity. It is there throughout, but explicit in the Communion rite in the Collect for the monarch, to be said alongside the Collect of the Day. It is there too in the overt references in the Prayer for the Church Militant. The impact of such propaganda should not be ignored; as we noted earlier, by the 1640s the Prayer Book had gained a key place in the religious consciousness of the people of England, hence the division caused by those preparing the populace for the second exile of the Book in 1645. Maltby notes:

> A goodly proportion of the English people became 'people of the book' – but as much of the Prayer Book as of the Bible. For conformists that association represented no conflict, but rather a happy alliance at best, a manageable partnership at worst.[19]

Conformity in this early 'Prayer Book period' is the key focus of Maltby's study and as such it explores developments in careful detail using specific local examples in Cheshire but also with reference to places elsewhere in England. She notes that conformity drew support from a cross-section of society.[20] Furthermore, she argues that the impact of conformity related not only to religious matters but also to the maintenance of the fabric of society as a whole.[21] This made the Prayer Book a key focus in the religious controversies of seventeenth-century England; it also meant that the settlement following the Restoration in 1660 had to be managed with great care. These sensibilities are clear in the politically couched language of Robert Sanderson's Preface to the 1662 Book. They are also clear in the coercive implications of the new Act of Uniformity. In her conclusion, Maltby quotes John Spurr: 'For all the talk of Moses and Aaron, ministry and magistracy, alliance of

---

18 Maltby, *Prayer Book and People*, p. 4.
19 Maltby, *Prayer Book and People*, p. 17.
20 Maltby, *Prayer Book and People*, p. 24.
21 Maltby, *Prayer Book and People*, for example pp. 170–2.

altar and sword, the Church of England did not enjoy the committed support of the governors of England in the 1660s.'[22]

The Church of England was formally restored to its place as the national church and this was enforced by law. Nonetheless, any monopoly would be short-lived on account of the energy and commitment of Christian dissenters. It was the 'Glorious Revolution' of 1689 that would finally replace a 'national' church with an 'established' church[23] and allow more toleration for dissenters, albeit with significant continuing disabilities in public life, including education. These mixed developments require us to view the formative nature of the Book of Common Prayer on English life, from 1662 onwards, with a degree of subtlety. There is no doubting its impact, but the existence of a continuing recusant Roman Catholic minority and a robust group of Protestant dissenters meant that the Prayer Book's undoubted impact on public life and the formation of a 'Christian society' was to be seen within this broader context. With Catholic emancipation in 1829, the influx of Irish immigrants following the famines of the 1840s, and also the rise of Methodism in the eighteenth century, the religious scene in England took on a more complex hue. Nonetheless, the predominance of the Church of England, its presence universal in country districts and its relationship to the Establishment (and indeed its own *established* role) allowed the Book of Common Prayer to play a crucial and transformative role over the next 300 years. The controversy surrounding attempts to revise the Book in the early twentieth century, exposed to detailed study in a later chapter, is testimony to the key influences still believed to issue from the Book of Common Prayer during the period right up to the outbreak of the Second World War.[24]

Apart from the conformity required by successive Acts of Uniformity, how and why has the Book of Common Prayer had the profound impact attributed to it by historical, sociological and theological commentators? Parts of the answer to these questions have emerged

22 Maltby, *Prayer Book and People*, p. 233. Quoting John Spurr, *The Restoration Church of England, 1646–1689*, New Haven: Yale University Press, 1991, p. 59.

23 Spurr, *Restoration Church*, p. 235.

24 For detailed explanation of the controversy over the 'deposited' 1928 Prayer Book, see the two *Joint Liturgical Studies*, 60 and 61: Donald Gray, *The 1927–28 Prayer Book Crisis; 1. Ritual, Royal Commissions, and Reply to the Royal Letters of Business*, and 61: *The 1927–28 Prayer Book Crisis; 2. The Cul-de-sac of the 'Deposited Book' … until further order be taken*, Norwich: Canterbury Press, 2005 and 2006.

incidentally already in this essay. One of the key factors was the publication of the liturgy in the vernacular. A number of scholars have referred to the implications of this key development and initiative going back to Cranmer's earliest work. David Loades, in stressing how the vernacular liturgy automatically made liturgy once again a collective act of worship, also draws out a political point. He argues that Cranmer's later revision of 1552 implicitly undermined the power of the clergy and gave more of a lever to laity in key positions in the nation. So Loades comments: 'To the lay councillors imposing it (the new liturgy), it represented a new structure of power, in which the church would be the department of state for ecclesiastical affairs, and the clergy would be civil servants.'[25] Politically sinister as this sounds, its positive implications have lived on despite all the vicissitudes of history that have intervened since that date. The Church of England continues to exercise this seminal role and it is fascinating that it is effectively a by-product of liturgical reform. In a speech before a group of leaders from different religious faiths, at Lambeth Palace, the Queen reflected:

> Here at Lambeth Palace we should remind ourselves of the significant position of the Church of England in our nation's life. The concept of our established Church is occasionally misunderstood and, I believe, commonly under appreciated. Its role is *not* to defend Anglicanism to the exclusion of other religions. Instead, the Church has a duty to protect the free practice of all faiths in this country.
>
> It certainly provides an identity and spiritual dimension for its own adherents. But also, gently and assuredly, the Church of England has created an environment for other faith communities and indeed people of no faith to live freely. Woven into the fabric of this country, the Church has helped to build a better society – more and more in active cooperation for the common good with those of other faiths.[26]

Loades points to one of the springing points for this remarkable role which would be assumed by the Church of England. It relates directly to the earliest initiatives to publish a vernacular liturgy. Without a doubt that same liturgical source has been one of the contributors to the 'better society' to which the Queen refers. The Queen also talks of the 'fabric of this country', thus picking up similar resonances to those

---

25 Loades, 'Revision of the Prayer Book', p. 83.

26 Speech by H. M. Queen Elizabeth II at Lambeth Palace, Wednesday 15 February 2012, www.archbishopofcanterbury.org/articles.php/2358/the-queen-attends-multi-faith.

of Judith Maltby in her analysis of the Book of Common Prayer and early conformity.

Alongside the shift of the liturgy into the vernacular stands the issue of how language is used. Rhetorical language is a key to this in conveying theological truth. So Uwe Michael Lang writes:

> Language is more than just a means of communication, it is also a medium of expression. Human speech is not just a utilitarian instrument that serves to communicate facts, and should do so in the most simple and efficient manner. It is also the means of expressing the workings of our mind in a way that involves our whole personality.[27]

In his essay Lang is looking particularly at the role played by Latin in the Roman liturgy, but he is also making a general point about the use of language, and notably the use of language in the liturgy. Others point to a similar significance of rhetoric in the Book of Common Prayer. Reflecting on the work of René Girard, David Jasper notes: 'The religious community, therefore, is bound upon the wheel of a sacred rhetoric whose power is either a deception or an absolute truth – the rhetoric allows no distinction to be made.'[28] Jasper notes a little further on: 'It is clear from his work that Thomas Cranmer had learnt well the techniques of rhetoric which made up one third of the foundation course for undergraduates at the Cambridge of his day.'[29]

Jasper argues that Cranmer makes good use of rhetoric, which he mines from the classical rather than the Jewish tradition. Sometimes the rhetoric is hortatory. Such, he argues, is the first exhortation in the 1549 Book, which he sees as powerful in its appeal for the people to approach the sacrament with a penitent heart. Such use of rhetoric, Jasper argues, allows 'a breaking down and reconstituting of language deeper and more recondite than is allowed by the extensive claims of recognized spirituality and theology'.[30] Jasper suggests there is almost a conspiratorial element in Cranmer's use of language. For example, in the Prayer of Oblation in the 1549 eucharistic rite, participants are made 'to admit that they are, in fact, unworthy to offer the sacrifice'.[31]

27 Uwe Michael Lang, 'Rhetoric of Salvation: The Origins of Latin as the Language of the Roman Liturgy', in Uwe Michael Lang (ed.), *The Genius of the Roman Rite: Historical, Theological and Pastoral Perspectives on Catholic Liturgy*, Chicago: Hillenbrand Books, 2009, p. 22.
28 David Jasper, *Rhetoric, Power and Community: An Exercise in Reserve*, London: Macmillan, 1993, p. 78.
29 Jasper, *Rhetoric, Power and Community*, p. 78.
30 Jasper, *Rhetoric, Power and Community*, p. 84.
31 Jasper, *Rhetoric, Power and ommunity*, p. 85.

Without using the language of conspiracy, Bridget Nichols also alludes to Cranmer's evocative use of language in the liturgy. She argues that such rhetoric is a product of his skill and creativity as a theologian and writer: 'what we have is Cranmer the liturgist quoting Cranmer the translator'. So she asks: 'How far is it possible to say that skilful translation and redeployment of original material is in itself a form of originality?'[32] Nichols finds a positive answer in quoting the historical scholar (himself a Roman Catholic), Eamon Duffy. Commenting on the 1973 translation of the Roman Missal, Duffy notes: 'Time and again the versions in the *Book of Common Prayer* render virtually exactly both the rhetorical force and the theological depth of the Latin originals. Time and again, alas, the 1973 English translations subvert both.'[33]

What we discover in these reflections is that both the vernacular translation with its corporate liturgical consequences, and the rhetorical use of language – both hortatory and laudatory – have also contributed to the impact of the Book of Common Prayer as an instrument in the 'formation' of both English piety and polity. In two successive articles, Nichols, this time with Jeff Astley, spells out the formative nature of the Prayer Book. First, reflecting on the mention of the Prayer Book in literature and then alluding to the book's history, both the explicit and implicit educative impact of the book is explored. They note:

Liturgy usually carries its learning lightly, 'transforming a theology into the cry of a community'. [Again quoting Jasper – my insertion]. The learning that takes place through the liturgy works primarily through a *hidden curriculum* of learning experiences that are not overtly labelled as acts of teaching, but which are potentially much more significant than overtly didactic exposition. The formative power of the liturgy is largely implicit. We learn our Christianity on our knees and on our feet through saying and singing prayers and psalms (and, of course, hymns); as well as by sitting and listening to readings, sermons and – not often these days – exhortation.[34]

This reverts us to the earlier emphasis on the liturgy as a 'divine given', as the *opus Dei*. The rhetoric is not merely in a self-conscious, humanly

---

32 Bridget Nichols, 'Cranmer's Intolerable Burdens: Plagiarism, Appreciation or Originality', *Ushow Library Bulletin and Liturgical Review* 9, August 1999, p. 13.

33 Nichols, 'Cranmer's Intolerable Burdens', p. 14.

34 Jeff Astley and Bridget Nichols, 'The Formative Role of the Book of Common Prayer', *Prayer Book Society Journal*, Trinity 2011, p. 9.

generated text. Instead it issues from the tradition itself, including Holy Scripture. In the second of their two articles, Astley and Nichols move on to the *performative* nature of the liturgy, crucial to understanding the power and the influence of the Book of Common Prayer. So Astley and Nichols comment directly: 'Worship comes to life and reveals its potential to form its participants, when it is performed.'[35] This is a thesis with a long history and once again it reinforces the divinely initiated element essential to the formative power of the liturgy upon both the Church itself and upon national life. It involves *mimesis*, that is, a rehearsing of the tradition itself and thus of God's encounter with the community both within Holy Scripture and subsequently within the tradition and experience. So, for example, in the Communion rite, the essence of salvation history is iterated in the saving acts of God in Jesus. This understanding has been classically expressed by Erich Auerbach, and his argument is essential to this aspect of the Prayer Book's formative power. Auerbach argues that mimesis is crucial for understanding *scriptural* texts. The issue there is not about 'crude history' but instead the performative living out of the truth. On scriptural narrative he notes that 'the moral, religious and psychological phenomena which are their sole concern are made concrete in the sensible matter of life'.[36]

Within the Book of Common Prayer, then, it is the liturgy performed that is transformative; it is a mimetic process.

In what sense, then, has the Book of Common Prayer, over the past 350 years (or perhaps more accurately 460 years) been transformative? How has it animated those who for one reason or another would describe themselves as Anglican? Anglican and Anglicanism have come to have a technical meaning in both ecclesiology and in ecclesiastical history; use of these terms is now almost universally assumed to relate to the churches or provinces of the Anglican Communion. Used in this technical sense it has a comparatively short history, perhaps to be traced back to the mid-nineteenth century and effectively to 1867, when Archbishop Longley convened the first Lambeth Conference largely in response to the Colenso crisis in South Africa.[37]

---

35 Jeff Astley and Bridget Nichols, 'The Formative Role of the Book of Common Prayer', *Prayer Book Society Journal*, Michaelmas 2011.

36 Eric Auerbach, *Mimesis: The Representation of Reality in Western Literature*, Princeton, NJ: Princeton University Press, 1991, p. 14. And see also Stephen Platten, 'Liturgical Living: Learning by Mimesis', *Anaphora* 5, Part 1, June 2011, pp. 23–38.

37 W. M. Jacob, *The Making of the Anglican Church Worldwide*, London: SPCK, 1997, pp. 158ff.

The term Anglican, however, could be said to have a longer and more diffuse meaning in more direct relationship to the Church of England.[38] Often the English ecclesiastical tradition is paired with the phrase *Ecclesia Anglicana*. Here it describes the essential qualities that have defined the western catholic inheritance as it was received and developed in England, both pre- and post-Reformation. It might be used in parallel with the term Gallican, which refers to the distinctive tradition of the western Catholic Church in France. In that sense, *Anglican* can refer both technically to that family of churches that make up the Anglican Communion worldwide but also to the distinctive nature of the way the Church of God has manifested itself in England, and to a certain degree in the Church of England. If this double identity holds water, then it could be said that, since the Reformation, it is the Book of Common Prayer that has animated both senses of the word Anglican. In different ways, the Book of Common Prayer (which has, as this present volume demonstrates, experienced its own internal development) has animated both Anglicanisms. The family of churches that form the Anglican Communion all owe their initial identity, either directly or indirectly, to the fashioning power of the Book of Common Prayer.[39]

Animation is itself patient of at least two different definitions. The first is simply to give life to something or someone. The second is the rather more specific meaning relating to the Latin word *anima*, which is the word translated into English as *soul*. Giving *soul* to something implies more than life and suggests a spiritual depth. So, for example, there has been talk of generating a real sense of spirituality in relation to the European Union and the nations that comprise it. The call has been for the discovery of a 'Soul for Europe'. In both these senses, the Book of Common Prayer has been responsible for the animation of the churches of the Anglican Communion and also in what it has given to England through the Church and as a nation, over a period of at least 400 years. Something of both these is conveyed in the introduction of Brian Cummings' new edition of the Books of 1549, 1559 and 1662. He writes: 'More than a book of devotion, then, this is a book to live, love and die to.' And then later:

---

38 Cf. here references in Maltby, *Prayerbook and People*, p. 9, and elsewhere.

39 This has been demonstrated and researched comprehensively in Charles Hefling and Cynthia Shattuck (eds), *The Oxford Guide to the Book of Common Prayer: A Worldwide Survey*, Oxford and New York: Oxford University Press, 2006. There is not space in this essay to develop this area, which is well covered in the volume noted above. See Christopher Irvine (ed.), *Anglican Liturgical Identity*, Joint Liturgical Study 65, Norwich: Canterbury Press, 2008.

It is a book of ritual, of practices and performances used to transform the activities of a life. Rituals, anthropologists now tell us, are what make the human animal different. Mankind is a 'ceremonial animal', Wittgenstein said. Ritual is the social act basic to humanity, the means by which we draw our lives together into a mutual practice.[40]

This brings together so much of our earlier argument in relation to the Book of Common Prayer and its formative impact on English society: mimetic, performative, social and the ritual that makes us human, to which Michael Stancliffe's essay directed us. The Book of Common Prayer is a text, but more than that, it is a performative text. This is true in as much as it is not simply a book of words. Instead these words are to be performed as liturgy; they are the basis for a series of rituals; they are in essence the script for a drama.[41] In the eucharistic rite the entire mystery of salvation is rehearsed every time the rite is celebrated. But it is not somehow rehearsed in isolation from the rest of our lives. It informs all that we do and are, and it also calls out of us a response. The word liturgy, deriving from the Greek word *leitourgia* (λειτουργία) has the resonance of *service* held within its meaning. Later in his essay, Michael Stancliffe writes of the primitive Church:

That does not mean, as the New Testament makes clear, that the early Christians passed their days mooning about in a pious dream, mumbling prayers and abstractedly doing their jobs with their hands while their minds were fixed on heaven. Very much the reverse. They celebrated perpetually in and through the service of their fellow men. That word 'service' means quite literally 'the work of a servant' – feeding the hungry, caring for the sick, supporting the weak, comforting the afflicted. That service was all part of the ritual, all part of the continuously repeated pattern of action and word whereby they celebrated the words and deeds of their Master and set forward the coming of his kingdom.[42]

But those texts that relate to rites of passage are also performative in an equally profound sense. In the rites of baptism, confirmation, holy

---

40 Cummings, *Book of Common Prayer*, p. xii.

41 Cummings, *Book of Common Prayer*, p. li. Quotes from the liturgical scholar Gregory Dix: '... rite is not speech alone. It is "primarily something done," not said.'

42 Stancliffe, 'Substance of the Liturgy', pp. 14–15.

matrimony and the burial of the dead, they especially focus Cummings'
phrase of the Book being 'a book to live, love and die to'. The fact
that the texts themselves emerged from a long and complex process,
over a period of more than a century, and even requiring debate in
Parliament, gives them a currency well beyond the devotional scripts
for those who choose to be there regularly worshipping in church. They
are scripts that have underlain the growth of our culture over a period
of 400 years and including two periods when the book was in exile.
Even in 1928, the proposals for a new revised prayer book were sharply
debated in both Houses of Parliament.

The performative nature of the Prayer Book rites runs at two different levels. First, as we have argued, they capture key moments in the
lives of individuals, families and communities. They act as rites of passage. So the calling of banns of marriage still reminds us that marriage
is the property not only of the couple, but also of the wider community.
Equally, within the rite, the responsibility of the community is under-
scored: 'Therefore if any man can show any just cause why they may
not lawfully be joined together, let him now speak, or else hereafter
for ever hold his peace.' This follows the preface, which sets out the
reasons for marriage and also a pattern of life destined to nurture a
healthy society. The promises required of the couple are equally rich in
setting a pattern for the flourishing of family life. 'Wilt thou love her,
comfort her, honour and keep her ... so long as you both shall live?'
Then moments later: 'With this ring I thee wed, with my body I thee
worship, and with all my worldly goods I thee endow.'

That this is part of an unfolding of an *entire life*, lived in the presence
of God, is made clear in the earlier rite of passage, that of confirmation.
The words pronounced by the bishop at the laying on of hands run:
'Defend, O Lord, this thy Child (or this thy *Servant*) with thy heavenly
grace, that *he* may continue thine for ever: and daily increase in thy
holy Spirit more and more, until *he* come unto thy everlasting kingdom.
Amen.' The Book of Common Prayer sets out a pattern for the whole of
life, which is implied to be a continuous journey, so we 'daily increase
in thy holy Spirit more and more'. At the burial of the dead this same
pattern is implied: 'In the midst of life we are in death: of whom may
we seek for succour, but of thee, O Lord, who for our sins art justly
displeased.' As Cummings puts it, Cranmer did not coin the words 'In
the midst of life we are in death'; but he knew them from the inside, and
he allowed them to live in others after him.[43]

---

43 Cummings, *Book of Common Prayer*, p. lii.

Alongside these rites of passage, we should not forget one other remarkable innovation of the Book of Common Prayer. Cranmer was determined, as we have seen from the 1549 Preface, that his book should be accessible and thus formative of all people. He thus condensed the monastic hours of prayer into two offices for the morning and the evening, with a pattern of prayer that recited the entire Psalter within the mornings and evenings of one month. The saying of these offices remains a requirement for all Church of England clergy, but far more than just those who are ordained regularly say these offices. Sometimes in twos and threes, lay people faithfully say Morning and Evening Prayer in parish churches in town and country throughout England. In cathedrals and in many college chapels the offices have been sung every evening for 450 years except for the break in the Commonwealth period.

So all these offices, prayers and rites are performative too of the story that is the foundation and framework of the Christian tradition that has helped shape European and English culture. In this sense, as Auerbach argues, they are mimetic.[44] Each rite rehearses in different ways elements of the story of Jesus Christ and of the religious culture from which that story sprang. Such performance and mimesis has been a powerful influence on the fashioning of our society. Modern linguistics has shown how crucial the structure, grammar and syntax of language are in fashioning human relationships and community.[45] Mimetic rehearsal of such language and texts plays a key role in the self-understanding of a community and nation. The significance of the Book of Common Prayer, then, extends well beyond our admiring it as a piece of linguistic construction. This also suggests that what we now call 'public theology', that is, the influence of religious faith in the political arena, will have been fashioned through the key part played in English culture by the Book of Common Prayer.[46] The cadences of the Prayer Book echo down the centuries. Let the final word on formation and transformation rest with Brian Cummings:

> Some of the praises of the book, of the glories of its language, have been misplaced. It is not a special form of language; it is the ordinary

---

44 Auerbach, *Mimesis*.

45 Diarmaid MacCulloch, *Thomas Cranmer: A Life*, New Haven and London: Yale University Press, 1996, p. 631.

46 Richard Harries and Stephen Platten (eds), *Reinhold Niebuhr and Contemporary Politics: God and Power*, Oxford: Oxford University Press, 2010. See in particular ch. 7: Stephen Platten, 'Niebuhr, Liturgy and Public Theology'.

language of its time, the vocabulary of the mid-sixteenth century, overlaid with the rhythm of the mid-seventeenth century. Yet it is a language with an unmistakeable power, employed freely by all other users of the English language, whatever their religious affiliation or whether they have one at all. Winnie, in Samuel Beckett's *Happy Days*, contemplates the absurdity and the futility of her life in the jetsam of her handbag, all the odds and ends spread out before her. 'For Jesus Christ sake, Amen' she says: 'World without end. Amen.'[47]

47 Cummings, *Book of Common Prayer*, p. lii.

2

The Tudor Prayer Books

That 'the whole realme shall have but one use'

GORDON JEANES

Uniformity is something people talk about in its absence. A uniformity that is complete is rarely even noticed, like the air we breathe. When the Convocation of the Province of Canterbury proposed in March 1542 that the Use of Sarum should be the standard liturgy throughout the realm, it must have seemed to be little more than administrative tidying up. But within a few years the notion of uniformity in the Church of England became one of conformity to a whole new pattern of worship, the legacy of which is still with us today and has been hotly debated down the centuries. Central to conformity has been the Book of Common Prayer in its various revisions, how it has been used or opposed, and how well it has performed its role as the vehicle of a nation's worship.[1]

Prayer Books and the liturgy before the Reformation

Before the Reformation there was no one prayer book. Religious life under the Tudor Henrys was resourced by a number of books that had evolved by way of convenience over the centuries: the Missal for the Mass, the Breviary for the daily prayers, the Manual for the occasional

---

1 This chapter is in many ways a brief summary of a much longer and more complicated story that can be followed in more detail in G. J. Cuming, *A History of Anglican Liturgy*, 2nd edn, Basingstoke: Macmillan, 1982, pp. 1–101; Charles Hefling and Cynthia Shattuck (eds), *The Oxford Guide to the Book of Common Prayer: A Worldwide Summary*, Oxford: Oxford University Press, 2006, pp. 9–55, 79–89. For recent studies of the Reformation, see for example Diarmaid MacCulloch, *Reformation: Europe's House Divided*, London: Allen Lane: 2003; F. Heal, *Reformation in Britain and Ireland*, Oxford: Oxford University Press, 2003.

offices, and the Processional for the processions that were a major event on Sundays and Holy Days. Bishops had their own book, the Pontifical. All these books followed a particular Use, the most common being those of Sarum and York, though there were others as well. In truth there was little difference between them, and if we could go back in time we might well have found that there was a greater difference between the text and the actual performance than there was between the texts of Sarum and York. The first printed service books were published as essentially private commercial ventures, their many rubrics and instructions evidently seen as a useful guide.[2]

The services were almost entirely in Latin, the exceptions being only a few lines such as the marriage vows, which were in English (and went into the Prayer Books with very little change). Latin was widely understood by the literate, but most of what was said by the priest at Mass was either silent or covered by the singing of the choir. Intellectual comprehension of the words of the service was a low priority. The experience of the Mass must have been a rich fusion of all the senses. The literate had prayer books that equipped them both in church and at home, but prayers learned by heart, often using the rosary, must have been the staple diet of most lay people. Lay communion was infrequent, possibly only annually at Easter. Lay devotion at Mass was supported not just by their own prayers but also by the vernacular intercessions known as *bidding the bedes* and, just before the priest made his communion, the Peace, in which all those present kissed the Pax, a religious picture. But the centrepiece of the Mass was the elevation of the consecrated bread as the Body of Christ, not simply a focus in the service but a cornerstone of many people's daily lives in that they would time their entry into church simply to witness the elevation.

The clergy have always bemoaned the ignorance of the laity, and educated lay people have always bemoaned that of the clergy. It is all but impossible to have any idea what was the level of education and participation, and whether it was any more or less inadequate than in other ages. Dissent was by no means unknown; in England, 'Lollardy' was feared and repressed by the authorities, but again it is hard to tell how common it was.

---

2 R. W. Pfaff, *The Liturgy in Medieval England*, Cambridge: Cambridge University Press, 2009, p. 417.

The English Reformation under Henry VIII and Edward VI

'Conformity' under Henry VIII was mainly conservative. Pilgrimages were prohibited and the Pope's name was deleted. Royalty and the royal supremacy were stoutly maintained – and there was much trouble over the elderly priest in Wells Cathedral who prayed for the wrong queen![3] But besides some readings from the English Great Bible (a translation that passed royal scrutiny) and the English Litany of 1544, Henry stonewalled the reforms that Cranmer and his allies were promoting. The Six Articles of 1539 and the King's Book of 1543 entrenched traditional teaching on the Mass and the sacraments.

With the accession of Edward VI, reform moved wholeheartedly forward, in the direction of the Reformed churches. What was unusual in England was the use of the liturgy as the central plank in reform. Martin Bucer and his fellow Continental exiles advising the government thought it a higher priority to train clergy as preachers of the Reformed theology. The use of the printed book as an agent of reform was very much a feature of the time, and a novelty historically. There had always been exemplars to be imitated, but attempts to enforce uniform practice had always been limited by the time and expense of manuscript copying. The medieval English uses enjoyed enormous prestige and a de facto uniformity at one level, but every liturgical manuscript was slightly different, generally incorporating a church's patron saint or a donor's favourite devotion. Customary practice was authoritative as well as any text. But the printing press and the Tudor government machine meant that for the first time a book could be produced that every parish in the land had to use by a specified date. This had applied in the first instance to the Bible, when the authorized version – I mean the Great Bible – was required to be set up and read in every church. Likewise under Edward VI the Book of Homilies, issued in 1547, ensured that Reformed teaching was heard in every church in the land when there was not a sermon by a licensed preacher (and they were not very thick on the ground).

The new liturgy was very much the work of one man: Thomas Cranmer.[4] This is not to claim that he composed every word of it. The

---

3 Letter of John Clerk, Bishop of Bath and Wells, to Thomas Cromwell, 21 February 1535; PRO, State Papers (Henry VIII), vol. 1, p. 427; Somerset and Dorset Notes and Queries, 2 (1891), pp. 265–6.

4 For Thomas Cranmer, see Diarmaid MacCulloch, *Thomas Cranmer: A Life*, New Haven and London: Yale University Press, 1996; A. Null, *Thomas Cranmer's Doctrine of Repentance: Renewing the Power to Love*, Oxford: Uni-

work of collaborators has been often suspected and sometimes identified. Committees and responses to questionnaires had their impact. But overall there is a notable unity both of style and of purpose.

The style of the writing was remarkably consistent from the very beginning, going back to the Litany, which saw the light of day in 1544. Much of the book was translation or adaptation of the medieval Latin books, but also of contemporary texts, Catholic, Lutheran and Reformed. Many of the traditional pieces had been translated beforehand in primers (personal prayer books), and the versions would continue to be honed in successive editions of the Prayer Book. But there is a deeply impressive tenor within the book as a whole, based not only on the words but the rhythm of the Latin liturgy. Perhaps it was the discipline of these originals that enabled Cranmer when composing his own texts to avoid the tedious prolixity of his contemporaries, and certainly the traditional format of congregational responses delivered the Church of England from the ministerial monologue. While many members of the Prayer Book Society compare Cranmer's prose favourably with that of later generations, scholars of Reformation liturgy also note with relief the alternatives that were not visited on the infant Church of England. However, the Prayer Book was not greatly appreciated by Cranmer's contemporaries who found his ambiguity irritating and, among the Reformers, the traditional elements more a scandal than a delight. The creative potential of such material was not acknowledged at the time.

As for Cranmer's purpose, it is clear that the Prayer Book embodied his personal theology. The Archbishop has often been labelled as influenced by one Reformer or another, but the truth is that he was his own man and the Prayer Book was his book. The Prayer Book proposed a Christian society under a Christian monarch. The congregation prayed for the King, and asked for deliverance from the Pope, every Sunday, Wednesday and Friday. The emphasis was on instruction in the Bible and the Reformed faith. Morning and Evening Prayer put Bible reading at their centre. Services included lengthy prefaces or exhortations setting out the teaching on the meaning of the rite or the desired response of the participant. (The preface to the marriage service is perhaps the most well known and well loved today.) With the regular hearing of the homilies, congregations were to be formed in correct belief and behaviour.

versity Press, 2006; G. P. Jeanes, *Signs of God's Promise: Thomas Cranmer's Sacramental Theology and the Book of Common Prayer*, London: T&T Clark, 2008.

Prayer was always 'common prayer', led by the priest in the name of the congregation whether or not they all joined in. It was usually concrete and honest rather than emotional or sentimental. It explored human frailty more accurately than it could express delight or joy; but overall it could measure the range of our ordinary lives and what we bring to God for healing, forgiveness and salvation.

The Christian society of the Prayer Book was a somewhat narrower one than that of the medieval world. Fewer books were to be seen in church after the reforms than beforehand: not simply the replacement of a library of service books by the Bible, Prayer Book and the Homilies, but also the condemnation of the private prayer books brought to church by the literate wealthy to say their own prayers during service time. Rosaries and religious pictures were also condemned as corrupt, and with them a host of personal devotions were extinguished. The church was a world of public discourse dominated by the words of the authorized books and those who read them out loud. Sometimes a preacher would deliver a sermon. Music was much simplified and reduced, leading many parish choirs to cease, but congregational hymnody was in its infancy with metrical versions of the psalms. The church building itself, stripped of its statues and images, its altars, lights and hangings, was a bare and empty space in which the congregation gathered in the nave for the services and the chancel used by those who received communion. But communion was not commonly celebrated. And the dead, so prominent in medieval liturgy, were notable for their absence. It is hard to say how many were bereft by these changes, and how many felt liberated.

Cranmer organized reform by stages, step by step.[5] The English Litany of 1544 was starkly simple but unexceptional. The 1548 *Order of the Communion* inserted vernacular devotions into the Latin Mass and introduced Communion in both kinds for the laity. The first Prayer Book of 1549 was conservative compared with many Continental reforms, but a radical move in a country largely unprepared. Its full title was *The Book of the Common Prayer and Administration of the Sacraments, and other Rites and Ceremonies of the Church after the Use of the Church of England.* That title covered the three types

---

5 For successive editions of the Prayer Book, a convenient text of 1662 with selected portions of 1549 and 1559 and a very detailed commentary is B. Cummings (ed.), *The Book of Common Prayer*, Oxford: Oxford: University Press, 2011. There are many older editions of the various prayer books. A detailed comparison of the texts of the successive editions can be found in F. E. Brightman, *The English Rite*, London: Rivingtons, 1915.

of services in the book. It was an ambitious collection of the whole of public worship into one volume: the 'common prayer' of Morning and Evening prayer through the year along with the Litany; the Communion service (preceded by Collects, Psalms, Epistles and Gospels for the year); then the life-cycle of baptism, confirmation, matrimony, visitation and communion of the sick, and the burial service. With thanksgiving after childbirth and the Ash Wednesday devotions (the Commination service), the Book was complete. At first glance it would seem to be little more than a translation and rationalization of the old services. Closer examination reveals the firm editorial hand of Thomas Cranmer himself. Almost everywhere one can detect a subtle but clear manipulation of the material to convey a Reformed theology of salvation, worship and the sacraments. And for all the medieval trappings – the ceremonies, the vestments and choirs, the stone altars in the chancels – no intelligent reader of the book or participant at the services was fooled. This liturgy denied the sacrifice of the Mass and the real presence of Christ in the consecrated bread and wine. The ceremonial high point of the Mass was now banned, and no longer did the priest lift up the consecrated bread to be venerated as Christ truly present, the very body that had suffered on the cross and been raised from the dead. Instead the Communion service ('The Supper of the Lorde and the Holy Communion, commonly called the Masse') was a sacrifice of praise and thanksgiving, and the bread and wine spoken of only as representing Christ's body and blood. For Cranmer, a sacrament was 'a sign of an holy thing', pointing to what it signified but not to be seen as linked with it. Christ was to be apprehended only spiritually by faith.

The first Prayer Book received a mixed reception. Like many archiepiscopal initiatives it seemed guaranteed to please neither traditionalists nor reformers. The people of Devon and Cornwall rose in revolt against what they called 'a Christmas game'; those with reforming sympathies were depressed by the extent to which medieval ceremonies were still embedded in the rites. Bishop Hooper was reconciled to vestments only by a period in prison. But reform proceeded at the speed determined by the government. Stone altars were demolished, to make way for wooden tables, which were to be placed in the middle of the chancel. The 1552 Prayer Book took reformation a stage further, with ceremonies further reduced, prayer for the dead extinguished, the mass vestments replaced simply by the surplice which was the common vesture for all services, and the Communion service (no longer commonly called the Mass) in particular radically revised to obliterate, if possible, old notions of the Mass and to set forth clearly the doctrine summarized in the new words of administration: 'Take and eate this, in remembraunce that Christ dyed for thee, and feede on him in thy hearte by faythe with thankesgeving.' The bread and wine were insignificant: what mattered was the spiritual feeding on Christ. (Kneeling communion was retained only on Cranmer's personal insistence, and by the insertion of the 'Black Rubric' added by the Council, affirming that kneeling signified only the humility of the communicant and not any adoration of the sacramental bread and wine.) In effect the second Prayer Book made explicit the doctrine that had been stated only ambiguously in the first.

The successive Prayer Books can be viewed in their legal form, attached to and enforced by Acts of Parliament, each one superseding what had been before. But it can be useful also to imagine them as successive stones thrown into a lake, each one having its own impact and distinct ripple that carried on even after its successors had taken its place. This we shall see when we move from Edward to the time of Elizabeth.

The Prayer Book under Elizabeth I

The 1552 Prayer Book enjoyed a life of less than a year. With Edward's death in July 1553 the reversal of religious policy under Mary was taken for granted and many churches did not even wait for government permission before reverting to the 'old religion'. But Mary's reign was short also; and we may speculate what might have happened if either Edward or Mary had lived and ensured a stable succession. In either case the religious policy was clear and would have been pursued with vigour.

There is therefore a certain irony about Elizabeth's religious policy, that it was the most uncertain in its beginnings and yet most influential because of the length of her reign.[6] Whether it be seen as a strength or a weakness of the Church of England, its identity as a 'broad church' dates from the range of responses to her initial hesitant settlement with the 1559 Prayer Book. The origins of that Book have been much debated. It is clear that compromise between traditionalists and evangelicals was impossible. If a new book based on 1549 was considered

---

6 For the Reformation under Elizabeth, see K. Fincham and N. Tyacke, *Altars Restored: The Changing Face of English Religious Worship, 1547–c.1700,* Oxford: Oxford University Press, 2007. W. P. Haugaard, *Elizabeth and the English Reformation: The Struggle for a Stable Settlement of Religion,* Cambridge: Cambridge University Press, 1968, has to be read in the light of later publications.

(and there is evidence that Elizabeth was attracted to it),[7] the Marian bishops were implacably opposed. They had been there under Edward and were not going there again. Not that Elizabeth had great affection for the Catholic establishment that had condemned her as illegitimate; but nor did she warm to the Marian exiles returning with their ideas for more advanced reform. John Knox in Geneva had written against 'the monstrous regiment of women', meaning Mary, but the book ended his career in Elizabeth's England. The Queen would work with the more moderate evangelicals who had lain low in England under her sister. The evangelicals regarded 1552 as the basic starting point; indeed many wanted to move beyond it and complete what, as they saw it, Edward and Cranmer had only begun. In the event the Prayer Book that was enforced was the 1552 Book with a handful of changes in a conservative direction: the petition in the Litany against 'the tyranny of the Byshop of Rome, and all hys detestable enormities' was removed (perhaps to keep adherents of the papacy within the fold of the established religion). A second change was in the Communion service, when the words of administration of the bread and cup combined those from 1549 and 1552 to produce a lengthy formula in which they are spoken of, however ambiguously, as the body and blood of Christ. And the Ornaments Rubric at the beginning of Morning Prayer required that 'the Minister at the time of the communion, and at all other tymes in hys ministracion, shall use suche ornamentes in the church as wer in use by aucthoritie of parliament in the second yere of the reygne of king Edward the vi.', and thus legally restored the medieval vestments and altars. (The Black Rubric about kneeling was not included. This was technically not part of the 1552 Prayer Book as authorized by Parliament but it could have been kept if the powers that be had wanted it.) These moves might have had an eye to the broad range of views among the English population or even to possible Lutheran allies abroad, but it is very likely that the Queen had a personal interest. Certainly she was fully prepared to battle with her supporters who disliked the crucifix and candles she maintained in the Chapel Royal.

The Royal Injunctions of 1559 provided for the orderly removal of stone altars and their replacement by a communion table. But other clauses of the Injunctions sounded conservative, even reactionary, reinstating the Rogationtide procession around the parish and requiring wafer bread for the Communion. This created an ensemble totally

---

7 B. Rowers, 'The Chapel Royal, the First Edwardian Prayer Book and Elizabeth's Settlement of Religion 1559', *Historical Journal* 43 (2000), pp. 317–44.

contrary to the spirit of the evangelical Reformers: the Communion celebrated by a priest in medieval vestments using not ordinary bread but a form of loaf reminiscent of the host in the Mass. How could this convey the Reformed doctrine that the bread and wine had no holiness in themselves but were signs enabling a spiritual feeding? Resistance was immediate and determined.

In their *Interpretations* of 1560 the bishops had to moderate the requirement on vestments, specifying the use of the cope for the Communion and the surplice otherwise; this was further moderated by Archbishop Parker in 1566, who required the cope only in cathedrals and collegiate churches and the surplice elsewhere. In 1565 Elizabeth demanded action to enforce conformity, and by the following year the bishops were now prepared to deprive and imprison the more extreme nonconformists. The use of the surplice became the litmus test; as John Jewel commented, it was 'as if the whole of our religion were contained in this single point'.[8]

One branch of reform, especially at the beginning of Elizabeth's reign, looked to further revision of the Prayer Book. In a meeting in 1563 of the Convocation of the Province of Canterbury, reforms were proposed with broad agreement from bishops and the lower house, including abolition of the cope and surplice and the sign of the cross at baptism, and replacing kneeling with seated communion. However, actual proposals in the lower house failed by one vote. The Queen was having none of it anyway. Reform failed in the 1566 Parliament, and again in 1571. In 1578 an unauthorized version of the Prayer Book, perhaps more accurately described as extracts from the Prayer Book, appeared bound with the Geneva Bible, omitting services disliked by the godly such as confirmation and the churching of women and referring to the minister rather than the priest.[9]

---

8 Jewel to Bullinger, 24 February 1567, *Zurich Letters* (1842), Parker Society (Cambridge: University Press), vol. 1, p. 185.

9 I examined two copies in the British Library: press marks 469.g.9. and 2.g.7. The publication seems to have carefully avoided being called a Prayer Book, lacking its mention in the title page. In the last rubric at the end of the communion it spoke of 'the order *in* this book appointed' rather than 'the order *of* this book appointed': a subtle disavowal of authority? The only substantive difference I have noted in the material is that the heading of the Catechism (confirmation not being included in the publication) reads: 'A Catechisme, that is to say, An instruction to be learned of euery childe, before he be confirmed, *or admitted to receaue the holy Communion*.' The Prayer Book makes no provision for admission to Communion other than by confirmation.

As time went on there was something of a draw between the Queen and the godly. Her attempts to reintroduce ceremonies and furnishings which were not in 1552 had come to nothing, but neither had the godly achieved further reform of the Book. This led to further polarization between those who chose to conform to royal authority and those who increasingly looked to the 'best reformed churches' in Scotland and on the Continent, and to the Stranger Churches in London that followed a similar liturgy.

The Admonition controversy

In 1572 The *Admonition to Parliament* was a systematic critique of the Church of England as only half reformed. The Prayer Book was attacked for continuing rather than extinguishing popish abuses. The authors were imprisoned, and Thomas Cartwright, Lady Margaret Professor in Cambridge, after taking up their baton found it wise to move to Geneva. The standpoint of the godly was, of course, far wider than simply arguments over particular issues in worship. It was about what sort of Church the Church should be, and the ways in which it should be modelled on the Church of the New Testament. The Genevan model (by now followed in Scotland) was the ideal form. Most of those who had been in exile under Mary had experienced it at first hand and conducted their religious lives according to its principles, and they were eager to share the experience with those who had not travelled so far, either geographically or spiritually. In the ordering of worship, the godly took the principle that nothing was allowed unless it was commanded by Scripture; and even what is admissible in Scripture is not to be allowed if it has been tainted by popery. Within the polity of the 'best reformed churches' not only was the word truly preached and the sacraments rightly administered but also the discipline properly applied. The Church of England under Elizabeth could claim the first two (though the word preached was rare, and the godly regarded the mere reading of Scripture without preaching to be a travesty). The third aspect, of discipline, was at best a pious hope.

But integral to the Genevan model was the ideal that the Church should be self-governing, freed from the shackles of the State, and that fitted badly with the royal supremacy. And the closer it was to the monarch, the less reformed seemed the Church. Bishops remained, and cathedrals and the whole medieval apparatus of government. As well as bishops, priests and deacons were recruited, ordained and employed in a manner only superficially reformed. The popish worship of the Prayer Book was only one of many abuses to be reformed.

In 1572, it was proposed in Parliament that the Genevan service book be allowed as an option. In 1584 and 1587 similar proposals were made for English versions of that book. But the Queen allowed no change. In the 1590s Archbishop Whitgift cracked down on the godly. Thomas Cartwright (back from Geneva) and others ended up in the Star Chamber. Three leaders of the small number who had actually separated themselves from the Church of England were executed. Potential reformers were bundled with dissident separatists in government propaganda. While the godly were a major part of the religious population, many steered clear of institutional reform, noted that the Queen was no longer young and hoped for better times under a new monarch. Others formed separate churches, and the Baptist and Congregational traditions date from this period. Enforced conformity failed.

Conformity

But there was also conformity, and much of it was genuine, positive and heartfelt. It is very difficult to tell from this distance the extent to which the Prayer Book was accepted or not. Much of the surviving literature inevitably speaks of controversy, and the church courts carry reports of nonconformity. On the other hand, there is ample evidence of support for the Prayer Book and indeed its popularity; that many copies were evidently bought and used, probably more at home than for following the service in church.[10] Christopher Marsh suggests a somewhat chequered assimilation of the Reformation in which the new ideas were taken on somewhat half-heartedly and often confused with, rather than removing, the old religion. He tells of the medieval guilds in Wisbech which, on their suppression, transferred their property, personnel and business to the new town corporation which, even in 1567, prayed for the soul of Edward VI and minuted the fact.[11] There are plenty of stories of old priests who would celebrate the Communion in a manner as close to the Mass as they could manage.

Such was the conservative end of conformity. Gradually, largely with the passing of a generation, the old patterns slipped away and new ones

---

10 J. Maltby, *Prayer Book and People in Elizabethan and Early Stuart England*, Cambridge: Cambridge University Press, 1998, pp. 24–30.

11 C. Marsh, *Popular Religion in Sixteenth-Century England*, Basingstoke: Macmillan, 1998, pp. 127–8.

were established. But it did not depend solely on the kind offices of the grim reaper. Eamon Duffy's voice of Morebath in Devon, Sir Christopher Trychay, a conscientious parish priest who had bitterly lamented the Edwardian reformation and sympathized with the Devon rebellion, had learned to preach a message acceptable to the authorities by 1561, and in 1573 uttered 'deo gracias' as he recorded the purchase of a new Prayer Book. As Duffy comments, 'The accommodating traditionalism of men like ... Christopher Trychay had its own integrity, making possible the marriage of the old ways and the new.'[12]

Others were more tenacious. The parish of Christ Church, Newgate, in London suffered an extended battle in the 1580s and 1590s between factions over whether to keep their professional choir or to use the money for preachers. By this date many considered the preachers to be most fitting for worship and that it was an 'absurd and preposterous imitacion of a cathedral church by some v singers'. But then, 'the said parish of Christ Church Newgate is well knowen to be very backward in matters of religion'.[13]

But if you were going to conform, the question arose, how do you interpret the book and the rules you are following? Parishes obeyed the royal injunctions reinstating the rogation procession around the parish boundaries and did so in the time-honoured fashion, as described disapprovingly by Bishop Grindal, when he commanded in 1560:

that the ministers make it not a procession, but a perambulation; and also that they suffer no banners, nor other like monument of superstition to be carried abroad; neither to have multitude of young light folks with them; but the substantial of the parish, according to the injunctions: the Ministers to go without surplices and lights; and to use no drinkings, except the distance of the place do require some necessary relief; and to use at one or two convenient places the form and order of prayers and thanksgiving appointed by the Queen's Majesty's injunctions.[14]

Likewise, the *Interpretations of the Bishops* demanded that the procession should include an exhortation to temperance.[15]

12 Eamon Duffy, *The Voices of Morebath: Reformation and Rebellion in an English Village*, New Haven and London: Yale University Press, 2001, pp. 175–7, 180.

13 Fincham and Tyacke, *Altars Restored*, pp. 93–7.

14 J. Strype, *The History of the Life and Acts of the Most Reverend Father in God Edmund Grindal*, Oxford: Clarendon Press, 1821, pp. 55–6.

15 *Interpretations*, Article 4, in W. H. Frere (ed.), *Visitation Articles and*

The Elizabethan churchmen are sometimes said to have been one with Cranmer in theology but in advance of him in their opposition to ceremonial. While this is generally accurate, one might insert a caveat on one aspect of sacramental theology. In his theology of the sacraments Cranmer had carefully separated the sign from the signified. All language of consecration had been airbrushed away in the Prayer Books, and in 1552 he avoided speaking of the bread and wine even indirectly as the body and blood of Christ.

For the most part the Elizabethan Church followed the principle that feeding on Christ was spiritual, not physical. However, many did not share Cranmer's aversion to linking sign and signified, nor did they object to the 1549 words of administration being added to the Communion: 'The bodie of our lord Jesu Christ which was geven for thee, preserve thy body and soule into everlastinge life.' It is notable that this alteration was not included among the many controversial items in the debates.[16] There was widespread acceptance of the language of consecration not just among conforming Anglicans but also among other Reformed theologians.[17] Bishop John Jewel, answering the Catholic Thomas Harding, had a clear sense of consecration and how it was achieved in the Prayer Book: quoting St Augustine ('Put the words of God (saith he) unto the element; and it is made a sacrament'), he wrote:

We pronounce the same words of consecration that Christ pronounced: we do the same that Christ bade us do: we proclaim the death of the Lord: we speak openly in a known tongue: and the people understand us: we consecrate for the congregation, and not only for ourselves: we have the element: we join God's word unto it; and so it is made a sacrament.[18]

Injunctions of the Period of the Reformation, vol. 3, London: Longmans, Green and Co., 1910, p. 60.

16 We know of at least one case where the priest avoided the 1549 words (Maltby, *Prayer Book and People*, pp. 48–9). The *Admonition* opposed the whole administration formula, but because it was addressed to each communicant individually while in the New Testament Jesus had addressed all together.

17 See for example *Confessio et Expositio simplex Orthodoxae Fidei & dogmatu Catholicorum syncerae religionis Christianae concorditer ab Ecclesiae Christi ministris qui sunt in Helvetia, Tiguri, Bernae, Scaphusij, Sangalli, Curiae Rhetorum & apud confederatos, Mylhusij item, & Biennae, quibus adjunxerunt se & Genevensis Ecclesiae ministri* ... Zurich, Christopherus Froschoverus, 1566, fo. 34v–36.

18 'Controversy with M Harding, Of Private Mass', in J. Ayre, *The Works of John Jewel*, Parker Society vol. 1, Cambridge: University Press, 1848, p. 123.

Jewel identified the words of Christ as the words of consecration, a common but not universal opinion in the medieval West. This would be enshrined liturgically in the changes made in the 1662 Prayer Book where the words of institution are enacted as words of consecration, but it also gave theological backing to the contemporary practice, that when the bread or wine for the communion ran out, the priest would say the relevant words of institution over them. This followed the regulations of the 1548 Order of the Communion, but these had been omitted in both 1549 and 1552, no doubt deliberately. My guess is that, in the absence of an explicit order otherwise, it remained common practice. In 1573 Robert Johnson was prosecuted for omitting the words when he brought extra wine to the communion. The indignation of the Queen's Commissioners, the Bishop of London and the Dean of Westminster (the former certainly no reactionary), strongly suggests that they believed Johnson to be breaching general or even universal practice. But Johnson knew his Prayer Book well. Edward Ratcliff described this as a contest between the Cranmerian Johnson and the Jewelite Commissioners. Although he was imprisoned, it is curious that the practice was never made statutory in any way until the Canons of 1604.[19]

The Bishop of London was no reactionary, but many would have so described the Dean of Westminster from 1561 to 1601, Gabriel Goodman. A deeply conservative man, he was considered too severe to be Bishop of London; in 1575 Archbishop Parker felt his 'sad and sure governance in conformity' qualified him for Norwich, but he stayed as Dean. He did not try to revive pre-Reformation worship, but he did not instigate further reform either, staying with the initial years of the Elizabethan settlement right up to his death in 1601. Westminster Abbey did not try to become a centre of preaching like St Paul's. Goodman continued to maintain the bells, bought an organ when a London parish wanted to dispose of theirs, and kept the copes and hangings left by the monks when their house was dissolved a second time. The royal associations allowed the Abbey to maintain a level of grandeur in its worship and a sense of historical continuity that would have been frowned on elsewhere, even in the cathedrals that had escaped the Reformation with their worshipping infrastructure largely intact.[20] At

19 E. C. Ratcliff, 'The English Usage of Eucharistic Consecration, 1548–1662 – II', *Theology* 60 (1957), pp. 273–80; R. Buxton, *Eucharist and Institution Narrative*, London: SPCK, 1976, pp. 89–92.

20 J. F. Merritt, 'The Cradle of Laudianism? Westminster Abbey, 1558–1630', *Journal of Ecclesiastical History* 52 (2001), pp. 623–46.

the very end of Elizabeth's reign the Abbey would become one of the godparents of the Laudian movement, at this point described by historians as 'avant-garde conformity'. But to most Elizabethans it would have seemed a small and insignificant coterie: Lancelot Andrewes and Richard Neile, court clerics dependent like Goodman on the patronage of the Cecil family, Richard Hooker writing in his vicarage in Kent, relics of the distant past perhaps, rather than embodying the potential of the Prayer Book for a future generation.

3

The Prayer Book in Early Stuart Society

HANNAH CLEUGH

This chapter explores the Prayer Book in the early Stuart Church of England, during the reigns of James I and Charles I. The period between the death of Elizabeth and the outbreak of the first Civil War in 1642 can be seen as 'book-ended' by attempts at Prayer Book reform, in very different directions and with very different results. During the first half of the seventeenth century, conformity to the Prayer Book remained the standard for public worship in the Church of England. Under James, a religious *via media* was maintained: churchmen of different theological perspectives received preferment, and in the Chapels Royal preaching and ceremonial were held in balance. With the accession of Charles I in 1625, however, the situation changed. Since around the turn of the seventeenth century, there had been a strand of theological opinion represented primarily by Lancelot Andrewes, John Overall, Richard Neile, John Cosin, Matthew Wren and William Laud, that sought to re-imagine the Church of England and her liturgy. Following Peter Lake and Anthony Milton, these will be referred to here as 'avant-garde conformists', reflecting that they were concerned with conformity to the Prayer Book and its provisions, but that their theological agenda led them to alter what that conformity represented.[1] This proved highly divisive, leading to bitter religious controversy throughout the 1630s. This reached crisis point when Laud attempted to impose a new Prayer Book (referred to as 'Laud's Liturgy') on the Scottish church in 1637, which led the following year to the Solemn League and Covenant against the Prayer Book and to the outbreak of war in the Three Kingdoms.

---

1 Diarmaid MacCulloch, *Reformation: Europe's House Divided, 1400–1700*, London: Allen Lane, 2003, p. 510. See also Peter Lake, *Anglicans and Puritans? Presbyterianism and English Nonconformist Thought from Whitgift to Hooker*, London and Boston: Unwin Hyman, 1988; and Anthony Milton, *Catholic and Reformed: Roman and Protestant Churches in English Protestant Thought, 1600–40*, Cambridge: Cambridge University Press, 1995.

Hampton Court and the Prayer Book of 1604

During Elizabeth I's long reign, the Prayer Book Protestantized England.[2] In the decades following the Settlement, regular worship in conformity to the Prayer Book encouraged the development of a distinctively Protestant English religious identity. Elizabeth's settlement of religion prescribed the Prayer Book as revised in 1559, which was, in reality, Cranmer's second Prayer Book (1552) with very few amendments.[3] However, the provisions of the Prayer Book were controversial from the outset, as the Vestiarian controversy of the 1560s and the Admonition controversies of the 1570s and 1580s indicated. The Reformation in Scotland had taken a very different course from that in England, so when, in 1603, the English throne passed to James VI of Scotland, Puritans saw the opportunity for reform of the Church of England. They anticipated that England could now see further reformation in the direction of the Scottish Church, and so of Geneva on which John Knox had modelled it. At last it seemed that the complaints of those who had objected about the 'popishe abuses yet remaining in the English church' – about the ceremonies contained in the Prayer Book, about bishops and non-preaching ministers – might now be heard. Thus as the new king rode southwards, he was greeted on the road by the 'Millenary Petitioners', determined to seize their opportunity. The Petition reiterated many of the demands that had been made in the course of Elizabeth's reign.[4]

James's response to the Petitioners was to convene a conference, which met at Hampton Court in January 1604. Details of the Conference are sketchy, and the official account of proceedings by William Barlow, Bishop of Chester, *The Summe and Substance, which it pleased his excellent maiestie to have with the lords, bishops, and other of his clergie at Hampton court* (London, 1604), has, as Arnold Hunt notes, long been recognized as 'a tainted source'.[5] The main instigators of the Millenary Petition, Arthur Hildersham and Stephen Egerton, were not

---

2 Eamon Duffy, *The Stripping of the Altars: Traditional Religion in England 1450–1700*, New Haven, CT: Yale University Press, 1992, p. 593.

3 See Gordon Jeanes, Chapter 2 in this volume.

4 No original copies of the Petition survive, but the list of demands is available in G. Bray (ed.), *The Anglican Canons 1529–1947*, Woodbridge, Suffolk: Boydell Press, Church of England Record Society, 1998, pp. 817–19.

5 Arnold Hunt, 'Laurence Chaderton and the Hampton Court Conference', in Susan Wabuda and Caroline Litzenberger (eds), *Belief and Practice in Reformation England: A Tribute to Patrick Collinson from his Students*, Aldershot: Ashgate, 1998, pp. 207–28.

invited to the Conference on account of their Nonconformity, thus the Puritan case was represented by Laurence Chaderton of Cambridge, John Rainolds of Oxford, John Knewstubbs, Rector of Cockfield, and Dr Thomas Sparkes, Rector of Bletchly. Hunt notes that the Conference was conducted such that the Puritans were doubtful that their cause had been given a proper hearing, chaired as it was by the King, in the form of a 'round table' rather than a formal disputation between opposing parties.[6] The demands of the Petitioners regarding the public worship of the Church and the required degree of conformity were largely unmet, as the 1604 Prayer Book re-imposed the 1559 text almost without alteration. The two significant changes to the 1604 text concerned the Catechism and the order for 'them that be baptized in private houses in time of necessity'.

The Catechism in the 1559 Prayer Book was minimal. The child was required only to 'rehearse the Articles of [his] belief' (that is, to recite the Apostles' Creed), and to know the Ten Commandments and the Lord's Prayer. In the 1604 version, this extended to include a brief treatment of the sacraments. This was the work of John Overall, Dean of St Paul's, and later to become Bishop of Coventry and Lichfield, then of Norwich. Overall was associated with the nascent 'avant-garde conformist' movement, and Anthony Milton has posited him alongside Richard Hooker as a possible 'inventor of Anglicanism',[7] but there is no hint of this theological tendency here. Rather, the section on sacraments in the Prayer Book Catechism is entirely reflective of the Elizabethan Protestant mainstream, deriving from Alexander Nowell's *Catechism*, which enjoyed semi-official status. The first version of it received unanimous approval by the Lower House of Convocation in 1562, and the Larger Catechism was published first in Latin in 1570 and then in English in 1573. There were already six versions of the Latin text in print by 1575, and by the Civil War, in its various versions (Latin, Greek and English) it had gone through more than 50 editions. Alongside the Prayer Book Catechism itself, Nowell's was one of the most widely used catechisms in early modern England.[8] Commenting

6 Hunt, 'Laurence Chaderton', p. 211.

7 A. Milton, '"Anglicanism" by Stealth: The Career and Influence of John Overall', in K. Fincham and P. Lake (eds), *Religious Politics in Post-Reformation England: Essays in Honour of Nicholas Tyacke*, Studies in Modern British Religious History, vol. 13, Woodbridge: Boydell Press, 2006, pp. 159–76.

8 Ian Green, *The Christian's ABC: Catechisms and Catechizing in England c. 1530–1740*, Oxford: Oxford University Press, 1996. Green offers a helpful discussion of the various versions of the text, and their interrelationship, listing these on pp. 690–2.

on the treatment of sacraments in the 1604 Prayer Book Catechism, Bryan Spinks has observed that there is 'no expression of the developing covenant theology with which many linked the sacraments', and the effect of the section was to conceal the theological developments and discussions that were taking place within the English Church by the beginning of the seventeenth century.[9]

A Puritan success? Private baptism

The other significant alteration between the 1559 and 1604 versions of the Prayer Book concerned the provision for private baptism. The presence within the Prayer Book of an order for private or emergency baptism had proved highly contentious throughout Elizabeth's reign. There were two reasons for the Reformed objection to the order: first was that the very fact of an order for emergency baptism seemed to call into question the central Protestant tenet of justification by faith alone, and particularly its corollary, predestination; second, the medieval insistence on the necessity of baptism for salvation meant that, when a child was likely to die, the emergency baptism was frequently performed by the midwife attending the birth. That the Prayer Book seemed to permit continuation of this practice was a substantial cause of the controversy surrounding the order. Writing to Heinrich Bullinger in 1566, Laurence Humphrey and Thomas Sampson had listed among 'Some blemishes which still attach to the Church of England' that 'Licence is also given to women to baptize in private houses.'[10] In like manner, the *Admonition to the Parliament* (1572) included the demand that '[Y]our wisedomes have to remove (as before) ignorant ministers, to take awai private communions and baptismes, to enjoyne Deacons and Midwives not to meddle in ministers matters, if they doe, to see them sharpelie punished.'[11]

The 'View of popishe abuses yet remaining in the Englishe churche' had gone much further, taking particular issue with the wording of the Prayer Book order:

---

9 Bryan Spinks, *Sacraments, Ceremonies, and the Stuart Divines: Sacramental Theology and Liturgy in England and Scotland 1603–1662*, Aldershot: Ashgate, 2002, p. 35.

10 H. Robinson (tr. and ed.), *Zurich Letters 1558–1602*, 2 vols, Cambridge: Parker Society, 1845, vol. I, p. 164; Lat. P. 97: '4. Mulierculis etiam domi baptizandi potestas facta est'.

11 J. Field and T. Wilcox, *An Admonition to the Parliament*, Hemel Hempstead, 1572, Aiiiv–Aivr.

And as for private baptisme, that wil abide the touchstone. Goe ye, sayth Christ and teache, baptising them, etc. Now teaching is devorsed from communions and sacraments. They may goe alone without doctrine. Women that may not speake in a congregation, may yet in time of necessitie, minister the sacrament of baptisme, & that is a private house. And yet this is not to tie necessitie of salvation to the sacraments, nor to nowsell up men in that opinion. This is agreable with the scriptures, and therfore when they bring the baptized childe, they are received with this special commendation. I certefye you that you have done well and according to due order, etc. But now we speake in good earnest, when they answer this: Let them tell us, howe this geare agreeth with the scriptures, and whether it be not repugnante or against the worde of God.[12]

Key to the Puritan objection to the Prayer Book provision was not simply a contested vestige of pre-Reformation practice, which might – like the sign of the cross in baptism or the use of the ring in the marriage service – be deemed 'superstitious': rather, the Prayer Book's Puritan critics were calling into question the very nature of the Church of England as a properly Reformed church. Reformed ecclesiology was predicated on the assumption that there were marks of a 'true church' and these were that the Word should be duly preached, and the sacraments duly administered. This understanding was affirmed in the nineteenth of the Articles of Religion ('Of the Church'):

> The visible Church of Christ is a congregation of faithful men, in the which the pure Word of God is preached, and the Sacraments be duly administered according to Christ's ordinance in all those things that of necessity are requisite to the same.[13]

Central to the objection to the Prayer Book order for private baptism was that it allowed that women, forbidden by Scripture from preaching, could yet administer the sacrament. Thus the prescribed liturgy seemed to allow a divorce of word and sacrament and thereby to call into question whether the Church of England did indeed exhibit both the necessary marks of a true church. The sensitivity surrounding this

---

12 Field and Wilcox, *Admonition*, Biiir.

13 *Articles agreed on by the Bishoppes, and other learned menne in the Synode at London, in the yere of our Lorde Godde, MDLII, for the avoiding of controuersie in opinions, and the establishement of a godlie concorde in certeine matters of Religion*, London, 1553, Biiir.

question was well reflected in the extensive defences of the Prayer Book practice mounted first by John Whitgift and then by Richard Hooker in the latter years of the sixteenth century.[14]

Against this controversial background, the amendment of the Prayer Book order at Hampton Court might be deemed a modest Puritan success. Little that was demanded by the Millenary Petitioners was conceded, but this long-standing Puritan demand was met, and, on Barlow's account, at the king's instigation. On the first day of the conference, the various points of the Prayer Book to be discussed were outlined:

> The third [point of discussion in the Prayer Book] was private baptism, if private for place, his majesty thought it agreed with the use of the primitive church; if for persons, that any but a lawful minister might baptize any where, he utterly disliked, and in this point his highnesse grew somewhat earnest against the baptizing by women and laikes.[15]

The question received extensive discussion, with the Archbishop of Canterbury (John Whitgift) reiterating the point he had made to Cartwright in the course of the Admonition controversy, namely that the Church of England did not, in fact, permit women to baptize. The principle of private baptism was upheld on the twin bases of antiquity and pastoral concern, but it was agreed that the rubric should be clarified to demand that the baptism be conducted by a lawful minister. Barlow recounts how, on the final day of the conference, in the presence of the bishops, deans, and 'doctors of the arches', James himself edited a copy of the Prayer Book to alter the rubric for private baptism.[16] Thus the 1604 version of the rubric read:

> The Pastors and Curates shall often admonish the people, that they defer not the Baptisme of Infants any longer than the Sunday, or

---

14 See, for instance, W. Whitgift, *The Defence of the Aunswere to the Admonition against the Replie of T.C.*, London, 1574, Tract IX 'Of the Communion-Book', pp. 503–11, and R. Hooker, *Lawes of Ecclesiastical Politie* V:62:16, in W. S. Hill (ed.), *The Folger Library edition of the works of Richard Hooker*, 6 vols, Cambridge, MA: 1977–1993 (hereafter FLE, *Lawes*).

15 William Barlow, *The summe and substance of the conference: which it pleased his Excellent Majestie to have with the lords, bishops, and other of his clergie … at Hampton Court, January 14, 1603 [1604]*, London: printed by Iohn Windet, for Mathew Law, 1604, p. 8.

16 Barlow, *Summe and Substance*, pp. 86–7.

other Holy day next after the child be borne, unless upon a great and reasonable cause declared to the Curate, and by him approved. And also they shal warne them, that without great cause, & necessitie, they procure not their children to be baptized at home in their houses. And when great need shall compel them so to doe, then Baptisme shalbe administred in this fashion. First, let the lawfull Minister, and them that be present, call upon God for his grace, and say the Lords Prayer, if time will suffer. And then the childe being named by some one that is present the said lawful Minister shall dip it in water, or power water upon it, saying these words,[17]

Further, the title of the order was altered to read, 'Of them that be baptized in time of necessity, *by the Minister of the Parish, or any other lawful minister that can be procured*', making very clear the change in official Church of England practice.

The doctrinal significance of this amendment was twofold: first, it addressed the particular objection about women administering the sacrament, and second, as Hunt points out, it denied the absolute necessity of baptism to salvation.[18] In this regard it went some way to answering the soteriological problem posed by the existence of such a rite. However, the extent to which this amendment could really be counted as a Puritan success is questionable. The canons issued following the Hampton Court Conference offered robust defences of contested points of Prayer Book practice, most notably of the use of the sign of the cross in the order for public baptism, but made no mention at all of the alteration of the text of the Prayer Book to demand that a minister should conduct private baptisms. Rather, the canons simply reiterated the demand first stated in the Advertisements for Due Order (1566) that the minster is 'not to refuse to christen or bury'.[19] Moreover, the evidence of visitation articles and injunctions of the years following Hampton Court implies that the amendment reflected a change in practice that was already widespread by the latter years of Elizabeth's reign.[20]

17 *The Booke of Common Prayer and administration of the sacraments according to the Rites and Ceremonies of the Church of England*, London, 1605, Riiiv.

18 Hunt, 'Laurence Chaderton', p. 224.

19 Bray (ed.), *The Anglican Canons*, p. 377.

20 The question does not appear in either Richard Bancroft's metropolitical visitation articles for 1605 or Richard Vaughn's for London in the same year, suggesting that the matter was not of immediate practical concern despite the long-running controversies surrounding the Prayer Book provision. See K. Fincham (ed.), *Visitation Articles and Injunctions of the Early Stuart Church*, 2 vols,

Altered conformity

The failure of the Millenary Petitioners has been seen as marking something as a watershed for Puritanism within the Church of England. As works such as the anonymous *Survay of the Booke of Common Prayer* published in Middelburg in 1606 indicate, the Conference did not signal an end to Puritan agitation about the Church of England and her prescribed liturgy. It did, however, constitute the final serious attempt at reform in the pre-Civil War period. The historian of Elizabethan Puritanism, Patrick Collinson, regarded Hampton Court as 'the end of the story' for the Elizabethan style of Protestantism, making clear as it did that there would be no further reformation. Faced with the choice to conform or to leave, most conformed.

By the time of the Hampton Court Conference, there was also another strand of reform beginning to develop within the Church of England. From around 1590, the theological movement that began as avant-garde conformity and matured as Laudianism was gaining traction with a small, but ultimately highly influential, group of churchmen. Their re-imagination of the Elizabethan Settlement, and of the Prayer Book and its worship, served to distance the Church of England from her sister Reformed churches, and would result – eventually – in the development of something which could be called a distinctive 'Anglicanism'.

Of key significance in this conceptual shift was Richard Hooker, who died in 1600, and whom Peter Lake credits with the 'invention of Anglicanism'.[21] Hooker, like other conformist writers of the Elizabethan Church, was concerned to defend the Church of England's retention of episcopacy in face of repeated calls that the English Church should adopt a fully Reformed polity. Hooker's defence of the Church of England was not, however, simply a defence of the status quo, but rather 'a new synthesis of what English Protestant religion ... ought to be'.[22]

In his *Laws of Ecclesiastical Polity* (published in 1600), Hooker sought to demonstrate not only that Presbyterianism was wrong, but also why it was wrong. In so doing, he questioned many of the assumptions of English (and indeed European) Protestant thought, particularly as pertaining to reason, Scripture, the Church, and the relations of these to one another. Hooker rejected the notion – axiomatic to the theological discourse of Reformed Protestantism – that Scripture was

Church of England Record Society, Woodbridge: Boydell Press, 1994 and 1998, vol. 1, pp. 8–10 and 28–38.

21 Lake, *Anglicans and Puritans?*, p. 227.
22 Lake, *Anglicans and Puritans?*, p. 146.

self-authenticating by the Holy Spirit. Rather, he argued, Scripture had been authenticated by the Church, and the message of salvation contained in it could only be understood with the aid of reason. In a move that was remarkable against the polemical backdrop of the sixteenth century, Hooker argued that the Church of Rome, far from being the Church of Antichrist, was a part of the true Church. He could thus draw benefit from the Church of England's discernible continuities with the pre-Reformation past. There was, therefore, no need 'to abolish out of the Church of England all such orders rites and ceremonies as are established in the Church of Rome'.[23] Thus, in Book Five of the *Laws*, in which he discusses the public worship of the Church, Hooker defends such controversial elements of the Prayer Book as the use of the sign of the cross in baptism. Hooker emphasized the value of prayer, and of reading, as opposed to that of preaching only,[24] and in this shift of focus set the tone of avant-garde conformist thinking on the subject, creating space between his theological agenda and that of his Puritan opponents.

Hooker would become vastly much more important for Anglicans in later decades and centuries than he was in the years immediately following his death. However, as his early critics recognized, Hooker changed the parameters of theological debate, developing a way of doing theology and a way of understanding worship that were at a remove from the mainstream of Reformed Christianity.[25] Far more immediately significant than Hooker in the growth of avant-garde conformity was Lancelot Andrewes, who was appointed Dean of Westminster in 1601. He was then bishop first of Ely then of Winchester, and died in 1628. In addition to his own approach to worship and ceremonial, and the reinterpretation of the Prayer Book that his writings (particularly his private ones) express, Andrewes's importance lies in his patronage for this new generation of churchmen, including John Buckeridge, John Cosin and William Laud.[26]

---

23 FLE, *Lawes* 4:4.3.

24 FLE, *Lawes* 5:22.6.

25 Hooker's views invited immediate criticism in *A Christian Letter*, published anonymously in Middelburg but written by the Puritan Andrew Willett. This in turn provoked a response by William Covel, *A Just and Temperate Defence of the Five Books of Ecclesiastical Polity written by M. Richard Hooker*, London, 1603. For a discussion of the debate, see Peter Lake, 'Business as Usual? The Immediate Reception of Hooker's *Ecclesiastical Polity*', *Journal for Ecclesiastical History* 52 (2001), pp. 456–86.

26 Peter McCullough's essay in this volume explores Andrewes's importance for the Prayer Book in detail. For his importance in the growth of avant-garde conformity, see Peter Lake, 'Lancelot Andrewes, John Buckeridge, and Avant-

The rise of avant-garde conformity within the Church of England has been well documented, as have the ceremonial policies that provoked such reaction after the accession of Charles I in 1625, and especially once William Laud was appointed Archbishop of Canterbury.[27] This provided the opportunity for Laud, Cosin, Matthew Wren and their associates to seek to impose upon the whole Church of England the ideas and practices with which they had experimented more or less privately since the early 1600s. Laud had tried out his policy of setting communion tables altar-wise and beautifying them when he became Dean of Gloucester in 1616, while Cosin's refurbishment of Peterhouse chapel in Cambridge gave full expression to Laudian aesthetic ideals.[28] Avant-garde conformists exploited the structures left over in England from the pre-Reformation Church, most particularly the system of cathedrals and their pattern of worship, and used these to re-imagine what English Protestantism should look like. Visitation articles and injunctions issued by avant-garde conformist and Laudian bishops indicate the extent to which they were concerned to ensure conformity to the Prayer Book, but it was their attempts to change the shape of conformity that proved so divisive in the Laudian Church.

A good example of this is in the arguments that surrounded the 'churching of women'. The Prayer Book provision for this had never been uncontroversial. Cranmer changed the title of the order from 1549 ('The Purification of Women after Childbirth, commonly called the Churching of Women') to 'The Thanksgiving of Women after Child Birth, commonly called the Churching of Women'. Altered also was one rubric reflecting the reformation of church architecture that occurred in the course of Edward's reign: the 1549 text had required that the woman come into the church and 'kneel down in some convenient place, nigh unto the quire door';[29] in 1552 she 'shall come into the church, and there shall kneel down in some convenient place, nigh unto the place where the table standeth'.[30] David Cressy interpreted

Garde Conformity at the Court of James I', in Linda Levy Peck (ed.), *The Mental World of the Jacobean Court*, Cambridge: Cambridge University Press, 1991, pp. 113–33.

27 K. Fincham and N. Tyacke, *Altars Restored: The Changing Face of English Religious Worship, 1547–c.1700*, Oxford: Oxford University Press, 2007.

28 Fincham and Tyacke, *Altars Restored*, pp. 115–16 and 230–1.

29 *The booke of the common praier and administracion of the Sacramentes and other rites and ceremonies of the Churche: after the vse of the Churche of Englande*, London: Richard Grafton, March 1549, Ee8r.

30 *The boke of common praier, and [ad]ministracion of the sacramentes,*

this change in location as transforming the role of the woman in the service,[31] but this is mistaken: the transformation had already taken place in the first Prayer Book and the two rubrics refer to more or less the same location in the church building. The change in title in the 1552 order reflected the way in which Cranmer had already re-imagined the service from one of purification to one of thanksgiving, and the order was carried through without further change in the 1559 and 1604 versions of the Prayer Book. It is interesting to note, *en passant*, that the churching of women is one of the few places in the Prayer Book where the priest is expressly permitted to use words other than those provided, should pastoral circumstance require as much.

Despite the thoroughgoing way in which the order had been reformed, critics regarded the churching of women as one of those 'peces of poperie' of which they wanted to see the Prayer Book purged, and it was a recurrent source of dispute at parish level. In an anonymous polemical work (which objected to much more about the Prayer Book than 'churching') published in Middelburg in 1601, and cast as a dialogue between a woman and 'a chauncelor', the woman says she would not submit herself to churching '[b]ecause I would be loth to shew my selfe either Iew or Papist'.[32] The order itself was rejected by many as 'superstitious', and a cause of particular objection was that it remained purification by another name, and that the proof of this lay in the customary requirement that, as the *Admonition* put it, the woman must 'come covered with a vayle, as ashamed of some folly'.[33]

The Laudian approach to the order would hardly have done much to address these concerns. The Prayer Book had never demanded that the woman wear a veil, but this was a matter of widely held custom, and one that was rather old-fashioned by the early seventeenth century when veils no longer formed part of women's headdress. In his injunctions of 1636 for his diocese of Norwich, Matthew Wren ordered

That the woman to be churched come and kneel at a side near the communion table without the rail, being veiled according to the cus-

and other rites and ceremonies in the Churche of Englande, London: Richard Grafton, 1552, Riv.

31 D. Cressy, 'Purification, Thanksgiving and the Churching of Women in Post-Reformation England', *Past and Present* 141 (November 1993), pp. 106–46, esp. p. 119.

32 *Certaine questions by way of conference betwixt a chauncelor and a kinswoman of his concerning the churching of women*, Middelburg, 1601, p. 7.

33 Field and Wilcox, *Admonition*, Ciiir.

tom, and not covered with a hat; or otherwise not to be churched but presented at the next generals.[34]

Through insisting on the veil, the Laudian hierarchy alienated women who would otherwise have been content to be churched: those who were well within conformist bounds in earlier decades, now found themselves counted, with Puritan activists, as beyond the establishment pale. When the contentious question of the veil was combined with a requirement to kneel at a controversial altar rail, it must indeed have seemed that Puritan suspicions about the Prayer Book were proved right. It is interesting that in the 1662 Prayer Book, the controversial veil was demanded while the other major cause of contention in the ceremony – the reading of Psalm 121 – was removed.

'Laud's Liturgy': the Prayer Book of 1637

The Millenary Petitioners of 1603 had hoped to see a convergence of the English and Scottish churches. The final episode in this chapter explores another attempt at the same aim, though in a rather different direction and with very different results. Laudians had long looked back with yearning to the earliest stages of the English Reformation – to the Prayer Book of 1549 and also to the texts of the later Henrician Church. In his first set of 'Notes' on the Prayer Book, published in 1619, Cosin presented 1549 as something of a golden moment in the sixteenth-century Reformation. In a really very odd passage in which he discusses the committal of the corpse, Cosin has the following to say:

> *The earth shall be cast upon the body by some standing by.* In King Edward's first Service-book it was here ordered, that the priest should cast earth upon the corpse. And though it be here altered more for respect of the priest's office, which was thought too high a function to take the grave-digger's spade in his hand, yet the custom prevails in most places at this day, and still the priest uses to cast earth upon the corpse, before the clerk or sexton meddles with it. No great fault, were it but to keep out that unchristian fancy of the puritans, that would have no minister to bury their dead ... [35]

34 Fincham (ed.), *Visitation Articles and Injunctions*, vol. 2, p. 158.
35 J. Cosin, *The Works of the Right Reverend Father in God John Cosin now first collected*, 5 vols, Oxford, Library of Anglo-Catholic Theology, 1843–55, vol. V, pp. 169–70.

Cosin makes the astonishing claim that the change in the rubric was not due to the desire to 'remove the corpse' from the funeral service, but rather to increase the status of the priest. This liturgical revisionism not only reflects Cosin's own devotional interest, but serves a polemical purpose – he is unable to resist taking a swipe at his 'Puritan' opponents, dismissing their views as 'unchristian fancy'. Continuing from his disparaging comments about those Puritans who 'would have no minister to bury the dead', he says:

> And this rubric, appointing the earth to be cast upon the body by some standing by, hath given them occasion to plead for it, that there is no need of any priest at a burial, that he is not a minister ordained for the dead, but for the living ... as if when a man is once dead, he belonged no more to the communion of saints or the mystical Body of Christ.[36]

For the same reason, he regrets that the celebration of Holy Communion following a burial was removed from the second Prayer Book. Commenting on the Collect, he says he can see no disadvantage in reviving the old custom and thereby showing 'that our Church is not ruled by Calvin'. For Cosin (and in line with Hooker's understanding), antiquity confers authority, and the Puritan critics of the Prayer Book are setting up false dichotomies in assuming that everything that is not explicitly warranted by Scripture is perforce 'popish and superstitious'.

It was these understandings that informed the Prayer Book known as 'Laud's Liturgy', but in whose formation Cosin and Wren were instrumental, which was introduced into the Scottish Church in 1637. Revision of the worship of the Scottish Church had been ongoing since the latter part of James's reign, and had proved controversial when in 1618 the General Assembly promulgated the Five Articles of Perth. These upheld confirmation by bishops, celebration of holy days, private baptism, private communion, and kneeling at the communion.[37] While these had proved controversial, the reaction to the Prayer Book of 1637 was violent, leading in 1638 to the formation of the Solemn League and Covenant against the Prayer Book, and ultimately to the outbreak of war.

The 1637 text drew heavily on that of 1549, especially – and controversially – in the order for Communion. Here, the institution narrative was renamed 'the prayer of consecration' and was followed imme-

---

36 *Works of Cosin* V, p. 168.

37 For an account of these liturgical revisions, see Spinks, *Sacraments, Ceremonies, and the Stuart Divines*, pp. 57–60.

diately by the prayer of oblation or thanksgiving. The manual acts from the Edwardian 'Black Rubric' were included, and the words of administration returned to the version of 1549.[38] The Laudian hierarchy attempted to impose in Scotland the liturgical revision they wished to see in England, and the attempt failed dramatically, at least in the short term. The theology of consecration articulated in the 1637 Book found expression in 1662, while the order of Communion based on that of 1549 would inform nineteenth- and twentieth-century attempts at Prayer Book reform.

Conclusion

By the turn of the seventeenth century England was a largely Protestant country, with a developing sense of a distinctively English Protestant identity. This was due in no small part to the effect of decades of worship in conformity to the Book of Common Prayer, and to the State and occasional prayers with which the Book was supplemented. But that version of Protestantism – what worship should look like, and where the Church of England stood in relation to Reformed Protestant Europe – remained contested ground. This is reflected in the attempts at Prayer Book revision and the diverse ways in which the Settlement of Religion was re-imagined during the reigns of James I and Charles I. The words of the Prayer Book had, in Eamon Duffy's resonant words, 'entered and possessed the minds' of English Protestants, becoming 'the fabric of their prayer, the utterance of their most solemn and vulnerable moments'.[39] When the Three Kingdoms collapsed into conflict in the middle of the seventeenth century, and the Prayer Book was proscribed in England and replaced with the *Directory for the Public Worship of God* (the 'New Directory'), it continued nevertheless to be widely used, and ordinary parishioners petitioned for its return.[40] Despite the controversies of the Laudian Church, the Prayer Book remained the basis of the religious identities and doctrinal understandings of the conformist parishioners of early modern England.

---

38 *The book of common prayer, and administration of the sacraments and other parts of divine service for the use of the Church of Scotland*, Edinburgh, 1637, N5r – N7v. The best account of the history of the 1637 Book remains G. Donaldson, *The Making of the Scottish Prayer Book of 1637*, Edinburgh: Edinburgh University Press, 1954.

39 Duffy, *Stripping of the Altars*, p. 593.

40 See Judith Maltby, *Prayer Book and People in Elizabethan and Early Stuart England*, Cambridge: Cambridge University Press, 1998.

4

Absent Presence

Lancelot Andrewes and 1662

PETER MCCULLOUGH

Lancelot Andrewes left behind perhaps the closest thing to a working critique of the 1559 Book of Common Prayer that was written not as public polemic, but as private notes about how he actually used it liturgically. These are his 'Notes on the Book of Common Prayer', first printed with other notes, principally by John Cosin, in William Nicholls's 1710 *Comment on the Book of Common Prayer*. Nicholls was working with one of four transcriptions of Andrewes's own notes now known today. Those that survive are, first, that made by Cosin in his heavily annotated 1619 copy of the Prayer Book, now known as 'The Durham Book'; second, a copy discovered by Archbishop Tenison among papers belonging to Laud, now still at Lambeth; and third, a copy found in a 1625 Prayer Book, now in the British Library.[1] All four attest that they were copied, as Cosin put it, 'out of my Lord of Winchester's, Bishop Andrewes', Service Book, written with his own hand'. In the nineteenth century Nicholls's printed text was collated with the manuscripts for the final volume of Andrewes's *Works* in the Library of Anglo-Catholic Theology.[2] It is from this text, which records all variants between the copies, that I will quote in this chapter. As for the date of the notes as originally written by Andrewes, the 1619 printing date of what became Cosin's 'Durham Book' is a rough guide. But since many of the annotations refer explicitly to Andrewes's practice in an episcopal chapel, they could date from as early as 1609, when Andrewes took up residence in Ely House in Holborn, with its fine medieval chapel (now St Etheldreda's, Ely Place). But they could just as

---

1 G. J. Cuming (ed.), *The Durham Book*, London: Oxford University Press, 1961; British Library, MS Harley 7311/7; Lambeth Palace Library MS 943/23.

2 Oxford: John Henry Parker, 1854, pp. 141–58; hereafter *Notes*.

easily derive from his successive episcopal chapel at Winchester House in Southwark, which he occupied in 1619.

Andrewes evidently annotated only four parts of his 1559 Prayer Book: the prefatory matter, Morning Prayer, the Litany, and the Holy Communion. This immediately shows Andrewes's preference for what he called in his sermons 'Full Service' or 'Great Service', where the three are part of one whole, Matins and Litany being in effect only preparative parts of the Eucharist. As one would expect from jottings, there are variations among the notes in both purpose and character. What is clear is that they were not private devotional or meditative glosses, on the model of his well-known *Preces Privatae*.[3] A minority might be called interpretative or historical glosses, such as the observation that the Litany's petitions for travellers, women in childbirth, the sick, children, prisoners and captives shows how *'affectionate mother church* ['Ecclesia pia mater'] *calls to mind the seven persons which are called in the statutes "miserabiles"'*, an antiquarian note that roots the Litany to the earliest Roman and then ecclesiastical law courts and their fundamental jurisdiction to protect the *personae miserabiles*.[4]

Another type is documentary proofs for those components of the service that were perennially objected to by more advanced reformers; their scholarly polemical weight is increased by being uniformly in Latin. So next to the *Gloria Patri* appended to the Lord's Prayer in Morning Prayer comes the tart proof, 'the Doxology was prescribed and retained by the holy fathers of the past against the poison of the Arians. Consult Hooker.'[5] Some of Andrewes's proofs for contested prayer book forms are scriptural. He marginally buttresses priestly absolution, for example, with citation of no fewer than five Old Testament and one New Testament texts.[6] Scripture comes to Andrewes's

---

3 Two exceptions only prove that rule, and they are directly related to the *Preces*: a schematic Latin paraphrase of the petitions of the Lord's Prayer (which also appears copied into Laud's private devotions); and a set of paralleled expansions or, rather, intensifications of clauses in the Confession at Morning Prayer (*Notes*, pp. 149–50). These, clearly, could have no public liturgical function.

4 'Ecclesia pia mater in hoc versiculo, septem personas, quas vocant canonici mizerabiles, commemorat, dignasque existimat duplice privilegio, viz.: solenni publicarum precum intercessione et carnium esu tempore quadragesimali' (*Notes*, p. 152).

5 'Doxologia a sanctis olim patribus contra virus Arianum praescripta et retenta. Consule Hookerum' (*Notes*, p. 150).

6 Ezek. 33.12; Job 33.23; Num. 6.24; 2 Sam. 12.13; John 20.23; the last of these ('Whose-soever sinnes ye remitt, they are remitted unto them') having been his text for what was, upon its delivery at court in 1600, a controversial sermon

aid too for some church furnishings and fittings, such as justifying the use for the Litany of a faldstool in the midst of the church with the note, 'See Joel [2.17], Let the Priests, the ministers of the Lord wepe betwene the porche & the altar, and let them say, Spare thy people, o Lord.'[7]

But for all of his annotations, the single most common documentary source is ancient conciliar authority, and that of a particular kind – one council, in fact, and that an obscure one, the Council of Laodicea. Although the date of such a council can only be inferred on the basis of shaky internal evidence (Andrewes uses the then accepted date of 368), its so-called canons had been incorporated in all the medieval and early modern compilations and accreted the usual commentaries and glosses. They are of particular interest to Andrewes here because of the number of excursus on choir offices, worship, vestments and the minor orders.[8] These are significant because many of the notes that we will encounter in further detail are striking for their Eastern Orthodox cast. When Andrewes was thinking liturgically, he did so eastward-facing, to ecumenical councils, Eastern liturgies, and even Eastern fittings. This is not just a case, though, of the familiar Reformed strategy of using anything but things Roman, but also what seems to me to be an instinctive, personal sympathy and preference. Indicative of this, particularly in his notes for the Holy Communion, Andrewes not only adds marginal section headings for the major parts of the liturgy (something not ventured in English prayer books until 1928, and familiar now in *Common Worship*), but he does so not in English or Latin, but Greek.[9] The extent to which this Eastern orientation meant that Andrewes in some degree turned his back on the 1549 Book of Common Prayer and the Sarum Rite – those two liturgies usually taken to be the direction of travel followed by Laudian revisers like Cosin in 1662 – is something I want to

which Laud emphatically titled in his posthumous edition of Andrewes, 'Of the Power of Absolution'; see *XCVI Sermons*, London, 1629, part 2, 49–65.

7 'Vide Prophetam Joel, de medio loco inter porticum et altare, ubi sacerdotes et prophetae ingemere et ingeminare ussi, Parce, Domine, Parce populo tuo' (*Notes*, pp. 149–50); I use here and elsewhere Geneva (1560) for biblical translations.

8 Henry Percival (ed.), *The Seven Ecumenical Councils*, Nicene and Post-Nicene Fathers, Series II, vol. 14, New York; Charles Scribner's Sons, 1916, pp. 123–44; hereafter cited by canon number.

9 So, for example, 'Hymn', 'Intercession', 'Confession', 'Absolution', 'Sursum Corda', are respectively Ὑμνολογία, Ὑπερέντευξις, Εξομολόγησις, Απολυτικον', and Ανάσχωμεν τας καρδίας (*Notes*, pp. 154, 157, 158).

trace in Andrewes's more substantive notes, and something that I think distances him from Cosin.

In fact, because Andrewes's notes are best known from Cosin's incorporation of them into his 'Durham Book', Andrewes's tracks have been somewhat covered over in prayer book scholarship by the younger man's. Cosin is often credited for proposals for, or even changes in, the 1662 Book that were not his ideas at all, but rather Andrewes's, by innocently using as annotational shorthand Cosin's 'Durham Book', where Andrewes lurks. Calling attention to this is not just a case of Andrewes's biographer keeping score by correcting attributions in Andrewes's favour. Rather, I hope that it is a worthwhile exercise in seeing how a scion of the Established Church – properly viewed as an arch-conformist disciplinarian, and a full two generations (40 years) older than Cosin – took a surprisingly flexible view of his Church's official formularies. And, further, that Andrewes's posthumous liturgical influence perhaps flowed not so much back into England in 1662, as into Scotland in 1637 and from thence – as his former pupil George Herbert put it – stood 'tip-toe in our land, / Ready to pass to the American strand'.[10]

Appropriately enough, one of the first of Andrewes's notes offers an epitome of his views on liturgical change. This is a matter of coincidence rather than design, as it is prompted by the prefatory 'Of Ceremonies, why some be abolished, and some retained', which dates from 1552 – specifically, the complaint that 'some be so newfangled, that they would innovate all things, and so despise the old, that nothing can like them, but that is new'.[11] Here one might expect the disciplinarian Andrewes, T. S. Eliot's idol for 'style and order', to, if anything, express emphatic agreement against innovators and innovation. But what he writes in the margin here is exactly the opposite; in two terse, numbered points, he gives an apologia for innovation:

(i) It is not said to be an innovation if it is simply made better, whether by alteration or addition.

---

10 George Herbert, 'The Church Militant' (ll. 235–6); *The Works of George Herbert*, ed. F. E. Hutchinson, Oxford: Clarendon Press, 1941, p. 196. Cosin was born in 1595, by which time Andrewes was not only 40, but also a senior residentiary at St Paul's, a royal chaplain, and DD.

11 *The Book of Common Prayer: The Texts of 1549, 1559, and 1642*, ed. Brian Cummings, Oxford: Oxford University Press, 2011, p. 215. Subsequent reference to the English Prayer Books (BCP) are from this edition unless otherwise specified.

(ii) That alteration which ruins well-placed things and does not perfect them is certainly schismatical innovation.[12]

Together these injunctions, one positive and one negative, assert the
worth of innovation, if of a specific kind, which might be boiled down
to an approving of alteration and addition, but not of excision. All
of Andrewes's subsequent notes fit exactly these principles: things
are added, or freely interpreted in a manner that Andrewes believes
strengthens or perfects what is already there, but he will not delete,
or otherwise 'ruin well-placed things'. These principles resonate with
Andrewes's views on the Reformation generally as found throughout
the sermons. His broad insistence that reform had gone far enough by
1559 might seem commensurate with Elizabeth I's own conservatism,
so aptly summed in her motto *Semper Eadem*, 'always the same'. But
Andrewes was willing to take one further step by holding that, even
with respect to the Queen and her 1559 Settlement, things had actually
gone a bit too far. As early as his 1590 doctoral thesis – which argued
that tithes were due to the clergy *jure divino*, unheard of since the reign
of Philip and Mary – he asserted that although the Henrician Reformation had not necessarily been wrong to dissolve monasteries and
chantries, it had behaved scandalously in appropriating their wealth to
the Crown and the laity instead of the Church. So, in that sense, Henrician alteration (and continuing Elizabethan impropriations) 'ruined a
well-placed thing', and missed a chance to perfect it.

In the commencement sermon related to his doctoral thesis, Andrewes
deployed the first surviving example of his lifelong attraction to Mary
Magdalen's anointing of Christ as a consummate model for how to
'anoint' or show love to the Church. Mary Magdalen's and the Church's
enemy were, he said, 'certaine *Court-Rattes* who would persuade
... *That CHRISTS head* [that is, the Church] *might be well enough
without Ointment*'. And that only those like Judas and the grumbling
disciples would ask, '*Utquid perditio haec? To what purpose is this
waste?*'[13] Three years later, before Elizabeth herself and her whole
court, Andrewes preached an entire Lent sermon on Judas' insidious

---

12 '(i.) Non est innovatio dicenda, si quid in melius simpliciter, seu altera-
tione, seu adjectione fiat. S. Ambr. lib. ii. de Officiis. (ii.) Alteratio, enim illa est
schismatica innovatio, quae bene posita destruit, non perficit' (*Notes*, p. 147).
The attribution of the first to Ambrose's *De Officiis* has stumped all editors, and
seems a red herring.
13 Lancelot Andrewes, *Selected Sermons and Lectures*, ed. Peter McCullough,
Oxford: Oxford University Press, 2005, p. 83.

question about waste and Christ's stern defence of Mary Magdalen's good work. In it he turned his guns on those who would reform Christ's body by taking things away while at the same time sneering at those who only wished, out of love, to add some little something to it, as in this passage, where all puns on 'reformed' were very much intended:

> The case is like, when they, that have wasted many pounds, complaine of that penny wast which is done on CHRIST's body, *the Church*. Or, when they, that in their whole dealings (all the world sees) are vn-reformed, seriously consult, how to reforme the *Church* ... GOD helpe us, when *Judas* must reforme *Mary Magdalen*.

Although Andrewes was there pressing against Elizabethan Erastianism, and the English Reformed tendency, as he saw it, to take away from, rather than add to, the Church, he was too much of a pragmatist to think that he could, in one argumentative step, turn Tudor Judases stuffing their money bags into pre-Reformation Mary Magdalens lavishing their boxes of ointment on the Church. So instead he appropriated (not, I think, without irony) Elizabeth's own mantra of doing neither, but just keeping things the same, as a kind of bare minimum, a position he found in no lesser authority than Christ's rebuke of Judas: '*Sinite illam*; Leave her alone.' Then, by implication calling to mind the pre-Reformation Church, he said,

> That, what our *Fathers* and *Elders* in the CHRISTIAN *Faith* bounteously employed on CHRIST; what they (I say) have that way dedicate, if we will not add to it and imitate them, yet we will let it alone, and not trouble them; and at least be not with *Judas*, if we like not or list not to be with *Mary Magdalen*.

He then pressed to the pointed summary:

> This (I say) under correction, is, as me thinketh, not unreasonable; that seeing, what superstition hath defiled, is removed and gone; touching that which is remaining, it be sayd, *Sinite illam* [Leave her alone].[14]

Andrewes's approach to liturgical change is precisely analogous to that he took to Mary Magdalen and her impulse to anoint Christ's body, the Church. At a minimum, Mary was to be left to her free-will gifts and

---

14 Andrewes, *XCVI Sermons*, pp. 289, 292.

good works, with no obligation for others to do the same if they were satisfied with the status quo. But of course, as the sermon proceeded, that was not to be Andrewes's final or ideal position. Rather, he said, 'the next and kindliest way, to have *Judas'* complaint redressed, is, to speake and labour, that *Marie Magdalen's* example may be followed'. So leaving things as they were was not a preferred option. Nor was innovation that beautifies – that enriches, that strengthens the Church – only just to be indulged. It was to be followed, 'not as *sufferable* onely, but as *commendable'*. And, incidentally, given the oft-remarked oddity that Mary Magdalen disappeared from the Calendar as a proper feast in 1552, only to reappear as such in the twentieth century, Andrewes's concluding commendations of her – 'In heaven ... *Marie Magdalen* shall looke cheerefully on Him, on whom she bestowed', and 'Yea, when the great and glorious acts of many *Monarchs* shall be buried in silence, this poore box of *Nardus* shall be matter of praise, and never die' – seem to me a glancing but pointed rebuke of her omission.[15]

Before leaving the 1559 prefatory matter, Andrewes paused to comment extensively on two things. First, he marshalled Laodicean canons to insist that Evening Prayer be kept on Saturdays, and then to expand, at even greater length, on the priest's obligation to promulgate not just saints' days, but also vigil fasts before them. In a 'rationale for vigils and feasts', Andrewes pointed out that since the commemoration of a saint or martyr was kept on the day of their glorification, it was appropriate then on the day before to commemorate 'by spending time in fasting, vigil, and prayers' how they 'suffered' in the days before their glorification. Andrewes went on in a further excursus to say that there should be neither vigils nor fasting preceding either Michael and All Angels or any saints' days which fell in Christmastide, Eastertide or Whitsuntide. As precedent for vigil fasts, he cited how they were 'brought into use by the Church and to us by statute'.[16] But vigil fasts are difficult to find in any of the Tudor canons, articles or official homilies, with the possible exception of Edward VI's 1547 proclamation calling for fasting 'upon fridays and saturdays, and the tyme commonly called Lent, and other accustomed times'. Vigil fasts were certainly not marked in the calendar in either 1552 or 1559 – but, following Andrewes's rota to the letter, were secured by Cosin for 1662, and supported by his 'Table of the Vigils, Fasts, and days of Abstinence', which did not appear first, as

---

15 Andrewes, *XCVI Sermons*, pp. 292, 298.
16 *Notes*, pp. 147–8.

usually said, in Cosin's *Devotions* of 1627, but at least a decade earlier in Andrewes's notes.[17]

Andrewes's first intervention in the actual text of a service comes at the beginning of Morning Prayer, with the explicit instruction before the opening sentences, 'Add to this place, because for an invitation to penitence they are admirable encomia of mercy and long-suffering, Ps. 78.38, Jer. 3.7. 12; Heb. 4' (probably v. 8, or v. 10).[18] There then follow six further sentences of Scripture, only one of which is appointed by the Prayer Book. That one (Luke 15.18), together with the first three, is representative of all of Andrewes's alternatives here in that they stress either the act of confession itself, or are, as he says, 'encomia of mercy and long-suffering', rather than the slightly more penal admonitions of some of the Prayer Book sentences. And that this was a feeling that anticipated that of later revisers like Cosin, Sanderson and Taylor is seen in their having taken some of the penal sting out of 1559's 1 John 1.8 ('If we saye that we have no synne, we deceyve ourselves, and there is no truthe in us') by adding to it v. 9 ('But, if we confess our sins, he is faithful and just to forgive us our sins, and to cleanse us from all unrighteousness').

It is at the end of the Litany, however, when Andrewes's notes become most interesting, because most innovative. And it is here too that we encounter proof that the largest proportion of the notes were designed to be put into practice, because they here become ceremonial instructions – written in the third person and the present tense, and read like a set of instructions for the succession of domestic chaplains who would have officiated in Andrewes's chapel, one of whom, not insignificantly, was Matthew Wren, a key figure in the revisions for 1662. It is crucial then to read the ceremonial notes alongside the annotated plan of Andrewes's chapel at Winchester House, found among Laud's papers after his arrest, used against him at his trial, and lavishly engraved for polemical use in William Prynne's *Canterburies doome* (illus., p. 62).[19] This is well known to scholars, and has been frequently

---

17 See Cummings (ed.), *BCP*, pp. 235, 756; Cuming (ed.), *Durham Book*, pp. 48–55.

18 'Add huc, quod ad invitandam poenitentiam egregia sunt misericordieae et longanimitatis encomia' (*Notes*, p. 148).

19 William Prynne, *Canterburies doome, or … the commitment, charge, tryall, condemnation, execution of William Laud*, London, 1646, pp. 122–5. See Nicholas Tyacke, 'Lancelot Andrewes and the Myth of Anglicanism', in Peter Lake and Michael Questier (eds), *Conformity and Orthodoxy in the English Church, c. 1560–1660*, Woodbridge: Boydell, 2000, pp. 5–33 (25–7); and Kenneth Fincham and Nicholas Tyacke, *Altars Restored: The Changing Face of English Religious*

cited as the paradigm for 'Laudian' fittings like the raised and railed altar, candles, incense and pictorial tapestries. But pairing it with the notes on the Prayer Book can I think tell us much more about what Andrewes was up to.

According to the key to the plan, seating in the body of the chapel was as one would expect in a cathedral choir or college chapel: the bishop in a return stall at the west end, across from him in the return stall on the *cantoris* side 'the chaplains seat where he readeth service' (that is, Morning or Evening Prayer), and as we've already seen, for the Litany, 'The Priest goeth from out of his seat into the body of the church, and (at a low desk ... called the fald-stool) kneels and says or sings the Litany.'[20] Two facing 'formes', simple stalls or even benches against the north and south walls, accommodated 'the familie', or members of the household.

But Andrewes's note at the end of the Litany takes us out of the realm of the usual; it needs to be considered part by part. First, '[*At the end of the Litany.*] Here the Minister riseth, and if there be a sermon an Introit is sung.'[21] Music ('an Introit is sung') should not surprise us; anthems sandwiching the sermon (to cover the progress to and from the pulpit) was common cathedral and royal chapel practice, here achieved by an introit sung from the 'music table' while the preacher processed to the pulpit. What is surprising here, though, is Andrewes's placement of the sermon after the Litany, and not after the Creed within the Holy Communion. In a lengthy later note on the Communion rite, he gives his justification for doing so. He acknowledges that 'after the end of the first part of the Liturgy (anciently called the Mass of the Catechumens) it is now our custom to have the sermon', but goes on to point out that 'the form of the rite which is to be celebrated comprises the third element of those which follow on from the sermon', and 'correctly, the sermon should be delivered before the Eucharist'. He then looks longingly back to the days of the 'ancient and primitive Church', when 'the sermon was held first thing in the morning' and all-comers were admitted; after the sermon they were dismissed for the second part, the Mass of the Catechumens, who were themselves in turn dismissed, leaving

---

Worship, 1547–c.1700, Oxford: Oxford University Press, 2007, p. 254. According to modern archaeology, the chapel interior measured 20m × 11.2m; see Derek Seeley, Christopher Phillpotts and Mark Samuel, *Winchester Palace: Excavations at the Southward Residence of the Bishops of Winchester*, London: Museum of London Archaeology Service and English Heritage, 2006, p. 27.

20 *Notes*, p. 151.
21 *Notes*, p. 152.

only the baptized for the Eucharist. All of which, his note concludes, 'is manifestly given according to the order of canon 19 of the Council of Laodicea'. The majority of this lengthy note was also retailed in Andrewes's Gunpowder Plot court sermon of 1615:

> It is well knowne, that, all the time of the Primitive Church, the Sermon was ever done, before the *Service* begun. And that, to the Sermon, Heathen men, Infidels, and Iewes, Hereticks, Schismatikes, *Energumeni, Catechumeni, Poenitentes, Competentes, Audientes*, all these, all sorts of people were admitted: But, when they went to service, when the *Liturgie* began, all these were voyded; not one of them suffered to stay.

But why did this matter to Andrewes in a household and in a wider culture where all adults present would have been baptized Christians? It was because the sermon was, always and emphatically for Andrewes, the most inferior part of Christian worship; so its runaway popularity with his contemporaries was to him an appalling inversion of priorities, or as he put it in the 1615 sermon,

> It were strange, that, that should be the onely, or the chiefe Service of GOD [with us], whereat, they which were held no servants of GOD, no part of the Church, might and did remaine no lesse freely, then they that were.[22]

He tried to rectify that in his own chapel by segregating sermon from Eucharist, something which even Cosin and the Restoration Laudians couldn't dare suggest, keeping as they did the rubric for sermon after the Creed at the Eucharist.

Andrewes's ceremonial note for the transition from Litany and sermon to Eucharist then continues thus: 'after the sermon they ascend with three adorations towards the Altar'; 'they' refers to the celebrant and a second minister, either deacon or priest. 'If', the note continues, 'both be priests, the one at one end, the other at the other, representing the two Cherubims at the mercy-seat: if one be but a Deacon, he kneels at the door.' This takes us into the *sacrarium* or sanctuary of Andrewes's chapel – behind a rail (consistently called in the notes and plan a 'septum') with a central gate (always called a 'door'). Keeping in mind that it was common parochial practice for the laity to enter a chancel for communion, the segregation of this space was not just for clergy, but

---

22 Andrewes, *XCVI Sermons*, p. 992.

even among them leaving deacons outside the rails is emphatic, and again is supported by quotation of Laodicea Canon 19 ('it is lawful to the priesthood alone to go to the Altar'). The plan specifies that the septum stood above 'two ascents', and the altar itself upon 'a footpace with two Ascents of Deal' – so, the sacred ministers' three 'Adorations' en route presumably being made at the bottom of the steps to the rail, at the bottom of the altar footpace, and then finally at the top in front of the altar. Bowing before a railed altar is now well known as a staple of Laudian ceremonial. So what strikes me most in this description is Andrewes's specification that once they arrive at the altar, the clergy stand at its north and south ends 'representing the two Cherubims at the mercy-seat'. Scripturally, of course, this takes us to the description of the Ark of the Covenant (illustrated in the Geneva Bible) with its 'Merciseat of pure golde', surmounted by 'two Cherubims of golde ... and the Cherubims shal stretch their wings on hie, covering the Merciseat with their wings, & their faces one to an other: to the Merciseat ward shal the faces of the Cherubims be' (Ex. 25.17–20). But liturgically, this takes us straight to Eastern Orthodoxy, where during the priests' entrance rite is sung the 'Cherubic Hymn', which begins, 'We, who in a mystery represent the Cherubim'; and where the altar area behind the iconostasis, restricted only to priests, is called the Holy of Holies, and the altar conceived as an explicit anti-type to the Mercy Seat over the Ark of the Covenant. Placing his sacred ministers in imitation of the Judeo-Eastern Orthodox cherubs is Andrewes's tidy solution to the perceived awkwardness of the Prayer Book requirement for the celebrant to stand at the north end of the altar. The priest's northward position is here snatched away from being anything like a host at a domestic table, presiding at a Genevan Lord's Supper. Rather, he and his ministerial partner are cherubs hovering over the body and blood that is the new covenant's mercy seat. So Andrewes told the court congregation in his 1620 Easter sermon that the 'two Angels, in white, sitting, the one at the head, the other at the feet, where the body of Jesus had lien' (John 10.12), 'may well referre to *Christ* himselfe, whose body was the true Arke indeed ... and is therefore heere betweene two *Angels*, as was the *Arke* (the type of it) *betweene the two Cherubims*'.[23] This Eastern iconography, though, while preserving a vivid doctrine of real presence, also subtly protects Protestant anxieties about priestly sacrifice. The Eucharist for Andrewes is sacrificial, there is no doubt, but he prefers, I suggest in a more Eastern way, to think of the priest

---

23 Andrewes, *Selected Sermons*, p. 231.

more as a minister of that sacrifice, which is always and for ever on the Mercy Seat, rather than as one who performs that sacrifice per se, a conception worked out in some detail in a 1598 sermon on Isaiah 6.6 (the seraphin's touching Isaiah's lips with the coal from the altar), where Andrewes explicitly used Chrysostom's Divine Liturgy to argue 'an Analogie and proportion between the Seraphim and the Priests, between the Altar and the Lords Table, between the burning Cole and the Bread and Wine', where just as 'the application of this Cole is by a Seraphin ... the same office that is here executed by an Angell is committed to the sonnes of men'.[24]

The iconography of priests as ministering angels continues in Andrewes's subsequent ceremonial notes, and exploits the vagueness of rubrics in the Prayer Book to add his own movement to an otherwise very stationary liturgy. The 1559 Book implies that the minister kneels with the congregation for the Decalogue, standing thereafter for the Collects of the day and for the sovereign. But Andrewes directs that

> the Priest ... descends to the door of the *Septum*, makes a low adoration towards the Altar; then turns to the people, and standing in the door, readeth the Ten Commandments, as from God, whilst they lie prostrate to the end, as to God speaking.[25]

This is the first of several embassies by the priest or deacon out from the sacrarium to the nave, either to or through the 'door' in the septum, which suggests the characteristic repeated issuings in and out of the iconostasis by an Orthodox deacon. Here with the Decalogue Andrewes conceives again of the priest as God's messenger or spokesman; a cue is there in the Prayer Book's inclusion of the short preamble to the Decalogue ('God spake these words and said'), but Andrewes's instruction on where and how to speak them goes several steps further (literally and metaphorically) than the rubric's, '*Then shall the priest rehearse distinctly all the Ten Commandments*'. And his instruction that the people respond 'as to God speaking' is an intensifying gloss on the Prayer Book's congregational response, 'Lord have mercy upon us, and incline our hearts to keep this law'. The 1662 Book edged only slightly in this direction by requiring that the priest shall, '*turning to the people*' (which implies a stationary priest), '*rehearse distinctly all the Ten Commandments*'. But the 'more explicit' 'performative

---

24 Andrewes, *Selected Sermons*, p. 142.
25 *Notes*, p. 154.

aspects' which Prayer Book commentators find in the Durham Book are Andrewes's, not Cosin's.[26]

Both 1559 and 1662 leave the priest in the same place then to stand for the Collects; but Andrewes sends his officiant back into the sanctuary: 'The minister makes adoration as before, ascends, and genuflects' before reading the Collects from the altar. Then follows the Epistle, which according to the prayer books, 'the priest shall read'. But here again, Andrewes's minister travels: 'Here the other Priest, or if there be none, he that executeth, descendeth to the door, adoreth, and then turning readeth the Epistle and Gospel.' This was done, according to the chapel plan, not just at the chancel steps, but at a raised lectern in the centre of the chapel: 'a footpace on three ascents on which the lectern standeth covered & thereon the great Bible'. And it was here too that the 'musique table' was put to further use, for here stood 'a Triquertrall Censor wherein the Clerks putteth frankincense at the reading of the first lesson' from a 'navicula like the keele of a boat with a halfe cover and a foot out of which the frankencense is poured'. For the Gospel reading, Andrewes put his money where his mouth was in a famous sermon on Philippians 2.10 ('That at the Name of Jesus every knee should bow'), but with an interesting qualification ignored by his acolytes in the 1630s as much as later: 'In the reading of the holy Gospel, and never else, is Adoration made at the name of Jesus; for then only is it in its right exaltation; and then men stand in a posture ready to make reverence.' On the point of standing for the Gospel, Cosin's desire for the same did result in a 1662 rubric, as it did for something else for which Andrewes in fact deserves the credit, and that is the return of the congregation's acclamation at the end of the Gospel, 'Glory to thee O Lord', something 'not peculiar to Cosin' (who asked for it unsuccessfully in 1661) but also found in the 1549 rite and the Scottish Book of 1637. The first to revive it in England was Andrewes, in his direct note 'Ad[d], Laus tibi Domine'.[27] Cosin did have more success in rubricating the congregation's need to stand for the Creed in 1662, but again, this had already made its way into the Scottish Book and that probably from Andrewes's note instructing the celebrant after the Gospel to return from the lectern, 'adore, ascend, and read the Nicene Creed, the people still standing'.[28]

---

26 Cf. Cummings (ed.), *BCP*, pp. 390, 769.

27 *Notes*, p. 154. See Cuming (ed.), *Durham Book*, p. 139.

28 'Adorat, ascendit, et legit Symbolum Nicaenum, populo adhuc stante'; *Notes*, p. 155.

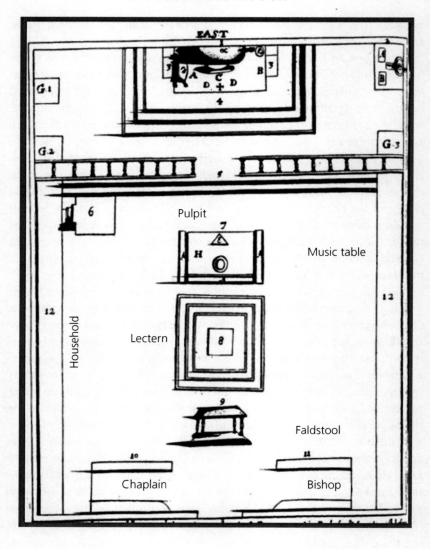

We now approach the part of the Prayer Book Holy Communion that has always drawn the harshest criticism – 1552's removal
of any express instructions for the Offertory, the 'redistribution and
remodelling of the Canon', the 'transposition of the devotions for communicants' to before rather than after the words of institution, and
of course the repositioning of the Gloria as a post-communion hymn.
What Andrewes does here seems to me an almost balletic dance around
his own principles of allowable innovation, where things can only be

added or improved, and nothing taken away. We have already noted that he firmly kept the sermon out of his eucharistic rite, planting it after the Litany. So where 1552 and 1662 have a rubric for the sermon after the Creed, Andrewes ignores it, and instructs his celebrant to bypass the pulpit for the altar in this note: 'the Priest adores. Then he removes the basin from the back of the Altar to the forepart.' Here we must pause. The 1559 rite had at this point followed the sermon with an exhortation to 'remember the poor'; then while the Offertory sentences were read, churchwardens were to collect alms from the congregation and place them 'in the poor men's box'. Cosin, following the Scottish 1637 rite, had in 1661 called successfully for the use of the more comely 'basin', or almsdish, which we find in Andrewes's chapel. Cosin had also fretted in 1661 about the lack of any instruction for how and when to prepare the holy table with the eucharistic gifts. Andrewes offered a model for how to deal with alms and altar at this point by in effect returning a ceremonial, rather than verbal, offertory to the English rite – slipping it into the white space, as it were, left in the 1552/1559 rite. For the celebrant, having reached down the almsdish 'from the back of the altar to the forepart', 'Then the Bishop ascends with treble Adoration, and lastly kneels down at the Altar.' So immediately following the Creed, the bishop voided his stall at the west end, processed the length of the chapel, made his adorations, and knelt at the altar. Thereupon, 'into his hands the Priest from a by-standing table on the south side, reaches first the Wafer bread, in a canister close covered, and lined with linen. 2dly. The Wine in a barrel on a cradle with four feet. These the Bishop offers in the name of the whole congregation, upon the Altar.' Now to be sure, there are touches of 1549 here, with its rubric for 'layeing the breade upon the corporas, or els the paten ... and puttyng the wyne into the Chalice ... and settyng both the breade and wyne upon the Alter'.[29] And Laudians, Ritualists, and Anglo-Catholics have for generations gone weak at the knees over Andrewes's evident revivalism. But I don't think there has been sufficient pause over the Eastern touches that are here, nor upon the liturgical substance of these accidents. For example, the chapel plan notes that the chalice was 'covered with a linnen napkin (called the Aire) embrodered with colored silkes'. According to the *Oxford English Dictionary*, this is the first usage of 'aire' in English, as '*Orthodox Church. A veil used to cover both the chalice and paten during the Liturgy*' ('aer, *n.*'). And more generally, Andrewes is here not just scratching the

---

29 Cummings (ed.), *BCP*, p. 27.

same itch that Cosin would feel to have some rubric for laying the altar, but is reconstructing the Offertory, excised in 1552, by having these things offered by the bishop 'in the name of the people upon the Altar', something not ventured even in 1662, but, again that found its way, slightly watered down, into the 1637 Scottish rite: 'The Presbyter shall then offer up, and place the bread and wine prepared for the Sacrament upon the Lord's table.'[30] Further, Andrewes heightens the ceremonial significance of the oblation of the eucharistic gifts by subtly redefining the pecuniary gifts. Andrewes's note proceeds: 'Then [the bishop] offers into the basin for himself, and after him the whole congregation, and so betake themselves to their proper and convenient place of kneeling.' His view of the hugger-mugger of churchwardens collecting alms and tithes to be dropped into the poor box was as withering as it was specific: 'This collection person by person, tumultuously running back and forth in the church, smacks of the Geneva fashion.'[31] Instead of this, his chapel congregants' offerings ceremonially join the bishop's own at the altar, presumably placed in the basin by the communicants en route to their kneeling places at the rail. Here Andrewes quotes Laodicea again to emphasize ritual position: 'Bishops and Priests only within the *septum*; Deacons at the door; the Laity without.' The unity and cohesion of this Offertory – innovative, but technically not breaking any 1559 rubrics – reflects the unique term used most frequently by Andrewes in his notes for the Eucharist itself: *sacra syntaxi*, the 'sacred gathering', a term not found in Andrewes's public writings or elsewhere to my knowledge in the period, but uniquely associated with the early Eastern Fathers, most prominently the homilies of that title by the seventh-century Anastasios of Sinai.

'The Priest meanwhile', Andrewes's note continues, 'reading the peculiar sentences for the Offertory.' Here Andrewes becomes not just ceremonially, but also textually, interventionist. For by 'peculiar sentences' he means not the appointed Offertory sentences in the BCP, but, he directs, 'Instead of these, read the peculiar Sentences for the Offertory *ut infra*', and helpfully supplies eight new ones in the margin.[32] The 1661 revisers did tinker with the 1552/1559 sentences: Puritans wanted two from Tobit axed; Wren and Cosin played with reorganizing the old sentences by theme. As the Wren/Cosin approach shows, the old sentences were a diverse bunch, not united by any common denominator

---

30 http://justus.anglican.org/resources/bcp/Scotland/Communion1637.htm.
31 *Notes*, p. 156.
32 Gen. 4.3, 4; Exod. 25.2; Deut. 16.16, 17; 1 Chron. 29.14, 17; Neh. 10.32; Ps. 96.7, 8; Mark 12.41.

about Christian offering. Andrewes's Offertory sentences, however, drive home the obligation of giving *to God alone*, and not necessarily only financial gifts. The emphasis is on the spirit in which offerings are given rather than their material value, and there is an emphatic step away from previous prayer books' calls for alms for the poor. Andrewes's Offertory is, like Mary Magdalen's ointment, about giving to God and God's Church, with no room given for Judas' objection, 'For, it might have been sold ... and given to the poor' (Mark 14.6). Not one of Andrewes's alternative sentences was taken up in 1662. But what is even more striking is that a full *five* of them were put in the 1637 Scottish Book. And 1 Chronicles' 'All things come of thee O Lord' was taken up in the 1928 American Prayer Book, and the English Proposed 1929 Book, and now stand in Order Two of *Common Worship*.

Andrewes's tighter temporal conjunction of the priestly offering of the elements with the collection of the people's offering, followed by these new Offertory sentences, are his own early solution to the incremental and complicated moves in Anglican rites after 1552 to enlarge the scope of the collection beyond offerings of alms or clerical tithes to general offerings and to unite those with the offering of the eucharistic elements in one greater act of oblation. Final proof of this comes at the end of the service, where, after the Gloria and before the blessing, Andrewes instructs that

> the congregation ariseth, and having made their adoration, they go towards their seats to a little private devotion. In their way, at the foot of the choir stands the *cippus pauperum* [poor men's box], into which every man puts a small piece of silver; whilst the Priest, standing still at the Altar, readeth the exhortatory sentences for alms, *ut supra*.

So on alms and oblations, Andrewes has his cake and eats it. Not to be accused of having, Puritan-like, cut anything appointed from the service, alms for the poor given to the soundtrack of the Prayer Book's appointed sentences, get redeployed at the end, poor relief being duly observed, but without sullying the greater offerings and oblations in the Eucharist.

There are other important touches to the service in Andrewes's notes. He insists on the discretionary Second Exhortation to Communion because of its emphasis on the need for confession and absolution. Next to 'draw near with faith' he jots laconically, 'Perhaps these words are not necessary, because they have already come near ... all have knelt at the rail.' The Confession was to be led by the priest after another of his trips out through the *septum* door, with absolution pronounced standing. The *Sursum corda* 'sequentia jubilans' ('follows jubilantly'). The Prayer of Humble Access (contrary to the rubric this time) is not to be read at what the rite called 'Gods borde', but by the priest back out again through the door, whereafter he turns, genuflects and approaches the altar for the consecration, but not before stopping at the credence table where 'the Priest, having made adoration, poureth water upon the napkin ready for that purpose, and cleanseth his hands' – justified with the belt and braces of 'as mystically shown in that Psalm, *Lavabo in innocentia manus meas*' and the more materialist 'it is so used good-manneredly and properly at great men's tables'.[33]

The ensuing note on the further preparation of the gifts is so startling in its descriptive detail that the reintroduction of the mixed chalice, last seen in the rubrics in 1549, almost goes unnoticed:

> *take the wafers from the canister and place them on the paten: then from the small tun pour the wine in a way that looks like blood gushing out; then out of the Tricanale mix in the water; do all of this standing as decently and decorously as possible.*[34]

Again we meet some real exotica in liturgical vessels here, but I want to set those aside to think about what they mean for that old question of the east- versus south-facing celebrant. Andrewes's quaint and possibly evasive 'standing as decently and decorously as possible' remark has overtones of the 1637 Scottish rubric that the priest stands at the consecration 'at such a part of the Table where he may with the most ease and decency use both his hands'. The plan of the chapel on page 62 is again of help here. It clearly shows on the north side ('3' and '8') a 'Kneeling stoole covered and stuffed' and 'A Cushion for the service booke', so for most things said at the altar this must have been the default position. But the placement of 'A' ('the silver & guilt Canister for the wafers like a wicker basket & lined with Cambrick laced'), 'B' ('the Tunne upon a cradle' holding the wine), 'C' (the chalice), two 'Ds' (patens) and the maltese cross ('the Tricanale being a round ball with a screw cover whereout issue three pipes … for the water of mixture')

---

33 *Notes*, pp. 157–9.

34 'Postea panes e canistro in patinam ponit: dein vinum e doliolo, adinstar Sanguinis erumpentis, in calicem haurit; tum aquam e Triconali scypho immiscet; postremo omnibus rite, et quam fieri potest decentissime atque aptissime compositis, stand pergit et peragit' (*Notes*, p. 159).

seems to me to make it impossible for the consecration to have been done from the north side, no matter how 'decently and decorously' the celebrant stood. The description of the 'Tricanale' is from the Chapel plan (Prynne, *Canterburies doome*, p. 122).

Andrewes also pipped the Scottish 1637 rite, Wren, Cosin and the 1662 rite to the post when it came to insisting on the manual acts in the institution narrative that had been removed in 1552.[35] But where a host of revisers, including the Scottish book, Wren, Cosin and Jeremy Taylor were adamant that the institution narrative should receive a congregational 'Amen', Andrewes is silent. But perhaps more to the point of real presence, he is adamant that following the words of administration ('The body/blood of our Lord Jesus Christ ...'), 'To this prayer of the Priest every communicant should say *Amen*; and then, and not before, take the Sacrament of him.'[36] The 1637 rite, Cosin and Wren all followed suit, but although 1662 included the congregational response to the institution narrative, the English rite demurred on the assent at reception until 1928.

Andrewes's last note to the Prayer Book was also one of his most original, and again typical of how he looked to the ancient East as well as back to 1549 for acceptable innovations. Following the post-communion thanksgivings ('we most heartily thank thee, etc.') but before the Gloria, Andrewes inserts this instruction: 'When the Psalm is ended, let the Deacon say, Let us give thanks to Him who has made us worthy to receive his holy Mysteries, &c.' The introductory clause, 'When the Psalm is ended' only makes sense if we assume that Andrewes's chapel musicians sang, as an anthem, a post-communion sentence – as provided in 1549 but excised thereafter.[37] What the deacon then says ('Let us give thanks, etc.') in some sense recapitulates the substance of the Prayer Book thanksgiving, so may have replaced it or been additional. But Andrewes seems most intent on having it, so much so that he sources it with a documentary note as Canons 13 and 14 of the eighth chapter of the fourth-century Apostolic Constitutions, that is, the portion of the Constitutions containing the elaborate version of the Antiochene Liturgy of St Hippolytus.[38] And with that ancient East-

---

35 *Notes*, p. 159; see Cumming (ed.), *Durham Book*, pp. 166–9; Cummings (ed.), *BCP*, pp. 402, 772.

36 *Notes*, p. 159; Cuming (ed.), *Durham Book*, pp. 172–3.

37 Cummings (ed.), *BCP*, p. 34.

38 *Notes*, p. 160; the full form in the dismissal in Chrysostom's Divine Liturgy is 'Stand upright. Having received the divine, holy, pure, immortal, heavenly, life-giving and dread Mysteries of Christ, let us give worthy thanks to the Lord.' *The Divine Liturgy*, Oxford: Oxford University Press, 1995, p. 48.

ern touch, Andrewes's communicants heard the Gloria, rose, dropped their alms into the poor box, and returned to their seats, and, the notes conclude, 'When all are composed in their seats, he [the celebrant] proceeds to the Blessing.'

Like those communicants, admirers of Andrewes took these things out into the world with them in the form of his notes. How they flowed into subsequent English revisions is easily accounted for by the collection and study of them by Cosin and Andrewes's former chaplain Wren. But how did they get to Scotland in 1637, where their force was if anything stronger? The easy answer is Laud, whose copy is still at Lambeth. But if Laud was the political force behind the Scottish Book, the liturgical force behind it was the Bishop of Dunblane, James Wedderburn. He is usually, and with reference to the 1630s, accurately considered one of Laud's creatures, so was it from Laud that he imbibed Andrewes? Filling a gap in the accounts of Wedderburn's early career provides a more likely answer. We know that, self-exiled from Scotland for his anti-Calvinism, he spent time in England in the 1610s, part of it as tutor to the children of the emigré Isaac Casaubon. And Casaubon's patron in his adopted home was Lancelot Andrewes. But Andrewes, we can now see, thanks to Ken Fincham's invaluable *Clergy of the Church of England Database*, was also Wedderburn's – the Scot being presented to two Cambridgeshire livings at the hands of Lancelot Andrewes, Bishop of Ely, in his episcopal chapel in Holborn. One can safely assume that in addition to those livings, Wedderburn took from Ely House the suavely adapted forms of the English rite and began the process, still ongoing even in *Common Worship*, of Andrewes's contribution to the ever-evolving and never truly fixed Books of Common Prayer.

5

The 1662 Prayer Book

BRIAN CUMMINGS

The new edition of the Book of Common Prayer of 1662 announced itself even in its physical form as an act not just of divine providence but of historical inevitability. In a large folio size, sometimes with extravagantly sized borders, and with the division of the page handsomely set off by red ruled lines, the new book published by His Majesty's Printers John Bill and Christopher Barker sported either one or sometimes both of two specially prepared engraved title pages by the young artist David Loggan. One of these, after an original by J. B. Gaspars, shows the ancient temple of the Lord nicely inhabited by some very debonairly cavalier families. It is, perhaps, a depiction of a homecoming, or a repossession of a lost ancestral seat. The other, only slightly less beautiful but even more monumental, reconstructs the spectacularly long full title of the book – 61 words dispersed over 25 lines of inscription, using three different fonts – as an imperial entablature of Roman proportions, an architectural border in which the title page becomes itself a reredos of authority and establishment. Having lasted now 350 years, the book may be accorded something of a success: '1662', like the 'First Folio' or 'the little red book', is one of those shorthand monikers that stands for a book of global significance or even a whole culture.

Robert Sanderson's Preface to the 1662 edition presented this feeling of entitlement as the most natural of emotions:

we have good hope, that what is here presented, and hath been by the Convocations of both Provinces with great diligence examined and approved, will be also well accepted and approved by all sober, peaceable, and truly conscientious Sons of the Church of *England*.[1]

These feelings match those that accompanied the event that heralded the revised Book of Common Prayer: the royal Restoration of King

---

1 *The Book of Common Prayer: The Texts of 1549, 1559, and 1642*, ed. Brian Cummings, Oxford: Oxford University Press, 2011, p. 211.

Charles II. On 29 May, the King's birthday, he entered London in a festival that lasted three days. The bonfires burned in Melton Mowbray for three days and nights. The people of Norwich enjoyed the merry-making so ebulliently the Corporation brought it to an end after a week. Oxford, it seems, was 'perfectly mad'.[2] The historian of the Restoration, Ronald Hutton, has remarked that 'no other English political event' has inspired such 'enduring enthusiasm'; he may or may not be the source of the 'living memory' he cites of Oxfordshire schoolboys being thrashed with nettles if they did not sport an oak apple to celebrate the anniversary.

However, as with much of the historical fanfare surrounding the Restoration, so with the inevitability of the 1662 edition, little is quite as it seems. Before his return to England, a deputation of ministers had requested that Charles abstain from using the Book of Common Prayer in his private chapel. In the Declaration of Breda, signed in the Netherlands in April 1660, Charles had recognized that 'the passion and uncharitableness of the times have produced several opinions in religion, by which men are engaged in parties and animosities against each other', and promised 'a liberty to tender consciences' in his new regime.[3] The Presbyterians, who were by no means few in number, were especially tender about the old Prayer Book, which they considered to contain 'many things that are justly offensive and need amendment'.[4] Indeed, in making their lists of offences, the Presbyterians were adding to a litany now more than half a century old. The Millenary Petition presented to the new king James in 1603 wanted the sign of the cross in baptism removed, along with interrogatories to infants in confirmation, and wedding rings; it demanded that women not baptize, and that the cap and surplice should not be enforced; that terms like 'priest' and 'absolution' should be suppressed; that people should not be taught to bow at the name of Jesus; that 'the Lord's Day be not profaned', but that rest on other holidays 'not so strictly urged'; and finally (a point on which all Anglicans might still agree to this day) 'longsomeness of

2 Ronald Hutton, *The Restoration: A Political and Religious History of England and Wales, 1658–1667*, Oxford: Clarendon Press, 1985, p. 126.

3 *Journals of the House of Lords, beginning anno duodecimo Caroli Secundi, 1660*, vol. XI, London, 1771, pp. 7–8; reprinted in *English Historical Documents*, ed. David Douglas, 10 vols, reprinted edn (London: Routledge, 1996), vol. VI, ed. Andrew Browning, pp. 57–8.

4 *Reliquiae Baxterianae: or, Mr Richard Baxter's narrative of the most memorable passages of his life and times; faithfully publish'd from his own original manuscript, by Matthew Sylvester*, London: for T. Parkhurst, J. Robinson, J. Lawrence & J. Dunton, 1696, pp. 234, 232.

service abridged'.[5] Most of these points were repeated in 1660 as they had been throughout the troubles of the 1630s and 1640s.

If some were looking for a resurrection, others came not to praise the book but to bury it. De facto, of course, the Book of Common Prayer was abolished by Act of Parliament on 4 January 1645, and was replaced by a new *Directory of Public Worship* organized in line with Puritan religious sympathies.[6] On 26 August it was further ordered that the Book of Common Prayer be prohibited 'in any private place or family'. For the first offence of use either in public in church or in private in the home the forfeit was £5, and for a third a year's imprisonment.[7] The revolution that did away with the monarch in 1649 also removed bishops, deans and cathedral chapters. The festivals of the church Calendar were banned, including, notoriously, Christmas Day; the buildings of the former cathedrals were vandalized and left as dilapidated symbols of lost ecclesiastical power. At Lichfield the roof had fallen in; Canterbury was a carcase of stone; Durham was used as a prison; St Paul's as a stable and shopping mall; St Asaph as a wine shop.[8] A fifth of clergy was deprived of livings, usually because of religious disobedience; the bishops quietly retired, and when they died they were not replaced.[9]

How far practice on the ground reflected Parliamentary ordinance is a matter of research and conjecture. No edition of the Book of Common Prayer was printed in English between 1645 and 1660. Yet one analysis of churchwarden's accounts of the late 1640s shows the illegal Book of Common Prayer still present in a third of churches examined; it also shows less than a quarter owning the new *Directory*. Whether this reflects local feeling or instead the time-honoured reluctance of churches to spend money on new books is less easy to assess. Practice certainly varied regionally. In rural communities, interregnum inventories show that prayer books were still lying around; but in London in 1659 only one copy was found.[10] However, the sense that it was a book on the way out and barely being kept alive is found not only among

---

5 Edward Cardwell, *A History of the Conferences and Other Proceedings connected with the Book of Common Prayer*, Oxford: Oxford University Press, 1840, p. 131.

6 C. H. Firth and R. S. Rait, *Acts and ordinances of the Interregnum, 1642–1660. Vol. 1 Acts and ordinances from 5th March, 1642 to 30th January, 1649*, London: HMSO, 1911, p. 582.

7 Firth and Rait, *Acts* I, p. 755.

8 Hutton, *The Restoration*, p. 143.

9 Hutton, *The Restoration*, p. 7.

10 Hutton, *The Restoration*, p. 172.

hot Protestants but among its most sacramentalist defenders. Matthew Wren, locked up in the Tower, remarked that there had never been a better opportunity to amend the errors in the old Prayer Book, since 'it hath been so long disused that not one of five hundred is so perfect in it as to observe alterations'.[11]

The new edition of 1662 is thus not an act of acclamation so much as one of conscious cultural retrieval. The culture of the Restoration that surrounds the 1662 Book of Common Prayer should therefore be seen, as the Restoration mood should be viewed in general, as one of profound paradox. The restored monarchy claimed merely to be setting the clocks back, undoing the unfortunate interlude and carrying on as normal. But in some ways it was as consciously revolutionary as anything seen in the 15-year radical interval. Part of this new revolution was a deliberate ideology of memory. The wonderfully entitled 'Act of Oblivion' of May 1660, or 'An Act of Free and General Pardon, Indemnity, and Oblivion' to give its full title, is a masterpiece of euphemism and culturally encoded commemoration and noisy forgetting. 'Out of a hearty and pious Desire to put an end to all Suits and Controversies that by occasion of the late Distractions have arisen', the Act declares, only one of the egregious faults of the civil wars – the regicide itself – is to be recalled and punished; all other actions are to 'be Pardoned Released Indemnified Discharged and put in utter Oblivion'.[12] Who was being remembered and who forgotten here? Disappointed Royalists, it is said, commented that the Act meant 'indemnity for [the king's] enemies and oblivion for his friends'. Yet we could also say that oblivion is not quite what it seems. The regicides were punished in the most outrageous way possible. Oblivion meant contradictory things at the same time. If we can forget the past perhaps it never happened. At the same time the new regime was involved in countless small acts of what psychologists would now call 'false memory'. Nostalgia for things Caroline meant the usual thing nostalgia brings: fabrication of a past that never was, that is simply too good to be true.

This, I think, is an important aspect of how we should view the movement to reinstall the old Book and simultaneously proclaim it as a new one. The 1662 edition is both consciously nostalgic – down to its appearance, in black letter – but it was also quietly radical and new-

---

11 G. J. Cuming (ed.), *The Durham Book*, London: Oxford University Press, 1961, pp. 287–8.

12 'Charles II, 1660: An Act of Free and Generall Pardon Indempnity and Oblivion', *Statutes of the Realm: volume 5: 1628–80* (1819), pp. 226–34, at http://www.british-history.ac.uk/report.aspx (accessed 29 February 2012).

fangled. It was designed to give a sense of uninterruptedness while it also enacted a suppression of any genuinely new alternatives. For those who resuscitated it, this was an act of emotion as much as will. And religious emotion is just as much evident in those who demurred. On the first return of the King it was not, contrary to the impression of hindsight, obvious either which religious party would succeed in promoting its ideal liturgy, or even, perhaps, what its own ideal precisely was. The first address of the Presbyterian ministers to the King welcomed 'your so wonderful and peaceable restoration unto your throne and government', and proceeded, in rather gingerly fashion, to broach the vexed question of episcopacy.[13] They clearly still hoped to effect a workable cleft between monarchy and episcopacy, reminding Charles of the defects of the bishops in 1640, and arguing for a theological distinction to be drawn between those who thought episcopacy 'a distinct order by divine right from that of the presbyter' and those prepared to see the bishops in a more practical role of administration.

On the liturgy in particular, in a section showing the clear influence of Richard Baxter, whose learning in the history of ritual balanced his instincts for reform, the Presbyterians proposed reform that combines coded critique with an intriguingly distinctive view of Christian worship, that should:

> be for the matter agreeable unto the word of God, and fitly suited to the nature of the several ordinances, and necessities of the church; neither too tedious in the whole, nor composed of too short prayers, unmeet repetitions or responsals; not to be dissonant from the liturgies of other reformed churches; nor too rigorously imposed; nor the minister so confined thereunto, but that he may also make use of those gifts for prayer and exhortation which Christ hath given him for the service and edification of the church.

The phrase 'repetitions or responsals' is an attack on the old Prayer Book. Yet it is also an appeal for a different kind of approach to church service. It was a common complaint of Puritans in general that ritualized prayer was not in tune with a genuine expression of faith in God. This is not only the usual suspicion of anything that smacked of Catholic survivalism. It is the assertion of what we might call a new language of the emotions, or to use the seventeenth-century term, the 'passions' or *affectus*. While the improper arousal of the passions was of course

---

13 Cardwell, *A History*, p. 277.

regarded since Augustine as the origin of sinfulness, Augustine was careful to say that it was not human affections that were themselves the problem. Christ redeems the world through love, after all. We can see the Presbyterian argument here as giving voice to this Reformed Augustinian sense of right affection. This is also grounded in a sense of history that it is deliberately claimed reaches back before liturgical history to the time of Christ.

This is a prelude to declaring that the Book of Common Prayer is in effect yesterday's book. It is as if the book is superseded and super-annuated: it is 'long discontinued', they say; and in a rather disingenuous phrase, infer 'if it be again imposed, will inevitably follow sad divisions, and widening of the breaches which your Majesty is now endeavour-ing to heal'. The King's own pronouncement on ecclesiastical affairs followed in October 1660. The first sentence affirmed that the 'the peace of the state' is bound up in 'the peace of the church'.[14] It made direct reference to Charles's own experience of Reformed churches in France, Germany, and especially the Low Countries. The 'notorious schisms' that English religion has recently undergone are therefore to be expunged and order restored. To this end, the Worcester declaration made a number of concessions to the Presbyterian wishes. A tone of godliness in tune with Puritan feelings is kept up throughout. Sensitiv-ities on the observation of the Lord's Day are observed; the power of the bishops is to be regulated; the godly insistence that only the pious be admitted to communion, long a bugbear among the Presbyterians, is also accepted, although it is linked to a traditional concept of confirm-ation. But if Baxter had hoped all this could be achieved in the context of a new book of common worship along Reformed Protestant lines, there is a sting in the tail. Charles puts his own feelings on the table:

> we do esteem the Liturgy of the Church of England, contained in the Book of Common Prayer, and by law established, to be the best we have seen; and we believe that we have seen all that are extant and used in this part of the world.

Instead of root and branch replacement, a different political solution is suggested now for the first time: what we might think of as a thor-oughly modern and English solution, a royal commission of the great and good, equally divided among the two sides, with the brief to look

---

14 *Journals of the House of Lords*, XI, pp. 179–82; reprinted in *English His-torical Documents*, VI, pp. 365–70, this ref. p. 365.

into any exceptions made to the Book of Common Prayer, to review them, and to make any necessary alterations or new additions.

The formal arrangements for the Savoy Conference that followed, named after the place where it met, are a classic of political practice, in the full sense of that word, and thus also conceal their most overt purposes. The warrant was issued on 25 March 1661. Even-handedness was on magnificent display. Twelve bishops were appointed, and twelve representatives from the Presbyterian Divines. Some of the bishops survived from before 1641 and were quite elderly, but they included John Cosin, newly Bishop of Durham, a student of liturgical history for decades, John Gauden, who wrote *Eikon Basilike*, and Henry King the poet. The Presbyterians were intellectually if not so distinguished, more original. As well as Baxter, who came armed with a full plan for a new reformed liturgy, there was the polymath John Wallis, a mathematician (he invented the symbol for infinity) and grammarian as well as theologian, and Anthony Tuckney, the Cambridge academic who caused a stir for promoting people on the basis of learning rather than godliness. The deputies to the conference also contained some notable talents, Peter Heylin and Peter Gunning on the Episcopal side, and John Lightfoot the Hebraist and rabbinical scholar for the Presbyterians.

Both sides imagined they were getting a much better bargain than was the case. It should be remembered that the Presbyterians were not anti-royalist; Arthur 'Two Sheds' Jackson waited at the head of the queue of clerics in May 1660 to present Charles II with a new copy of the Bible. The Presbyterians thought they had gained the upper hand by having revision discussed at all. Yet it soon became clear that the base standard for discussion was the existing Book of Common Prayer, and any hopes to negotiate it away were already gone. On the other hand, those on the Episcopal side who thought that they had carte blanche to reverse the tide of Puritanism and return the Book of Common Prayer to a more serious ritual engagement with the past were also disappointed. Power lay in the hands of Gilbert Sheldon, Bishop of London and, as Master of the Savoy, the chair of the committee. Sheldon was a friend and intellectual ally of Edward Hyde, Earl of Clarendon, the Lord Chancellor. While a firm conservative in politics, Clarendon, like many conservatives, was wary of too much theological curiosity, and probably thought there were as many trouble-makers among the liturgical fusspots as among the zealous Reformers.

The lesson from the Savoy Conference, a good lesson for anyone having to deal with politicians, is that neither the explicit brief for reform nor the covert encouragement to reactionary tide-stemming was ever the intention of the conference's designers. And even if they had designed differently, the best policy with any issue that arouses passions on both sides is to satisfy neither party and even to leave well alone. The 1662 revision can be seen to be a triumph for announcing large-scale revision while keeping things the same. Yet it is in this achievement of restoring the Book at all that the result of 1662 was in its way radical, while a lot of the small changes were nonetheless significant.

The complexity of the Presbyterian position can be ascertained via its leader, Baxter, who had wrestled for some 30 years with the Book of Common Prayer. He was episcopally ordained as a deacon in 1638, even though he circulated among friends experimenting with nonconformism. In Shropshire before the Civil War he considered a prescribed liturgy lawful, although he also considered the existing Book had 'much *disorder* and *defectiveness* in it'. He was particularly concerned at the '*promiscuous giving of the Lord's Supper to all Drunkards, Swearers, Fornicators, Scorners at Godliness &c.*'.[15] But when he encountered religious radicalism at close quarters in the New Model Army in 1645 he was equally disconcerted. Acting as an army chaplain, he endorsed the principle of baptism and rejected the antinomian belief in the exclusive exercise of free grace characteristic of the Ranters. His 1649 publication, *Aphorismes of Justification*, argued against strict predestination and incorporated human co-operation with grace, leading to accusations of Arminianism, popery, and even Pelagianism.

It was during the 1650s, under the Commonwealth, that Baxter achieved national prominence as a result of his ministry at Kidderminster. Here he attempted a middle way between radical Puritanism and Prayer Book worship. He tolerated written liturgy but himself used extemporary prayers; he advised communicants to remain seated during the sacrament, but he did not refuse to administer it to those who knelt. He did not observe Christmas but he liked church music; 'God would not have given us, either our Senses themselves, or their usual objects, if they might not have been serviceable to his own praise', he said.[16]

If Baxter does not conform to the cliché of the Puritan, something similar can be said about the conformist bishops on the other side, even their champion, John Cosin. It is obvious enough which party he belonged to, on which he never swerved the slightest. He was librarian and secretary to John Overall, the precursor of establishment Arminian-

---

15 *Reliquiae Baxterianae*, i.13.
16 Richard Baxter, *The Saints Everlasting Rest*, Henry Fisher, 1825, p. 757.

ism, until his death in 1619. He was already a historian of the Book of Common Prayer by this time, going through Martin Bucer's *Censura* of 1551 in detail, and comparing the current text in detail with a copy of 1549. After 1623, when he became chaplain to Richard Neile, the Bishop of Durham, he became associated with northern dioceses especially, as a prebend at Durham, Archdeacon of the East Riding in 1625, and Rector of Brancepeth in 1626. Through Neile he encountered both the arch-Arminian controversialist Richard Montague, and the rising star, William Laud. Geoffrey Cuming, perhaps the finest twentieth-century historian of Anglican liturgy, sums up brilliantly the two sides of Cosin: 'a passion for uniformity in the performance of divine service and a love of beautifully carved woodwork'. Those who want to see the latter alas are deprived of his personal project in the stalls at Brancepeth, destroyed by fire 20 years ago, but you can still see the whopping font cover at Durham Cathedral, like a mahogany version of a Saturn V rocket. At Peterhouse in Cambridge, where he was Master in the 1630s, he gave full expression to the ceremonies of the Book of Common Prayer both in matter and in spirit: he installed the new altar at the east end, with crucifix and candlesticks; and he encouraged signing with the cross, kissing the book, and bowing at the name of Jesus, all of which was vilified by the Puritans.

If the Commonwealth brought fame to Baxter, to Cosin came exile. But if his opponents imagined he would be only too happy to be in Catholic Paris, this is not the case. He found his new hosts 'exceeding uncharitable and somewhat worse' in their exercise of religion. He compared them unfavourably with the Geneva camp (which is a serious insult with Cosin) for threatening damnation on anyone who did not accept their articles of faith. He disliked the way that his companions and servants were proselytized, in the case of his footman, he said, involving a female French honey-trap; it caused him great personal distress when his son defected to Catholicism in 1652. What is interesting is that in Paris he became more decidedly Protestant, even while maintaining his Prayer Book beliefs. He perfected his view that praying for the dead was natural and human, and endorsed by the 1549 Book of Common Prayer; he was horrified that he was not allowed to use the English funeral rite in France, and forced (he said) to bury his friends as if they were dogs. Crucially, on the Eucharist, while he ratified his belief in the real presence, he argued that the 'body and blood are neither sensibly present'; they are present only to those 'prepared to receive them', and then only in the act of receiving. This is intriguingly close to Cranmer's mature position, and it influenced Cosin's minute attention to the question of consecrated and unconsecrated bread in the 1662 text, a strikingly ambiguous lacuna in 1552.

The Savoy Conference began on Easter Monday, 15 April 1661, and ended on 25 July. The senior bishop, Accepted Frewen, Archbishop of York, gave way immediately to Sheldon, on the grounds that he best knew the King's mind. Sheldon, like any good chair of a committee, made his shrewdest move in an initial point of procedure. The Conference convened, he said, at the request of the Presbyterians, and thus they should begin by making a list of their complaints and suggestions. The bishops, he moved, had nothing to do until the Presbyterian case was presented.[17] So subtle was this, the Presbyterians agreed. They thereby showed their hand entire, first. As a result they were cast in the role of innovators (in the negative sense); the substantive part of the conference consisted in going through their objections one by one and arguing them down.

The Presbyterians produced the so-called *Exceptions* on 4 May. This consisted of 18 larger points and then many pages of detail. In their Preface, they made the argument, not unreasonable, that the work was over a hundred years old, and had been written for different times.[18] The barely concealed sub-text was that it was out of date; it is not so different an argument from the one used in the 1960s to promote the need for new forms of liturgy for modern times. Article II of the *Exceptions* expanded on this, in a fascinating attempt to place the 1549 edition in a historical context:

> our first reformers out of their great wisdom did at that time so compose the Liturgy as to win upon the papists, and to draw them into their Church-communion, by varying as little as they well could from the Romish forms before in use.

This is damnation via historicization. However fit for purpose it was for its times, it is now too close to the Roman rite. This vein is continued in Article III, which complains about 'the repetitions, and responsals of the clerk and people, and the alternate reading of the psalms and hymns'. This produces 'a confused murmur' in the church, as each side is confused as to who should say what; unspoken is the Puritan antipathy to formality of prayer and ritual, and the desire to free up 'the gift of prayer' (especially longer formats) and to allow improvised petition-

---

17 Geoffrey Cuming, *Godly Order: Texts and Studies Relating to the Book of Common Prayer*, London: SPCK/Alcuin Club, 1983, p. 146.

18 Cardwell, *A History*, p. 303.

ing of God for daily needs. The Collects were too short. The existing Book of Common Prayer injuriously gave no room to any departure from the set script, although in Article VI, the Presbyterians carefully noticed that the 1549 Book had given latitude for local variation. Other Articles address four different kinds of traditional Puritan complaint: the observance of holy days; too much use of ceremonial, bordering on superstition; a number of points of doctrine, the main of which are an objection to the concept of absolution, and a resistance to assuming the whole of the congregation as being regenerate and destined for heaven; and lastly, a plea for clarity of language and expression (appealing again to the idea that the Book is outdated). One of the main pleas here was for the use of the King James translation to replace the Great Bible text, which had never been changed since 1549, not even by King James.

As well as the general points, the Presbyterians produced 78 objections to particulars, once again including points of doctrine, ceremony and defects in wording: an example of the last is the use of the word 'worship' in the marriage vows, now no longer comprehensible. Yet when the *Answer to the Exceptions* was produced a month later, Sheldon's cunning was evident. Crucially, he avoided any sense of a general and mutual discussion from first principles. The bishops painted the Presbyterians into a corner marked by their own exceptionalism. As for the idea that the Book of Common Prayer produced dissension: on the contrary, since it was banned, 'We have had continual dissentions which variety of services must needs produce, whilst every one naturally desires, and endeavours not only to maintain, but to prefer his own way before all others.'[19] Common prayer is the key to common order. This is subtly joined to a dismissal of the idea of extemporary prayer: 'great care may be taken to suppress those private conceptions of prayers before and after sermon, lest private opinions be made the matter of prayer in public'. Therefore, responsals are justified precisely as a way of avoiding Puritan fondness for long prayers: they work 'by quickening, continuing, and uniting our devotion, which is apt to freeze or sleep, or flat in a long continued prayer or form' (339). In a waspish side-note, the bishops record how the 'long tedious prayer' of the nonconformists is continually interrupted by the loud 'Amens' of the Puritan congregations, 'mutual exultations, provocations, petitions, holy contentions and strivings', which, it is suggested, are as much a way of showing off their own piety as stirring up the zeal of others.

---

19 Cardwell, *A History*, p. 336.

In conclusion, the bishops made 17 bullet-point concessions. They conceded just one general principle, the use of the King James Bible, something they wanted in any case. Some of the agreement is faint to the point of derisory. They agree that when a reading is not from an epistle it should not be called an epistle; that longer time be allowed for those wishing to take communion to notify the minister; that the font can be moved if the congregation cannot hear well. They do allow that the words 'with my body I thee worship' be changed to 'with my body I thee honour'; but in the eventual 1662 Book of Common Prayer, the old wording was restored. The doom of the Presbyterians was not just in the text of the new Book, but in the exclusion from ministry of those who would not swear to its uniformity. Baxter foresaw this clearly. Yet we should not take the defeat of the Presbyterian party as the overwhelming victory of the Episcopalians. Traditionalists also wanted to revise the 1552 Prayer Book as it had come down in its 1559 and 1604 forms. Wren, Bishop of Ely, spent 18 years in the Tower revising the Book of Common Prayer page by page. Cosin saw Wren's *Advices* soon after returning from Paris in 1660. He then combined his own researches with Wren's in compiling the so-called Durham Book, a 1619 Prayer Book which Cosin drenched in his own ink. Closest to Cosin's heart was the form of the Communion. As early as 1628 in his *Collection of Private Devotions*, he had reprinted part of the Canon from 1549 as a private prayer to be said at consecration. A back-to-1549 movement became the Laudian dream. In annotating the Durham Book, Cosin came across a solution he had not seen before. In the 1637 Scottish Book of Common Prayer, which was famously flung across St Giles's Kirk and caused the rebellion that led to the first Civil War, James Wedderburn reintroduced the epiclesis (the blessing of the elements) from the 1549 Canon, restored the Prayer of Oblation to its original function, and excised what he called a 'Zwinglian tenet' from the 1552 sentences, that the sacrament is a bare sign of remembrance. Cosin made full use of the Scottish Book (while never mentioning it) as well as 1549 in the Durham Book, and made plenty of room for Laudian furniture and vestment.

Sheldon's politics outmanoeuvred Cosin as well as Baxter. Neither Clarendon nor Sheldon was much of a ritualist, but both were realists, and they knew that the 1549 Canon smelt trouble. It did not even come into discussion: Sheldon's whole object was to restore the book in use in 1642, which was in effect 1552. Nevertheless, the Durham Book was the practical starting point for the revised book of 1662, which now began in earnest. William Sancroft, Cosin's chaplain, entered in the

Savoy concessions to the already copiously annotated margins. He also incorporated some of Wren's and Cosin's earlier work in improving the rubrics in about 80 places, and the spoken text in 66.[20] It was only in September 1661 that Sheldon first saw the Durham Book, and Cosin was now brought in to help in the final stages. The existing book was so crammed and even incomprehensible that a 1634 edition was found and a 'fair copy' made, although it is not a transcription, omitting old material and adding new. The Durham Book Canon was copied in, but as an alternative version on a separate sheet; 1549 was being quietly buried in the margin.

In November 1661, Convocation passed in 16 hours' sitting every jot and tittle of the new book. In all, 4,500 words were removed and some 10,500 added. Still the Presbyterians came back for more, and got some, although even the little they had sometimes was taken away again. Benedicite was removed, then restored again. The Apocrypha stayed, after argument, a little victory for *Bel and the Dragon*. However, some Laudian details in Communion rubrics went; the words 'offer' and 'sacrifice' were exposed to some minute censorship; the 'Sacrament of the Body of Christ' changed to 'the consecrated bread', and then finally 'the bread'. Cosin lost most of his thanksgiving for the departed.

The 1662 edition, we can say, even so was full of small improvements, as well as the containment of controversial points. The rubrics were altered in many places with much greater clarity emerging; the Collects, so often now attributed to the sole authorship of Cranmer, were embellished and smoothed over, often through the introduction of scriptural quotation; the service for burial, in Sanderson's version, has greater dignity and pathos than 1552. Yet anybody who compares the various versions now might still be surprised how close 1662 is in substance to 1552. It is more of an old book than a new book. Fittingly, perhaps, the most famous of its novelties, 'A General Thanksgiving', was composed by Edward Reynolds, counted among the Presbyterians at Savoy, although also a bishop. If that makes him sound all things to all men, he was more a man of consistent principle of fair-mindedness. He was a preacher of Lincoln's Inn in 1622 and rector of Braunston in Northamptonshire for 30 years from 1631. Yet he preached a fast sermon in the House of Commons in 1642, took the covenant in 1643, and helped write parts of the *Directory of Public Worship* that replaced the Book of Common Prayer in 1645. He became Dean of Christ

---

20 Geoffrey Cuming, *A History of Anglican Liturgy*, London and New York: Macmillan, 1969, p. 157.

Church in 1648, where he hoped to heal divisions, but he refused the oath of subscription and resigned in 1650. Reynolds was the leader of the moderate Presbyterians throughout the 1650s, but he does not conform to the modern stereotype of the Civil War Nonconformist. That is more our fault than theirs. He was learned in Greek literature, and he wrote a *Treatise on the Passions*. It is in the spirit of that work that Reynolds provides an emotional register for Christian worship: 'We bless thee for our creation, preservation, and all the blessings of this life, but above all for thine inestimable love.' He prays that we do this 'not only with our lips, but in our lives'. It is a sentiment that owes much to the Puritans, and the General Thanksgiving as a whole is the nearest thing in the Book of Common Prayer to the kind of long prayer the Presbyterians wanted to see throughout; by a delicious irony, which would not have been lost on Reynolds, it is now the prayer most beloved of BCP traditionalists.

6

Common Prayer in the Eighteenth Century

WILLIAM JACOB

By 1700, the Prayer Book, as revised in 1662, was largely accepted in parishes as the common prayer of the Church. This was a gradual process, with significant resistance in the 1660s and 1670s,[1] but proposals in 1689 by the Commission established by William and Mary to introduce revisions to the Prayer Book sought by trinitarian dissenters, came to nothing. By the later seventeenth century, younger clergy and gentry, influenced by liturgical practices in their Oxford and Cambridge college chapels, were introducing dignified and formal worship to parish churches. Similarly, under the influence of post-Restoration reorderings of cathedral choirs, college chapels and parish churches rebuilt after the Great Fire in the 1670s in the City of London, parish churches were gradually reordered, with chancels restored to liturgical use and altars in railed enclosures, standing in front of elaborate reredoses, against the east walls of chancels. Much of the Laudian project of the 1630s had happened by 1700.[2]

In the late seventeenth and early eighteenth centuries, a renewed confidence in the Church of England saw the establishment of the Society for the Promotion of Christian Knowledge (SPCK), and the Society for the Propagation of the Gospel (SPG), which led to the Prayer Book being translated into Tamil. The East India Company commissioned a Portuguese translation of the Prayer Book in 1695 for use among Portuguese settlers on its estates.[3] Erastus Jablonski, chaplain to Frederick I,

---

1 For the reception of the restored Prayer Book in, for example, Wiltshire, see Donald A. Spaeth, *The Church in an Age of Danger: Parsons and Parishioners 1660–1740*, Cambridge: Cambridge University Press, 2000, pp. 188ff.

2 See Kenneth Fincham and Nicholas Tyacke, *Altars Restored: The Changing Face of English Religious Worship 1547–c.1700*, Oxford: Oxford University Press, 2007, ch. 8.

3 See W. M. Jacob, *The Making of the Anglican Communion Worldwide*, London; SPCK, 1997, pp. 85–8.

Elector of Brandenburg, who granted the title 'bishop' to the presiding ministers of the Reformed and Lutheran churches in his dominions, commissioned a High Dutch translation of the Prayer Book published in Berlin in 1704, in the hope that its use might induce the English bishops to consecrate these 'bishops' for the Prussian Church.[4]

The Prayer Book served as the primer for prayer, worship and doctrine for the great majority of the population, only about 6.7 per cent of whom, it was estimated, dissented from the Church of England. It was a major vehicle, in association with the parish church, for expressing communal identity. When most people regarded their parish church as their place of worship, and most people attended services, the liturgy brought together the households and 'all sorts and conditions of men' in a parish, and provided a means of expressing community solidarity and resolving conflicts and differences.[5] The Prayer Book's liturgies, and the ways in which they were conducted, functioned as a social mortar for holding together and reinforcing community and social networks and doctrines.[6]

The Prayer Book provided a programme for people's lives, with daily prayer and liturgies to mark the different phases of life – birth, marriage and death – and an annual cycle of fasts and celebrations. Its liturgies provided instruction about the Christian faith and, especially in the Catechism, a book of instruction for children and the young. Usually bound in with it, to provide a compendium of belief and practice, were the Thirty-Nine Articles of Religion, setting out in detail some key doctrines held by the Church, a metrical Psalter, to provide a hymn book for the Church, often the Authorized Version of the Bible as well, to enable people to say Morning and Evening Prayer at home, and sometimes even a model form for making a will, in the event of urgent necessity. It was an invaluable aid for Christian discipleship at home, as well as at church. A quite high proportion of the population could read and so had access to it, and many people, through hearing it regularly, in any case knew it by heart. Diaries and commonplace books show that some people at least read daily services at home, and it provided a

---

4 George Every, *The High Church Party 1688–1718*, London: SPCK, 1956, pp. 113–19 and 140–5.

5 For a discussion of this in the period before 1640, with particular reference to seating in churches, see Christopher Marsh, '"Common Prayer" in England 1560–1640: The View from the Pew', *Past and Present* 170 (2001), pp. 66–94.

6 For a fuller discussion of this, see Jeremy Gregory, '"For all sorts and conditions of men": the social life of the Book of Common Prayer during the long-eighteenth century: or bringing the history of religion and social history together', *Social History* 34 (2009), pp. 29–54.

vocabulary and phrasebook for personal prayers. The Prayer Book also provided a handbook for clergy in their pastoral ministry, providing words to use at childbirth, baptism, marriage, in sickness and at death, and prayers of intercession and thanksgiving to use on behalf of their parishioners.

Sunday morning liturgy – Morning Prayer, the Litany and Holy Communion, to the end of the Prayer for the Whole State of Christ's Church, when there was not a celebration of Holy Communion – was probably the only time most of a community met together. The internal layout of churches was designed to accommodate the whole community, set out in their order in society, including provision for the poor, and often separating men from women.[7] The Occasional Prayers at Morning or Evening Prayer might include personal requests for intercessions and thanksgivings. At Bath Abbey a visitor one Sunday in 1766 noted 'one Gentleman, and twelve men and ten women ... returned public thanks for the Benefit received by the Bath-Water'.[8] After the Creed, public notices of interest to the whole community, especially banns of marriage, were read, and public penances were performed by those sentenced by the consistory court, to reconcile them to the community against whom they had offended. Bread charities were often distributed to the poor after Sunday morning services. In summer or Lent, during or after Sunday afternoon Evening Prayer, children rehearsed, before the congregation, what they had learned of the Catechism at school or at home.

Liturgical observations were part of communal life. People liked to begin May Day festivities, the local fair day, often the saint's day to whom the parish church was dedicated, or a meeting of a parish friendly society, with Morning Prayer.[9] On rogation days, in May, in towns as well as villages, a significant proportion of the population processed round the parish boundaries, to identify in which parish a person paid rates, or tithes, or had a right to claim poor relief, and at salient points they stopped for a lesson from the Bible and a collect to

---

7 For the internal layouts of churches during the period, see Nigel Yates, *Buildings, Faith and Worship: The Liturgical Arrangement of Anglican Churches 1600–1900*, Oxford: Clarendon Press, 1991, chs 3, 4, 5 and 6, and for a discussion of the social ordering of church seating, see W. M. Jacob, '"This congregation here present ...": Seating in Parish Churches during the Long Eighteenth Century', *Studies in Church History* 42 (2006), pp. 294–304.

8 *Letters from Bath 1766–1767 by the Revd John Penrose*, ed. Brigitte Mitchell and Hubert Penrose, Gloucester: Alan Sutton, 1983, pp. 125–6.

9 See W. M. Jacob, *Lay People and Religion in the Early Eighteenth Century*, Cambridge: Cambridge University Press, 1996, pp. 68–9.

be read, as well as for refreshments.[10] Often on St Thomas's Day (in the Prayer Book Calendar 21 December), after Morning Prayer, winter charities of coal, clothing or money were distributed to the poor.

Most ordination candidates were advised to use Charles Wheatly's *The Church of England Man's Companion: A Rational Illustration of the Book of Common Prayer of the Church of England*, first published in 1710, as their liturgy textbook. It provided a useful handbook for clergy, both for understanding and conducting the liturgy, and exercising pastoral ministry. It became the standard work for the rest of the century. One hundred and ten years later a subsequent standard work, *The Book of Common Prayer according to the use of the United Church of England and Ireland with Notes selected and arranged by Richard Mant*, drew heavily on Wheatly, and seldom differed from him.

Wheatly illustrates the deep knowledge of patristic sources that underlay Anglican self-understanding in the late seventeenth and throughout the eighteenth centuries, and the general desire to conform the Church of England to the model of the 'primitive Church', in doctrine, liturgy, the design of churches and in pastoral practice. Wheatly assumed Morning and Evening Prayer would be said in parish churches daily, and if a congregation was lacking he recommended the priest to 'say them in the family where he lives'.[11] In most small villages clergy lamented that they could not raise weekday congregations, but in towns, certainly on the traditional 'station' days and during Lent, there were daily services. Sixty-six churches in the City of London in 1714 had daily services.[12] James Newton, Rector of Nuneham Courtney in Oxfordshire, walked to Abingdon to weekday services, and noted when visiting London, on Wednesday 25 April 1759, at St James's Piccadilly there was 'a large congregation'. John Penrose, a visitor to Bath in 1766, noted one Wednesday at the Abbey, 'every seat quite full'.[13] Provision was sometimes made for daily services in places of work. [14]

---

10 See Jacob, *Lay People and Religion*, pp. 70–1.

11 Charles Wheatly, *A Rational Illustration of the Book Of common Prayer*, 3rd edn, London, 1720, p. 80.

12 J. Wickham Legg, *London Church Services in and about the Reign of Queen Anne*, London: The Society, 1906.

13 *The Deserted Village: The Diary of an Oxfordshire Rector, James Newton of Nuneham Courteney 1714–1786*, ed. Gavin Hannah, Gloucester: Alan Sutton, 1992, p. 26, and *Letters from Bath*, p. 34. For a more detailed discussion, see Jacob, *Lay People and Religion*, pp. 61–3.

14 See, for example, *The Law Book of the Crowley Iron Works*, ed. M. W. Flinn, Durham: Surtees Society, 167 (1952), p. 162.

Wheatly noted that elements in the liturgy omitted in the 1552 Prayer Book and thereafter had 'continued since the First Prayer Book', for example, saying or singing psalms antiphonally, and for the 'whole congregation to make obeisance' at the name of Jesus, to turn east to say the Creed, and to respond to the announcement of the Gospel in the Communion service with 'Glory be to thee O Lord', and at the end, 'Thanks be to God for his holy Gospel'.[15]

Wheatly illustrated a high sacramental doctrine in his commentary on the Holy Communion service. He suggested that the Ante-communion should be regarded as the Mass of the catechumens, but suggested that if clergy indicated their intention to celebrate Holy Communion every Sunday and holy day by placing the elements on the altar at the Offertory, there might be enough people for a weekly or monthly Communion rather than only three or four times a year as in most villages.[16] In towns there was usually a monthly celebration. He criticized views he attributed to Bucer and Calvin. He regretted the omission of the invocation of the Holy Spirit in the Prayer of Consecration, but suggested that the words 'Hear us O merciful ...' imply such an invocation, and that consequently the elements are consecrated 'and so become the Body and Blood of our Saviour Christ'. Nor did he see why signing the elements with the sign of the cross should be 'laid aside', as signing with the cross was preserved in baptism. He regretted the separation of the Prayer of Oblation from the Prayer of Consecration, and emphasized the reverent consumption of what remained of the consecrated elements. He drew attention to the communal nature of the Communion by urging that, at the Offertory 'all communicants' should 'come from the more distant parts of the Church as near to the Lord's table as they can'. The generosity of lay people throughout the century in giving silver for use at Holy Communion, and costly fabrics for the communion table, suggests that this high sacramental doctrine was widely held.[17]

Baptism was urged by Wheatly as a public event, at the font, during Morning or Evening Prayer. He urged that babies should be 'dipped'

---

15 Wheatly, *A Rational Illustration*, pp. 130, 140, 268 and 278.

16 For a discussion of the reasons why in small communities celebrations of Communion were so infrequent, see Jacob, *Lay People and Religion*, pp. 57–60.

17 Wheatly, *Rational Illustration*, pp. 278–324, and Jacob, *Laypeople and Religion*, pp. 209–13, and William Jacob and James Lomax, '"A Broad Church": Sacred Silver in the Seventeenth and Eighteenth Centuries', in *Treasures of the English Church: A Thousand Years of Sacred Gold and Silver*, London: Paul Holberton Publishing, 2008.

in the font, and that 'sprinkling' should be the exception. Nearly all clergy complained of pressure from lay people for their children to be baptized 'privately' at home.

The major theological preoccupation of the late seventeenth- and early eighteenth-century Church of England was the Church's congruity with the 'primitive' Church of the first four centuries to defend it against attacks by Roman Catholics and Puritans, who both denied it was part of the true Church. This infused most aspects of the Church's life, even the design and layout of churches, as the context of the Prayer Book liturgy. William Beveridge's *Collection of Canons Received by the Greek Church*, published in 1672, in Volume Two of which he described the typical layout of an early Christian church, initiated a strong interest in the layout and design of early churches. William Cave's *Primitive Christianity* in 1673 also discussed the interrelationship between liturgy and architectural form in the early Church. George Wheler's *An Account of Churches and Places of Assembly of the Primitive Christians*, published in 1689 and based on his visit to Greece, Asia Minor and the Holy Land, used the evidence of Eusebius, and his own experience of archaeological sites, to reconstruct the plans of early churches in Tyre, Jerusalem and Constantinople. His plan and elevation for an ideal early church probably influenced the design of his chapel of ease in the expanding suburb of Spitalfields, east of the City of London. These writings influenced the 1711 Commission to Build Fifty New Churches in the populous suburbs of London, and especially Nicholas Hawksmoor who, drawing on Joseph Bingham's *Origines ecclesiasticae, or, Antiquities of the Christian Church*, produced a sketch for an ideal church, entitled 'The Basilica after the Primitive Christians', with a subheading, 'Manner of Building the Church – as it was in ye fourth century in ye purest times of Christianity'.[18] The design and layout of large numbers of churches built or rebuilt throughout the eighteenth century were modelled on the basilicas that Christians took over or built in the fourth century.

Reading the Fathers also influenced the pastoral and devotional life of the Church. Samuel Wesley, Rector of Epworth, quoted Tertullian's description of 'the first Christians who often met together *ad conferandum Disciplinum*, and to pray and sing Hymns to Christ as God'.[19]

18 For a full discussion of the architectural background, see Pierre de la Ruffinière du Prey, *Hawksmoor's London Churches: Architecture and Theology*, Chicago: University of Chicago Press, 2000, pp. 32–40 and 60–9.

19 Samuel Wesley, *The Poor Communicant Rightly Prepar'd: or a Discourse Concerning the Blessed Sacrament* (1700), Appendix: A Letter Concerning Reli-

He and many other clergy, encouraged by SPCK, established religious societies for young men in their parishes, to encourage deepening their spirituality, studying the Bible, and engaging in charitable activities. Society members often funded a priest to say daily prayers in church, committed themselves to attend Holy Communion more frequently, and sometimes donated communion silver. Their good works might include funding a charity school to teach poor children the Catechism and to read the Bible and the Prayer Book, and to sing psalms in church. Society members sometimes themselves formed a choir to sing canticles, metrical psalms and hymns in their parish church.[20]

Religious societies contributed to an explosion of music in churches. Services were probably monotoned by the celebrant, while parish clerks led the responses and gave a note, with a pitch pipe, for the tune for the congregation, and 'lined' the psalms. In addition to psalms set for the day, metrical psalms and texts from either *The Whole Book of Psalms, Collected in English Metre, By Thomas Sternhold and John Hopkins*, first published in 1556, or *A New Version of the Psalms of David* by Nicholas Brady and Nahum Tate, published in 1696, were usually sung between the Sunday morning services, or after the sermon. There was much criticism of the standard of music in parish churches, and from *c.*1715, encouraged by the publication of Thomas Bisse's *The Beauty of Holiness in the Common Prayer*, there was a determined effort at all levels to improve the quality of music. In town parishes on Sundays, singers usually sang the versicles and responses, settings for the canticles and an anthem, and the responses to the Commandments, the Sanctus and Gloria at Holy Communion. During the eighteenth century most town churches acquired organs, sometimes, as at Holy Trinity Hull in 1711, and Doncaster parish church in 1748–40, funded by public subscription. Organists often played a short piece after the psalms, to provide time for reflection. Otherwise, from mid-century there might be a group of instrumentalists, perhaps including a bassoon, a violin and a cello. Rural parishes also often had groups of singers. A very great deal of music was published during the century, both for town and village singers, and many town churches published their own hymn and

---

gious Societies, no pagination. For religious societies, see Jacob, *Lay People and Religion*, pp. 77–92.

20 See, for example, *The Christian Sacrifice of Praise: Consisting of Selected Psalms and Hymns with Doxologies and Proper Tunes for the Use of the Religious Society of Romney, Collected by the Author of the Christian's Daily Manual*, (1724). Hawksmoor's 'The Basilica after the Primitive Christians' provided space for a charity school in the undercroft. See de la Ruffinière du Prey, *Hawksmoor's London Churches*, pp. 63–4.

tune books.[21] Bishops and some clergy were very concerned that singers might dominate services by attempting to emulate cathedral choirs, and in any case discouraging congregational participation. There were many disputes between clergy and singers.

Hymn collections, other than metrical psalms, developed among Anglicans in the early eighteenth century initially for private or small-group devotional use, which is how John and Charles Wesley intended them to be used. There was a considerable market for printed collections of hymns. John Wesley's *A Collection of Hymns for the People Called Methodists*, in its various editions, was probably intended for personal and society use, but his *A Collection of Psalms and Hymns for the Lord's Day*, published in 1784, was intended for corporate worship.[22] It was generally thought that the law did not permit hymns to be sung during services, which is why they were placed before and between services, but a York consistory court case found this was not so.[23] Some Evangelical clergy began to introduce hymns into services instead of metrical psalms. James Hervey at Collington was noted in the early 1750s introducing two of Isaac Watts's hymns, which the clerk gave out line by line. In 1761 John Berridge compiled a collection of hymns, drawn chiefly from the Wesleys and Watts, for use at Everton.[24] Many Bristol parish churches began to sing hymns in worship in the 1760s.[25] However, some clergy and many laity strongly opposed this innovation. Where there was no choir, the parish clerk, who usually chose the tunes, continued to line out the psalms.

Although the Prayer Book was the nation's primer for prayer, worship and doctrine, as evidenced by the extent to which its language and formulae influenced people's private prayers, it was not without

21 See Nicholas Temperley, *The Music of the English Parish Church*, vol. 1, Cambridge: Cambridge University Press, 1979, pp. 88–97 and 104–242; Nicholas Temperley, *Studies in English Church Music 1550–1900*, Farnham: Ashgate, 2009. Hilary Davidson, *Choirs, Bands and Organs: A History of Church Music in Northamptonshire and Rutland*, Oxford: Positif Press, 2003, provides an illustration of the level of provincial musical activity.

22 Robin A. Leaver, 'Psalms and Hymns' and 'Hymns and Sacred Poems: Two Strands of Wesleyan Hymn Collections', in *Music and the Wesleys*, ed. Nicholas Temperley and Stephen Banfield, Urbana, IL: University of Illinois Press, 2010.

23 Temperley, *Studies in English Church Music*, pp. 105–7.

24 See Thomas K. McCart, *The Matter and Manner of Praise: The Controversial Evolution of Hymnody in the Church of England 1760–1820*, Drew Studies in Liturgy Series, no. 5, Lanham, ML and London: Scarecrow Press, 1998, pp. 30–69.

25 Jonathan Barry, 'Charles Wesley's Family and the Musical Life of Bristol', in Temperley and Banfield (eds), *Music and the Wesleys*.

criticism. Practically, people regretted the length of Sunday morning services, and complained of the number of repetitions of the Lord's Prayer, the *gloria patrie* after every psalm, the Nicene Creed as well as the Apostles' Creed, and the archaic language of the liturgy, such as the intercession to administer justice 'indifferently'. Other people had more radical proposals about how to 'more perfectly reform the Church of England's liturgy' to make it, and the Church's theology, closer to the practice and theology of the 'primitive Church'. Serious research about Eastern liturgies and texts from the early Church began in the late seventeenth century, especially on the oldest then-known liturgical text, the *Apostolic Constitutions* dating from the fourth century, which was then thought to be of apostolic origin.

Research about ancient liturgies led scholars in two directions. One was developed by a few radical 'Nonjurors', who, after the accession of William and Mary, declined the oath of allegiance and effectively separated themselves from the Church of England, with their own succession of bishops. In 1718, they adopted a revised eucharistic liturgy based on the 1549 rite. Subsequently Thomas Brett produced a new eucharistic liturgy strongly influenced by the *Clementine Liturgy* of the *Apostolic Constitutions* and Eastern liturgies. Adopting this in 1734 caused the Nonjurors to split into three factions: using the Prayer Book, the 1718 revision, and adopting Brett's liturgy, respectively. The Scottish Episcopal Church's *Communion Office*, adopted in 1764, was deeply indebted to Brett's liturgy mediated through Thomas Rattray's *The Ancient Liturgy of the Church of Jerusalem.*[26]

A second line of inquiry was developed by scholars, researching the New Testament and early liturgies with access to material unknown to the English Reformers. This raised questions about the New Testament evidence for the doctrines of Christ and the Trinity. William Whiston, Isaac Newton's successor as Lucasian Professor of Mathematics, who was deprived of his chair for questioning the biblical evidence for the Trinity, held the *Apostolic Constitutions* to be of apostolic authorship and to have the same authority as the New Testament. In 1713, he published *The Liturgy of the Church of England reduc'd nearer to the Primitive Standard*, recommending, as a first step, returning to the 1549 Prayer Book but, in the longer term, that the *Apostolic Constitutions* should be adopted to provide a basis for intercommunion

---

26 See W. Jardine Grisbrooke, *The Anglican Liturgies of the Seventeenth and Eighteenth Centuries*, London: SPCK, 1958, chs 3, 5, 6 and 7; Robert D. Cornwall, 'Thomas Brett 1677–1744'; and Rowan Strong, 'Thomas Rattray, 1684–1743', in *Oxford Dictionary of National Biography*, online.

between Anglicans, Roman Catholics, Lutherans and Dissenters. However, although he substituted 'altar' for 'table', provided for chrism in baptism, anointing the sick and for 'extended communion' for the sick, he addressed all prayers to the Father, provided a new Collect for Trinity Sunday and omitted the Proper Preface, and the Athanasian Creed, and part of the Nicene Creed as unscriptural and unknown in the 'primitive' Church.[27] A friend of Whiston's, Samuel Clarke, Rector of St James's Piccadilly in London, in his *Scripture Doctrine of the Trinity*, published in 1712, also outlined possible changes in the Prayer Book. In annotating a copy of the Prayer Book, Clarke amended all passages citing the Trinity, to equate 'God' with 'Father'. Whether this was an academic exercise, or represented his practice at St James's, one of the most fashionable and prestigious parish churches in the rapidly developing West End of London, attended by many visitors, is unknown.[28] Benjamin Hoadly, Bishop of Winchester, a friend of Clarke's, in 1735 published *A Plain Account of the Nature and End of the Lord's Supper ... to which are added forms of prayer*, in which he sought to recover the meaning of the Lord's Supper for Christ and his first followers, and concluded it to be a memorial of a sacrifice, in which Christ's followers joined to acknowledge him as their master and their confederation with one another.

Whiston, Clarke and Hoadly, while seeking to recover the earliest Christian understanding of the Eucharist and the Church, ignored the role of the Holy Spirit in the development of the Church's understanding of the nature of God as Trinity and of worship during the patristic period and later. Their publications provoked much debate. The orthodox defence was magisterially stated by Daniel Waterland, Master of Magdalene College, Cambridge, in his *Review of the Doctrine of the Eucharist as laid down in Scripture and Antiquity* in 1737, in which he set out understandings of the Eucharist as it had developed within the life of the Church.[29]

However, proposals to revise the Prayer Book more in conformity with Scripture continued. In 1749, the anonymous *Free and Candid Disquisitions relating to the Church of England*, associated with John Jones, Vicar of Alconbury in Huntingdonshire, proposed revising

---

27 Grisbrooke, *Anglican Liturgies*, ch. 4, and Stephen D. Snobelin, 'William Whiston 1667–1752', *Oxford Dictionary of National Biography*, online.

28 Bryan D.Spinks, *Liturgy in the Age of Reason: Worship and Sacraments in England and Scotland 1662–c.1800*, Farnham: Ashgate, 2008, p. 142.

29 For Waterland, see B. W. Young, 'Daniel Waterland', *Oxford Dictionary of National Biography*, online.

the Prayer Book to conform with only the Bible. He also argued for removing the repetitions in Morning Prayer, the Litany and the Holy Communion, for using a selection of psalms, dropping readings from the Apocrypha, omitting the Athanasian Creed, omitting Sternhold's and Hopkins' metrical psalms in favour of hymns from Isaac Watts, and recommended commissioning a new translation of the Bible. Several more proposals for revising the Prayer Book were published in the 1750s and 1760s.[30] The authors all held that the biblical evidence was that, while the Son and the Holy Spirit were divine beings, they were subordinate to the Father. Although they accepted the Trinity and the Apostles' Creed, they wished to drop the Athanasian Creed. How widespread sympathy with these views was is not easy to determine.

The most serious attempt to remove the Athanasian Creed from the Prayer Book was by Francis Blackburne, Archdeacon of Cleveland, and Theophilus Lindsey, his stepdaughter's husband, the Vicar of Catterick. They promoted the Feathers Tavern Petition to abolish subscription to the Thirty-Nine Articles of Religion, but with only just over 200 signatures, it was ignominiously rejected by the House of Commons in 1772. Lindsey resigned his living and established a 'reformed' Church of England, opening Essex Street Chapel in London, using *A Liturgy, Altered from that of the Church of England, to Suit Unitarian Doctrine*, based on Samuel Clarke's unpublished manuscript amendments to the Prayer Book, which his son had given to the British Museum in 1768. It was drawn to Lindsey's attention by his brother-in-law, John Disney, Vicar of Swinderby in Lincolnshire, who subsequently transcribed Clarke's amendments, and gave a copy to his friend Dr Samuel Prevost, in February 1787, three days before his consecration as Bishop of New York. As Lindsey moved in a more Unitarian direction, he periodically revised his liturgy until, in 1789, he omitted the Apostles' Creed. His liturgy was popular with Presbyterian ministers and congregations who were moving towards Unitarianism, for a formal liturgy permitted a layman to lead the worship if a minister was unavailable. Five Presbyterian liturgies based on Lindsey's revisions of Clarke's amendments to the Prayer Book were published between 1776 and 1791.[31]

---

30 For a discussion of these, see Marion J. Hatchett, *The Making of the First American Prayer Book 1776–1789*, New York: Seabury Press, 1982, pp. 19–35.

31 For an account of the influence of the Prayer Book on Unitarian worship, see A. Elliott Peaston, *The Prayer Book Reform Movement in the XVIIIth Century*, Oxford: Basil Blackwell, 1940. For Lindsey, see B. W. Young, 'Theophilus Lindsey', *Oxford Dictionary of National Biography*.

Many of the details of these proposed changes to the Prayer Book, including removing repetitions from the Sunday morning liturgy, and the suggestions to omit the Benedictus from Morning Prayer and the Magnificat and Nunc Dimittis from Evening Prayer, as being unsuitable for public worship because they referred to particular events and people, had their origins in either the Savoy Conference in 1661 or the 1689 Commission established to revise the Prayer Book.[32]

Anglican Evangelicals do not seem to have been much interested in liturgical revision, but they introduced hymns allowing emotion to be expressed in public worship. Several Evangelical clergy, for example Martin Madan, with his *A Collection of Psalms and Hymns extracted from Various Authors*, in 1760, and Augustus Toplady, with *Psalms and Hymns for Public and Private Worship* in 1766, published collections of hymns.[33]

John Wesley, when he revised the Prayer Book for the Methodists in North America, after the American War of Independence, because they needed to form an independent Church, published in America in 1784 *The Sunday Services of the Methodists in North America: with other Occasional Services* (published in London in 1786 as *The Sunday Services of the Methodists and other Occasional Services*). He noted in the Preface, 'I believe there is no liturgy in the World either in ancient or modern language which breathes more of a solid scriptural rational piety than the Common Prayer of the Church of England.' This did not prevent him adapting it for use by his ministers elsewhere than in parish churches. Most of his alterations too followed the recommendations of Puritan divines at the Hampton Court Conference in 1604, the Savoy Conference in 1661 and the 1689 Commission. These included replacing 'priest' by 'minister' throughout, omitting all the repetitions in the Sunday morning services, dropping all holy days, apart from Christmas, Good Friday and Ascension Day, and numbering Sundays after Christmas up to 15, concluding with Passion Sunday, excluding lessons from the Apocrypha, and the Benedicite at Morning Prayer, omitting private baptism, confirmation, the visitation of the sick and churching, and omitting the Gospel canticles as being personal, while retaining

---

32 See Spinks, *Liturgy in the Age of Reason*, pp. 48–53, and Hatchett, *Making of the First American Prayer Book*, pp. 13–16. The Commission's proposals were never published or debated, but summaries of them seem to have been widely available.

33 Spinks, *Liturgy in the Age of Reason*, pp. 162–170, and J. R. Watson, *The English Hymn: A Critical and Historical Study*, Oxford: Clarendon Press, 1997, pp. 265–9.

the psalms provided as alternatives. He replaced 'Morning Prayer daily throughout the year' with 'Morning Prayer every Lord's Day', and similarly for Evening Prayer, and recommended the Litany to be said on Wednesdays and Fridays, and extempore prayer on other days.

In the Holy Communion, Wesley omitted the rubrics but retained the manual acts, omitted the alternative Collect for the king, the Nicene Creed, the exhortations, the word 'absolution', the Proper Preface for Christmas day, modified the Trinity Sunday Preface, omitted 'all meekly kneeling' at receiving communion, and the 'prayer of thanksgiving'. He replaced 'bishops and curates' with 'all ministers of the Gospel' in the prayer for the Church, 'us' for 'you' in the absolution, permitted extempore prayer before the blessing in which he inserted 'may', and permitted singing hymns. He omitted godparents in baptism, required the baby to be 'dipped' in the water, or 'sprinkled', omitted the word 'regenerate' and the sign of the cross, and reference to rings in marriage, and the committal in the burial of the dead. He added a preaching service, comprising just a Collect before preaching, but recommended that on Sundays this should not replace attendance at the parish church. The Ordination service was headed 'The Form and Manner of Making and Ordaining Superintendents, Elders and Deacons', the place of a bishop being taken by a superintendent.[34]

The American War of Independence also necessitated a revision of the Prayer Book for the continuing episcopal clergy and congregations in the former colonies. They feared that more than minor amendments to the Prayer Book would divide the Church. There is no evidence that they used Wesley's revised Prayer Book, but the adaptations to the Prayer Book by the First Episcopal Church in Boston, under the influence of the second edition of Lindsey's liturgy, had been circulated to Philadelphia, New York and probably Connecticut. The Scottish bishops had also sent their Communion Office of 1763 to the Connecticut clergy as part of their concordat for consecrating Samuel Seabury in 1784.[35] In 1784, the Connecticut clergy and Seabury initially adopted revisions

34 See John C. Bowmer, *The Sacrament of the Lord's Supper in Early Methodism*, London: Dacre Press, 1951, pp. 207–12; A. Raymond George, 'The People Called Methodists: The Means of Grace', in *A History of the Methodist Church in Great Britain*, vol. 1, ed. Rupert Davies and Gordon Rupp, London: Epworth Press, 1965; and A. Elliott Peaston, *The Prayer Book Tradition in the Free Churches*, London: James Clarke & Co., 1964, pp. 39–54.

35 For a detailed account of the revision of the Prayer Book for use in the Protestant Episcopal Church in the United States, see Hatchett, *Making of the First American Book of Common Prayer*, upon which this account is largely dependent.

common to those of Clarke and Lindsey, and the Boston clergy and laity adopted these proposals with minor amendments. Seabury, however, rapidly backed off these proposals. In 1785 'a general convention' at Philadelphia, to which the parishes in the 'southern' states sent representatives to consider how to form a church, set up a committee to review the liturgy. This recommended a series of amendments largely reflecting the proposals to revise the Prayer Book in 1689 and in the various liturgies published in the 1750s and 1760s, and it was agreed a Book embodying these recommendations should be published. During the six months that took, anxieties about its radicalism grew. Seabury in particular distanced himself from it, and misleading reports were circulated in England. It was published in Philadelphia in April 1786 as *The Book of Common Prayer, and Administration of the Sacraments, and Other Rites and Ceremonies, As Revised and Prepared for the Use of the Protestant Episcopal Church*, noting, on the title page, it was for trial use. Compared with earlier proposed revisions it was liturgically and theologically conservative. The Eucharistic doctrine of the Prayer Book and expressions of trinitarian doctrine were retained. 'Minister' was substituted for 'priest' throughout, but absolutions, apart from that in the Visitation of the Sick, were retained, and provision was made for a 'special confession'. The Benedicite and Gospel canticles were retained. The Nicene and Athanasian Creeds were omitted, and 'descended into hell' omitted from the Apostles' Creed.

The English bishops, who requested to see the Book before consenting to consecrate as bishops the two priests elected as 'superior ministers' by their state conventions, merely asked that 'descent into hell' be restored in the Apostles' Creed, and that the Nicene and Athanasian Creeds should be retained, even though their use be 'Discretional'. Seabury was deeply critical of it, and also of the process of approving it, objecting to the involvement of representatives of the laity. Because of Seabury's opposition and objections by the New England states, the Book did not win general consent.

When the Convention reconvened in Philadelphia in September 1789, including New England representatives, and Seabury, a committee was appointed to prepare a further revision. The result was a Book largely based on the Proposed Book, but more radical in several ways. In the Holy Communion, the summary of the law was permitted as an alternative to the ten commandments, the Gospel acclamations were included, either the Apostles' or Nicene Creed was permitted, a more scriptural Proper Preface for Trinity Sunday was provided, most significantly, the Scottish Prayer of Consecration of 1763 was adopted, probably not under Seabury's influence, and a hymn was permitted after the consecration. Reference to baptismal regeneration was restored but godparents and use of the sign of the cross were made optional. A form of Family Morning and Evening Prayer was included, based on Bishop Gibson's *Family Devotions*. The book was ratified by all the state conventions, although Connecticut resolved always to use the Nicene Creed at the Holy Communion.

Although the Prayer Book remained unaltered throughout the century, despite criticisms of its repetitions and archaisms, and proposals for significant revisions by scholars wishing to make it more scriptural or more closely aligned to early liturgies, in Scotland and the United States and in the Methodist Church adaptations were made to meet different situations, and reflecting different theological nuances. Probably the revisions proposed for use in the Church of England would not have secured general approval. However, the Church of England, unlike the Methodist Church and the Episcopal Church in the United States, had no forum for considering these matters. The convocation were not granted royal letters of business to permit debates after 1717, until 1852, and neither the bishops nor any ministry of the Crown wished to risk attempting to revise the Church's liturgy in Parliament.

7

The Transition from 'Excellent Liturgy' to being 'Too Narrow for the Religious Life of the Present Generation'

The Book of Common Prayer in the Nineteenth Century

BRYAN D. SPINKS

On 25 April 1797, William Van Mildert, Rector of St Mary-le-Bow, London, preached a sermon entitled 'The Excellency of the Liturgy, and the Advantages of Being Educated in the Doctrine and Principles, of the Church of England'.[1] The sermon was preached in accordance with the trust established in the will of John Hutchins, citizen and goldsmith, that, on 25 April every year, some able minister of the Church of England was to be engaged to preach a sermon in St Mary-le-Bow that enforced and recommended 'the excellency and use of the Liturgy of the Church of England, and to set forth the advantages which do, and may reasonably be expected to accrue to such poor Children as are educated in the Doctrine and Principles of the said Church'.[2] In his sermon, Van Mildert, who later was to become Bishop of Durham and its last Prince Bishop, praised the Book of Common Prayer for preserving the most happy medium between extremes, and for being distinguished by the spirit of piety as well as perspicuous and beautiful simplicity.[3] He asserted:

---

1 Elizabeth Varley, *Last of the Prince Bishops: William Van Mildert and the High Church Movement of the Early Nineteenth Century*, Cambridge: Cambridge University Press, 1992.

2 William Van Mildert, *The Excellency of the Liturgy, and the Advantage of Being Educated in the Doctrine and Principles, of the Church of England*, London, 1797. The notice is printed after the text of the sermon, but not paginated.

3 Van Mildert, *Excellency of the Liturgy*, p. 11.

Our Liturgy, indeed, in its present state, is a most valuable repository of Christian knowledge. It serves as a manual of faith and practice; nor can any person be thoroughly conversant in it, without finding his understanding enlightened, his thoughts spiritualized, and his heart improved.[4]

Brushing aside the calls for emendations and abbreviation, he claimed:

Upon the preservation, therefore, of our excellent Liturgy in its present improved state, must depend, in a great measure, the preservation of the Church of England.[5]

Through the 'long eighteenth century', the 'excellent' liturgy had managed to remain unscathed in the face of the exotic proposals and experiments of the Nonjurors and the theologically heterodox emendations urged by the Newtonian theologian Samuel Clarke and his later followers.[6] Events of the nineteenth century took a different turn. Many churchmen continued to extol the Prayer Book in language comparable to van Mildert's, and it remained the only lawful liturgy for the Church of England. The Victorian era, however, saw new and irreversible assaults on the Book's liturgical adequacy as well as on the manner in which the services were performed. The Report of the Royal Commission on Ecclesiastical Discipline of 1906 would indeed note that there was:

no justification for any doubt that in the large majority of parishes the work of the Church is being quietly and diligently performed by clergy who are entirely loyal to the principles of the English Reformation as expressed in the Book of Common Prayer.[7]

But more tellingly the Commission noted:

the law of public worship in the Church of England is too narrow for the religious life of the present generation. It needlessly condemns much which a great section of Church people, including many of her most devoted members, value; and modern thought and feeling are

---

4 Van Mildert, *Excellency of the Liturgy*, p. 13.
5 Van Mildert, *Excellency of the Liturgy*, p. 15.
6 Bryan D. Spinks, *Liturgy in the Age of Reason: Worship and Sacraments in England and Scotland 1662–c.1800*, Farnham: Ashgate, 2008, pp. 105–58.
7 http://anglicanhistory.org/pwra/rced11.html (accessed 20 January 2012).

characterized by a care for ceremonial, a sense of dignity in worship, and an appreciation of the continuity of the Church, which were not similarly felt at the time when the law took its present shape.[8]

The consequences of that particular observation, which would end the hegemony of the Book of Common Prayer, were to unfold in the twentieth century. The focus of this chapter is upon the ecclesiastical movements and events of the nineteenth century that led to this latter observation of the Royal Commission, paying particular attention to the voices of those who lived through what was to be a century of drastic liturgical change.

The excellent liturgy

The esteem with which Van Mildert held the Prayer Book was echoed by many writers throughout the nineteenth century. During 1802 in Wakefield Parish Church, Thomas Rogers gave a series of lectures on the service of Morning Prayer which were published in 1816. In the Introduction, Rogers eschewed any originality for the substance of his lectures, and explained that they were intended to impress upon the minds of the recipients 'a due sense of the excellency and utility of the Liturgy of our Church'.[9] He exhorted his readership:

> These excellent compositions of the Common Prayer, have a strong claim to your serious attention, not only for the plainness and simplicity of their style, and the admirable order in which they are arranged, but for their direct tendency to produce and establish in you that humility and spirituality of mind which every real Christian would wish to possess, when approaching the throne of Grace ... Suffer me to exhort you, as members of the Established Church, to hold fast the form of sound words.[10]

Similarly, Charles Simeon, the noted Cambridge Evangelical, preached four sermons on the Book of Common Prayer, which were published in 1812 under the title *The Excellency of the Liturgy in Four Discourses*.

---

8 http://anglicanhistory.org/pwra/rced11.html (accessed 20 January 2012).

9 Thomas Rogers, *Lectures Delivered in the Parish Church of Wakefield in the Year 1802 on that part of the Liturgy of the Church of England contained in the Morning Prayer*, London, 1816, p. xi.

10 Rogers, *Lectures*, pp. iv–v.

Presumably having in mind Evangelical scruples over regeneration in the baptismal rite, and the words 'sure and certain hope of the resurrection' in the burial rite, Simeon admitted that the liturgy was not absolutely perfect. He nevertheless considered:

> as one of the highest excellencies of our Liturgy, that it is calculated to make us wise, intelligent, and sober Christians; it marks a golden mean; it affects and inspires a meek, humble, modest, sober piety, equally remote from the coldness of a formalist, the self-importance of a systematic dogmatist, and the unhallowed fervour of a wild enthusiast. A *tender seriousness, a meek devotion* and an *humble joy*, are the qualities which it was intended, and is calculated, to produce in all her members.[11]

As his title reinforced, Simeon defended what he termed the 'unrivalled excellence' of the Book of Common Prayer.[12] John Skinner, the incumbent of Camerton, Somerset, claimed that 'even those who could not read might easily join in the excellent Liturgy of the Church'.[13] In a sermon preached in 1822, he contrasted the educated clergy of the Church of England with many uneducated local Methodist preachers, and rhetorically asked, 'Is it the same thing to attend the crude, undigested effusion of a cobbler or a collier, under the name of prayer, as the beautiful service of our Liturgy?'[14] Joseph Leech, the Bristol newspaper publisher, on his rides to services in the villages around Bristol in 1845, encountered a cleric en route to preach at Iron Acton, who in conversation purportedly asserted:

> One page of our beautiful liturgy, uttered in the spirit that God requires, and the Church directs, 'with a lowly, penitent, and obedient heart,' would fall like refreshing dews on the soul, and leave us in a holier, happier frame of mind than a hundred discourses. The best and most elaborately prepared sermon is to my mind a poor, bald,

---

11 Charles Simeon, *The Excellency of the Liturgy, in Four Discourses. Preached Before the University of Cambridge, in November 1811*, Cambridge, 1812, p. 54. See also Andrew Atherstone, *Charles Simeon on The Excellency of the Liturgy*, Alcuin Club/GROW Joint Liturgical Study 72, Norwich: Hymns Ancient and Modern, 2011.

12 Simeon, *Excellency of the Liturgy*, p. 23.

13 John Skinner, *Journal of a Somerset Rector 1803–1834*, ed. Howard and Peter Coombs, Oxford: Oxford University Press, 1984, p. 269. An entry for 1824.

14 Skinner, *Journal of a Somerset Rector*, p. 213.

and meagre composition, compared with the touching beauty and true piety of a single sentence of the Litany.[15]

Leech himself told the account of a particular individual who had been brought up in the Dissenting tradition, but at the age of 18 first encountered 'our inimitable Liturgy',

> which came upon him with its piety breathing and comprehensive petitions, the simple and beautiful majesty of its addresses to the Almighty, the contrite humility which pervades its penitential confessions, and the fervour with which it enables faith to express itself – all these, presented to him for the first time in the full force of freshness and novelty, made such an impression on him that from that day forward he was a churchman, declaring that he could never again bear to listen to the bald and erratic extemporisings of Dissent.[16]

In his 1848 sermons on the Prayer Book, Frederick Denison Maurice stated that 'I hope you will never hear from me any such phrases as our 'excellent or incomparable Liturgy' because it was not there to be praised but used.[17] Although he rejected the term 'excellent', Maurice held that the Prayer Book was at the heart of English national identity and of English morality and, along with many other nineteenth-century churchmen and churchwomen, he regarded the liturgy as essential to the English Church.[18]

---

15 Joseph Leech, *Rural Rides of the Bristol Churchgoer*, ed. Alan Sutton, Stroud: Nonsuch Publishing Ltd, 2004, pp. 171–2. Journalistic licence is no doubt at work here, giving voice to Leech's own views.

16 Leech, *Rural Rides*, p. 195.

17 Frederick Denison Maurice, *The Prayer-Book considered especially in Reference to the Roman System. Nineteen Sermons preached in the Chapel of Lincoln's Inn 1848*, London: Macmillan and Co., 1893, p. 6.

18 See further, Andrew Braddock, *The Role of the Book of Common Prayer in the Formation of Modern Anglican Church Identity. A Study of English Parochial Worship, 1750–1850*, Lewiston: Edwin Mellen, 2010. For a contemporary argument that the Prayer Book was 'implicated in establishment, development, and consolidation of the national identity of early modern England', see Timothy Rosendale, *Liturgy and Literature in the Making of Protestant England*, Cambridge: Cambridge University Press, 2007.

The Book as used

John Skinner of Camerton recorded in his journal for Sunday, 6 January 1828, 'I read the prayers as usual.'[19] But what was 'usual'? Contemporary journals and diaries such as Skinner's, and the newspaper articles of Joseph Leech, allow us to flesh out the Prayer Book services as performed during the first part of the nineteenth century.

The rubrics of the 1662 Book of Common Prayer insisted that Morning Prayer, the Litany and Ante-communion were to be celebrated every Sunday, and the three rites were celebrated consecutively. Communion itself was in most churches only quarterly. When communion was administered, only those wishing to receive stayed for that part of the service. The surplice was worn for all services, but although not sanctioned by rubric, it had become the custom for the priest to remove the surplice and put on a black gown for preaching the sermon. At evening service, the catechism was expounded, and because it was a shorter service, it may account for the higher attendance. William Holland, incumbent of Over Stowey, Somerset, noted in 1800 that 'In Country Parishes there are always more in the afternoon than in the morning', which was also the experience of the Revd Francis Witts in the 1820s at Upper Slaughter in the Cotswolds, and of Joseph Leech around Bristol in 1845.[20] The 'occasional' services were often celebrated on Sundays too. William Holland recorded on 1 April 1804, Easter Day:

> Not many at Church but a good many at the Sacrament, two or three and twenty. The Church at Asholt very full indeed. I received three children into the Church first and then I read the Baptism over again for another child, the elder of the first three was ten years old. The Duty of this day almost fatigued me, I had prayers twice, a Sacrament, two Sermons, two Christenings, and a Churching and so I went into Mr Blake's and they gave me a glass of mead and I drank tea there.[21]

Francis Witts had a christening and churching after morning service on Sunday, 12 April 1807, at Erchfont, and the following Sunday a

---

19 Skinner, *Journal of a Somerset Rector*, p. 309.

20 Jack Ayres (ed.), *Paupers and Pig Killers: The Diary of William Holland A Somerset Parson 1799–1818*, Gloucester: Alan Sutton Publishing, 1984, p. 33; Francis E. Witts, *The Complete Diary of a Cotswold Parson. Vol. 2, The Curate and Rector*, Chalfont: Amberley Publishing, 2008; Leech, *Rural Rides, passim*.

21 Ayres (ed.), *Paupers and Pig Killers*, pp. 95–6. Though Holland wrote Asholt, the name today seems to be Aisholt.

burial after the evening service.[22] On Sunday, 20 September 1820, John Skinner recorded that after Evening Prayer he buried a child who had died from the measles.[23] Morning and evening services usually needed the assistance of the church clerk who led the congregational responses, and sometimes led the singing where there was no parish band or singers. Most parishes had a clerk, and a good many also had the singers and band.

At St George's, Somerset, Joseph Leech stated that the vicar was 'an admirable reader, impressive without ostentation', and at Slimbridge, where two curates occupied the reading desk and divided the duty, the service combined 'the utmost solemnity and simplicity'.[24] Leech also described the dignity of a service at St John's, Torquay, at which three priests and Bishop Henry Phillpotts officiated. Of Phillpotts, Leech observed:

> At the rehearsal of the Commandments he advanced to the steps of the altar, and facing the congregation, read, while the three clergymen knelt towards the East. His delivery of the Decalogue was beautifully judicious: without any appearance of acting, no acting could yet be employed to produce more effect: conscious of his want of strength, there was an earnest and emphatic effort to make up for his physical debility, as was evinced by the impressive shake of the head and the upraised hand at the close of almost every period.[25]

Not all clergy and churches, though, were meticulous about dignity, decency and good order. Henry Moule, Vicar of Fordington in Dorset told Francis Kilvert something of the state of things when he had first arrived in that parish in the late 1820s:

> No man had ever been known to receive the Holy Communion except the parson, the clerk and the sexton. There were 16 women communicants and most of them went away when he refused to pay them for coming. They had been accustomed there at some place in the neighbourhood to pass the cup to each other with a nod of the head. At one church there were two male communicants. When the cup was given to the first he touched his forelock and said, 'Here's

22 Witts, *Complete Diary*, vol. 2, pp. 109, 111.
23 Skinner, *Journal of a Somerset Rector*, p. 138.
24 Leech, *Rural Rides*, pp. 221, 232.
25 Joseph Leech, *The Church-Goer's Rural Rides*, 3rd edn, Bristol, 1851, pp. 245–50, p. 247.

your good health, Sir'. The other said, 'Here's the good health of the Lord Jesus Christ'.

One day there was christening and no water in the Font. 'Water, Sir!' said the clerk in astonishment. 'The last parson never used no water. He spit into his hand.'[26]

In his 1845 visit to Bleadon church, Joseph Leech recorded:

The Rev. David Williams was in the reading-desk when I entered, going through the service, just as you would suppose the service to be gone through in such a church as I have described. He seemed to be suffering from flatulency, for at every other verse he was obliged to pause, afterwards wiping his mouth with an old brown hand-kerchief, and occasionally varying the act by using the sleeve of his surplice (which was far from clean) for the purpose. There was no singing or musical service whatever, the Rev. Gentleman objecting to it, as I have heard, on the grounds that it affects his head, but he has never complained of it affecting his heart ... he has occasionally paused in the midst of the Psalms, to correct the clerk for reading too fast or too loud, but by way of reprisals the clerk has sometimes had to correct the parson for reading the wrong psalm, an incident of this kind having occurred, I think, on Whitsunday last.[27]

At Yatton church, Leech complained of the speed with which the parson read the service. He commented:

There is an old joke of an Oxford spark saying he would give any man the Creed and beat him before he came to the end of the Litany. I really believe from the rate at which he read, the incumbent of Yatton might do this with ease: I attempted to keep up with him, but finding the pace impossible I closed my book, and listened with resignation ... I cannot bear to hear the beautiful prayers of the church, which so abound in fervent appeals, in deep devotional and penitential expressions, and awful epithets, being skipped through by clergyman and congregation, as if they were performing a mere daily task, the primary object of which was expedition.[28]

26 William Plomer (ed.), *Kilvert's Diary 1870–1879. Selections from the Diary of the Rev. Francis Kilvert*, New York: Macmillan, 1947, pp. 279–80.
27 Leech, *Rural Rides*, pp. 297–8.
28 Leech, *Rural Rides*, p. 180.

Perhaps with such incumbents in mind, Richard Cull, a tutor in elocution, had in 1840 published *Garrick's Mode of Reading the Liturgy of the Church of England*. David Garrick, the famous eighteenth-century actor, had instructed some clergy in the art of speech delivery, and the manuscript notes of one cleric were published in 1797, and now republished by Cull. Cull noted:

> It is a subject of deep regret that this prominent duty (publicly reading service) is commonly so ill performed, even by Clergymen of high mental endowments and of great acquirements, and the object of the present work is to supply the Clergy with some principles to guide them in their public reading.[29]

Thus with the opening three words of the exhortation to confession at Morning Prayer, 'Dearly beloved brethren', the advice Garrick had given was:

> Here, make a pause much longer than the comma, or, indeed, than the time which is thought to be necessary after a semicolon. – Then proceed with a *solemn dignity* of tone, and with a *tenor* of *smooth, regular* delivery.
> *the scripture moveth us in sundry places to acknowledge* –
> Not ac*know*ledge (the second syllable very long,) as it is pronounced by many.[30]

In the original Preface that was reprinted by Cull, the intention was to redress 'the slovenly and irreverent manner in which the Common Prayer was read by the generality of Divines'.[31]

But parish clerks had a crucial role too. Joseph Leech, on his 1844 visit to Redcliff church, opined:

> I don't know whether or not parish clerks may be out of my province: if it were not taking a liberty, however, I would meekly beg that the rev. the vicar might devote a spare hour to teaching the clerk to deport himself with more reverend humility in his business: he lolled upon the left hand with an air of the utmost complacency, and casting a side-long glance towards the ceiling said, 'We beseech thee to

---

29 Richard Cull, *Garrick's Mode of Reading the Liturgy of the Church of England*, London and Cambridge, 1840, p. vii.
30 Cull, *Garrick's Mode of Reading*, pp. 67–8.
31 Cull, *Garrick's Mode of Reading*, p. 63.

hear us, good Lord,' as if it did not greatly concern him whether his prayers were complied with or not.[32]

Writing in 1803, William Jones, incumbent of Broxbourne, Hertfordshire, complained that the deputy parish clerk, a tailor called Mr Rogers, kept losing his place in the book and fumbling over words:

> Upon the whole, he made a sad, bungling piece of work of it, & if he acquits himself no better in his tailoring capacity than he does in supplying a Church-clerk's place, he must be what is called a miserable hand, a mere *botcher*. The whimsically wretched mistakes he made, & which I have heard too many fixed in that high office make, in reading the psalms, etc, are incredible … In some parishes, one might suppose that miserable reading was considered as a first-rate qualification in a parish-clerk. They *jabber*, as fast as they can pelt out the words, right or wrong.[33]

The parish musicians and singers, using the metrical psalms of the old version of Sternhold and Hopkins or the new version of Tate and Brady, often preferring the folk music style of 'fuguing', could make or mar the service.[34] Although the pipe organ and barrel organ were becoming more common in the early nineteenth century, most churches used a medley of instruments. Although hymns were not unknown, they were regarded by many bishops as expressions of Methodism, and discouraged.[35] At Abbott's Leigh in 1845, Leech noted that in the West Gallery there were a big fiddle, a flute and a bassoon, 'together with sundry persons who perform on these musical implements, severally and respectively – I wish I could add respectably'.[36] William Holland recorded on Sunday, 15 April 1804, that at Asholt church (Somerset),

> A disagreeable fellow was playing his fiddle in the Church when I came in, without tune or harmony, intending I presume to accom-

---

32 Leech, *Rural Rides*, pp. 41–2.

33 O. F. Christie (ed.), *The Diary of the Revd. William Jones 1777–1821. Curate and Vicar of Broxbourne and the Hamlet of Hoddesdon 1781–1821*, London: Brentano's, 1929, pp. 149–50.

34 See Christopher Turner (ed.), *Georgian Psalmody 1. The Gallery Tradition*, Corby Glen: SG Publishing in association with Anglia Polytechnic University, 1997.

35 See Thomas K. McCart, *The Matter and Manner of Praise. The Controversial Evolution of Hymnody in the Church of England 1760–1820*, Lanham, ML: Scarecrow Press, 1998.

36 Leech, *Rural Rides*, p. 243.

pany the Psalm Singers. I however ordered him to stop his noise which he would hardly do and then he began trying his discordant hautboy.[37]

John Skinner had to ban his singers when they arrived intoxicated, and who, 'being offended because I would not suffer them to chant the service after the First Lesson, put on their hats and left the Church'.[38]

Joseph Leech, noting that in some 'primitive' parishes the custom was to write the psalms to be sung on a slate which was hung over the gallery, recalled one occasion at Isle Brewers:

the clerk, when he has partly given out the psalms, discovered that the usual telegraph had not been lowered; his announcement, therefore, when interrupted, ran thus: 'Let us sing to the praise and -----, I say (looking up to the gallery), why don't thee hang out the slate there?' I mention this incident only to illustrate that parish orchestras look for the most part upon themselves in the light of mere parish musicians, and have little or no sense of the solemnity of their situation or of that portion of the service which appertains to them.[39]

But there were success stories too. Holland spoke well of the singers and two flautists in 1805, and in December they had new instruments from London.[40] Leech's visit to Thornbury, Christmas 1844, reveals that this church had an organ and organist, as well as a gallery choir. The voluntary was 'dashing', and followed by the Gloria sung by the gallery singers, though perhaps this was because it was Christmas, and because the Mayor and Corporation were in attendance.[41] Furthermore, at least some cathedrals maintained a reasonable choral tradition.[42] However, even while Leech was making his 1845 visits, the liturgical practices of parish churches across the country were beginning to undergo considerable change. Isaac Williams, in his prefatory thoughts to his poems published in 1842, wrote:

---

37 Ayres, *Paupers and Pig Killers*, p. 96.

38 Skinner, *Journal of a Somerset Rector*, p. 200. Cf. p. 162.

39 Joseph Leech, *The Bristol Church Goer: His Visits to Bitton, &c.*, Bristol, 1849, p. 16.

40 Leech, *The Bristol Church Goer*, pp. 120, 125.

41 Leech, *Rural Rides*, pp. 207ff.

42 William J. Gatens, *Victorian Cathedral Music in Theory and Practice*, Cambridge: Cambridge University Press, 1986.

The Church, 'tis thought, is wakening through the land
And seeking vent for the o'erloaded hearts
Which she has kindled, – pours her forth anew, –
Breathes life in ancient worship, – from their graves
Summons the slumbering Arts to wait on her,
Music and Architecture, varied forms
Of Painting, Sculpture, and of Poetry.[43]

Williams alluded rather obliquely here to what were, in fact, the double tsunami of Tractarianism and the Ecclesiologists, the aftershocks of which would completely alter the inherited pattern and forms of Church of England worship.[44]

The Prayer Book assailed

It is doubtful whether those who gathered at Hadleigh Rectory and planned the Tracts for the Times could have foreseen the liturgical revolution that would ensue. Calls for shortening the Prayer Book services had already begun in the latter decades of the seventeenth century, and periodically throughout the eighteenth century. Such calls were renewed at the beginning of the nineteenth century by those viewed as representing a more liberal voice – Connop Thirlwall, Charles Wodehouse and Edward Berens. They argued for an abridgement of the morning services, the omission of the Athanasian Creed and rubrics such as mentioning the dipping of children in baptism.[45] The Tractarians initially called for no changes at all, only the enforcement of the rubrics regardless of whether or not they had long fallen into abeyance. In Tract 3, Newman argued that only rationalists and Evangelicals wanted alteration to erode the Church, and he returned to this theme in Tracts 38 and 41. In Tract 9, Hurrel Froude turned his attention

---

43 Isaac Williams, *The Baptistery, or, The Way of Eternal Life*, Oxford: John Henry Parker, 1842, p. x.

44 Nigel Yates, *Anglican Ritualism in Victorian Britain 1830–1910*, Oxford: Oxford University Press, 1999; Nigel Yates, *The Anglican Revival in Victorian Portsmouth*, Portsmouth: Grosvenor Press for Portsmouth City Council, 1983; Dominic Janes, *Victorian Reformation: The Fight over Idolatry in the Church of England 1840–1860*, New York: Oxford University Press, 2009; Teresa Berger, *Liturgie – Spiegel der Kirche: Eine systematische-theologische Analyse des liturgischen Gedankenguts im Traktarianism*, Forschungen zur Systematischen und ökumenischen Theologie 52, Göttingen: Vandenhoeck & Ruprecht, 1986.

45 R. C. D. Jasper, *Prayer Book Revision in England 1800–1900*, London: SPCK, 1954.

to the plea for shortening services. He retorted that they had already been shortened at the Reformation. Furthermore they were intended for daily use, but now had become weekly. The logical trend would be that they would become monthly and then disappear altogether. The Tractarian ploy was to observe the rubrics diligently so that bishops in turn would enforce them. However, when High Church bishops such as C. J. Blomfield of London in 1842 and Henry Phillpotts of Exeter in 1845 – neither of whom were Tractarians – attempted simply to enforce the wearing of the surplice for preaching, they met with protest, and resistance.[46] The Ornaments Rubric that had lain dormant since 1559 was to become a storm centre, and was appealed to for support of practices from lighted candles on the altar to full eucharistic vestments and incense. The Tracts also made appeal to the pre-Reformation medieval services, and later Tractarians would begin to interpret the Prayer Book through the lenses of the medieval liturgies, and even replace Prayer Book formularies with those of the medieval rites or the contemporary Catholic rites. Newman had begun using the Roman Breviary in 1837, a practice that Pusey adopted in 1839.[47] Pusey defended baptismal regeneration in Tracts 67–69, and in Tract 81 defended the concepts of real presence and sacrifice in the Eucharist, which many regarded as smuggling popery into the Church of England.

If the Oxford Tracts were one assault, the Cambridge Ecclesiologists were another. The evangelical Francis Close astutely observed:

as Romanism is taught *Analytically* at Oxford, it is taught *Artistically* at Cambridge – that it is inculcated theoretically, in tracts at one University, and it is *sculptured, painted* and *graven* at the other ... in a word, that the 'Ecclesiologist' of Cambridge is identical in doctrine with the Oxford *Tracts for the Times*.[48]

---

46 L. E. Ellsworth, *Charles Lowder and the Ritualist Movement*, London: Darton, Longman and Todd, 1982, p. 8, citing their Diocesan Charges. The Revd Dr John Allen Giles recorded in March 1855, 'A letter from Mr Adams told me that Mr. Newman the new curate at Bampton now preached in his surplice, which was thought a novelty and was much talked about.' Leech had remarked that the Revd Williams at Bleadon had kept his surplice on for the sermon, but like many others, simply because it saved the necessity of changing. Elsewhere it became a liturgical controversy. David Bromwich (ed.), *The Diary and Memoirs of John Allen Giles*, Taunton: Somerset Record Office, 2000, p. 319; Leech, *Rural Rides*, p. 298.

47 Ellsworth, *Charles Lowder*, p. 10.

48 F. Close, *The Restoration of Churches is the Restoration of Popery. A Sermon*, London, 1844, p. 4.

In May 1839 John Mason Neale and Benjamin Webb had founded the Cambridge Camden Society, later to become the Ecclesiological Society. While by no means the first to promote neo-Gothic architecture,[49] the Society's publications promoted this style as the only true Christian style, and their principles would be embraced by William Butterfield and Richard Carpenter. Christopher Webster observes:

> Within a generation, Anglican churches and the worship within them, were indeed undergoing a far-reaching process of transformation and *The Ecclesiologist* could claim with a good deal of justifiable pride in its last edition in 1868 'we have the satisfaction of retiring from the field as victors'.[50]

Both Neale and Webb were concerned with the interiors as well as exteriors, and strengthened the growing criticism of box pews and rented pews.[51] But they were also interested in ceremonial. Neale and Webb published the translation of Durandus of Mende's *The Symbolism of Churches and Church Ornaments* in 1843, and members edited *Hierurgia Anglicana* between 1843 and 1848, recording the survival of pre-Reformation ornaments and rituals in the Church of England. These works coalesced with the convictions of Tractarians, such as J. R. Bloxam, who has been described as 'the real originator of the ceremonial revival in the Church of England'.[52] Geoffrey Brandwood notes that although Webb never adopted vestments or incense, Neale, after he started the sisterhood of St Margaret's, East Grinstead, did, and he also introduced exposition of the sacrament.[53]

---

49 For varied styles, including Gothic revival, see M. H. Port, *Six Hundred New Churches. The Church Building Commission 1818–1856*, Reading: Spire Books, 2006; Nigel Yates, *Buildings, Faith, and Worship: The Liturgical Arrangement of Anglican Churches 1600–1900*, Oxford: Oxford University Press, 1991.

50 Christopher Webster, '"Absolutely Wretched": Camdenian Attitudes to the Late Georgian Church', in Christopher Webster and John Elliott (eds), *'A Church as it Should Be': The Cambridge Camden Society and Its Influence*, Donington: Shaun Tyas, 2000, pp. 1–21, p. 2. Cf. *The Ecclesiologist* 29 (1868), pp. 315–16.

51 See Trevor Cooper and Sarah Brown (eds), *Pews, Benches and Chairs: Church Seating in English Churches from the Fourteenth Century to the Present*, Ecclesiological Society, Donington: Shaun Tyas, 2011.

52 A. Symondson, 'Theology, Worship and the Late Victorian Church', in C. Brooks and A. Saint (eds), *The Victorian Church: Architecture and Society*, Manchester: Manchester University Press, 1995, p. 195.

53 Geoffrey K. Brandwood, '"Mumeries of a Popish Character" – the Camdenians and Early Victorian Worship', in Webster and Elliot, *A Church as it Should Be*, pp. 62–97, pp. 76–77.

Few churches adopted such extreme Catholic ceremonial in the 1850s, but the wide ripple effects should not be underestimated. For example, the *Essex Standard* newspaper of 21 February 1845 carried an article under the title 'Rubrical Changes at Witham', which began:

> The changes in the performance of Divine service introduced in this county immediately after, and some of them in accordance with the suggestions and directions of the Bishop of the Diocese, were carried out more extensively at Witham than in other places; and on the chancel of the church being repaired, a cross and other matters, novel in Protestant churches, were introduced. These changes occasioned the most uncomfortable sentiments in the minds of the parishioners; but, as in the generality of instances, the objections to these unwelcome changes were suppressed, partly from respect to the minister, and partly from the commendable wish to avoid disputes. Recently, however, it has been respectfully intimated to the Vicar, the Rev. John Bramston, that a return to the old form of service was desirable: and it was suggested that a private meeting of the Vicar and his leading parishioners should be held on the subject. This was done, and in the evening of the 10th instant between 20 and 30 of the principal inhabitants met Mr. Bramston at the house of one of the churchwardens, when the various points were discussed in a friendly spirit. Upwards of twenty objections were presented to the reverend gentleman, including the preaching in the surplice, the offertory, the cross erected at the altar, the credence or side table for the elements of the holy communion, the placing of the alms basin on the altar at All Saints Church, the manner of singing in the morning service, the minister turning from the people during prayer, the performance of baptism in the congregation, the application of the alms for other purposes than those of the poor of the parish, and other points.[54]

Bramston, later to be Dean of Winchester, was no extreme ritualist.[55]

---

54 *Essex Standard*, 21 February 1845, 'Rubrical Changes at Witham', no pagination, but 2nd sheet. The paper also printed the sermon that Bramston preached the following Sunday defending the changes. He took his text from 1 Cor. 14.1, 20, 26, 33, 40. Sheets 3 and 4.

55 Witham Church did not regularly use eucharistic vestments until 1968 when they were introduced by Canon Leslie John Derrett. During my curacy at St Nicolas, Witham, 1975–78, I borrowed High Mass vestments for festivals, though the ceremonial was hardly a High Mass by Knott's *Ritual Notes* standard. William Van Mildert had been curate of Witham. Revd John Suddards was Team Rector of Witham for ten years, and in 2011 left for Thornbury, one of the

He inherited from his predecessor the scheme to build a new church in the town centre, since the old parish church of St Nicolas was some distance away. The building committee rejected George Gilbert Scott in favour of the Norwich architect John Brown, a decision that cost them dearly.[56] However, when the new All Saints Church was opened, Bramston seems to have taken the opportunity to introduce, both there and at St Nicolas, some of the newer more moderate fashions in worship.

Others did similarly. In 1850, Lady Charlotte Guest complained of the Revd Walter Ponsonby:

> Ist., the intoning of the service, 2ndly., the print of a crucifix and dead Christ on the Altar of the Mortuary Chapel, 3rdly., the total disuse of the gown which, however unimportant of itself, I looked upon as a badge of party. I remonstrated on the Popish tendency of his formalities.[57]

Ponsonby 'referred to his obligation to follow the rubric, and seemed greatly shocked and hurt at being suspected of anything like a Romanising tendency'.[58]

Benjamin Armstrong, Vicar of Dereham 1850–88, noted the changes made in 1855 at St Ethelburga's, Bishopsgate:

> Mr. Rodwell has Holy Communion every Sunday; a surpliced choir; intones the service; has nothing but Gregorian tones; rings the Sanctus bell in service; preaches in his surplice; kneels east and, in short, has adopted the whole feature of Catholicity of which our system is capable.[59]

Surpliced choirs and good music, and even the wearing of the surplice for sermons in one or two places, predate the Tractarian Movement, but there is little doubt that the movement gave them further impetus;

---

churches visited by Leech. Sadly, John Suddards was murdered at Thornbury in February 2012.

56 Janet Gyford, *A History of Witham*, Witham: Janet Gyford, 2005, pp. 73–5.

57 The Earl of Bessborough (ed.), *Lady Charlotte Guest: Extracts from her Journal 1833–1852*, London: John Murray, 1950, p. 238.

58 Earl of Bessborough, *Lady Charlotte Guest*, p. 239.

59 Herbert B. J. Armstrong (ed.), *Armstrong's Norfolk Diary. Further passages from the Diary of the Reverend Benjamin John Armstrong*, London: Hodder and Stoughton, 1963, p. 54.

they also became a part of worship even in churches that most certainly disowned Tractarianism.[60]

In 1869 Armstrong visited the rector of Whissonsett, and noted:

He showed us his banners, eucharistic vestments and scarlet cassock and laced cotta for the thurifer! Who could ever suppose that such things would be used again and in the heart of Norfolk! The object of the Ritualists is to make our services as glorious and beautiful as any in the world.[61]

Armstrong made changes at a slower pace at Dereham. In 1861, he introduced a surpliced choir at all services, but didn't preach in his surplice until 17 May 1868, though he still wore his black gown when preaching in Norwich Cathedral in 1871.[62] On 7 December 1873 he celebrated choral Communion, and thought that it was probably the first time in Dereham since the Reformation.[63] In October 1870 he had recorded with pride and satisfaction:

To-day I have completed twenty years in this parish. Preached on retrospection, drawing a comparison between the state of things now and twenty years ago. Nothing could be worse than the state of the Church in 1850. Then, the altar was a miserable mahogany table with a covering fifty years old; there was a vile yellow carpet; a Grecian reredos with daubs of Moses and Aaron; no painted glass, and the rail for the communicants intersecting the sedilia. Look at it now – an altar and super-altar of full dimensions, with flower-vases always replenished with flowers; candlesticks and candles (now introduced); three altar-cloths changed at the seasons; the windows painted; a stone reredos highly painted and with a central Cross; a rich carpet; credence table; Bishop's chair, etc, etc.[64]

On the other hand, St Barnabas, Jericho, Oxford, had been built in 1869 to showcase Tractarian ceremonial from the start. Francis Kilvert described a service that he attended in 1876:

60 Leeds Parish Church 1818 had a surpliced choir, and was followed by St James's Ryde under Richard Sibthorp. Michael Trott, *The Life of Richard Waldo Sibthorp*, Brighton: Sussex Academic Press, 2005.

61 Trott, *Life*, p. 119.

62 Herbert B. J. Armstrong (ed.), *A Norfolk Diary: Passages from the Diary of the Rev. Benjamin John Armstrong*, London: George Harrap and Co. Ltd, 1949, pp. 82, 135, 163.

63 Armstrong, *A Norfolk Diary*, p. 177.

64 Armstrong, *A Norfolk Diary*, p. 156.

The large Church was almost full, the great congregation singing like one man. The clergy and choir entered with a procession, incense bearers and a great gilt cross, the thurifers and acolytes being in short white surplices over scarlet cassocks and the last priest in the procession wearing a biretta and a chasuble stiff with gold ... The poor humble Roman Church hard by is quite plain, simple and Low Church in its ritual compared with St. Barnabas in its festal dress on high days and holidays.[65]

Some fourteen years later, the young Ursula Bethell wrote:

We went together to the afternoon service at St. Barnabas ... What wd. you have said to it! The Altar with a gorgeous canopy over it & seven red lamps always burning before it – & many candles & crucifixes. The clergyman decked out to a degree – he was robed & unrobed several times during the service by two little acolytes who always stood by him – & he looked like the pictures of Roman Catholic Priests. While singing a hymn they marched round the church – many men clothed in red holding banners & crucifixes – & then a boy with incense which filled the church![66]

The new good taste in Church architecture and furnishing meant that whereas at the Reformation the question had been, 'How could Gothic interiors be adapted for the celebration of Prayer Book liturgies?', now the question was 'How could Prayer Book liturgies be adapted for Gothic and neo-Gothic interiors and furnishings?' A committee of the Lower House of the Canterbury Convocation rightly noted in 1866, 'some advance in Ritual is the natural sequel to the restoration and adornment of Churches which has so remarkably prevailed during the last twenty-five years'.[67]

Dale Adelmann has documented the other important contribution of the Ecclesiologists, and that is the revival of quality choral worship.[68] Both Webb and Neale subscribed to the Musical Antiquarian

---

65 Plomer (ed.), *Kilvert's Diary*, p. 365. St Barnabas was funded by Thomas Combe, Printer to the University, and a Tractarian supporter, who was connected with Magdalen College where Bloxham was a Fellow. See Roy Judge, 'May Morning and Magdalen College, Oxford', *Folklore* 97 (1986), pp. 15–40, for the intersection of Bloxham, Combe and Holman Hunt.

66 Peter Whiteford (ed.), *Vibrant Words: The Letters of Ursula Bethell*, Wellington, New Zealand: Victoria University Press, 2005, p. 5. Letter dated 1890/91.

67 Cited in Ellsworth, *Charles Lowder*, p. 84.

68 Dale Adelmann, *The Contribution of Cambridge Ecclesiologists to the*

Society, from which evolved the Motet Society with its concern for sacred music. This, together with the work of the Revd Thomas Helmore at the recently opened St Mark's Training College, Chelsea, saw the encouragement of plainsong. John Hullah, a member of the Camden Society from 1843, gave classes on sight singing at Exeter Hall from 1841. The year 1850 saw the publication of the *Hymnal Noted*, which drew heavily on the hymns of the Sarum use. Neale translated many pre-Reformation hymns, and would be a main contributor to the hugely successful *Hymns Ancient and Modern*, 1861. This hymnal, conceived on a journey on the Great Western Railway, bore a Tractarian stamp, though the collection drew on a variety of traditions and centuries.[69] However, music was able to cross boundaries in ways that Tractarian theology and Ecclesiologist ceremonial could not, and *Hymns Ancient and Modern* was used in many churches that would never have regarded themselves as remotely connected with Tractarianism. Charles Box, a noted musician, described services at various London churches he visited in 1882. At Holy Trinity, Gray's Inn Road, morning service 12 March:

> First portion of prayers read; second intoned. Venite and Psalms chanted. Te Deum (Hopkins' Service in G); Anthem, 'Turn Thy face from my sin' (Atwood); Versicles and Litany (after Tallis). No Communion service. Hymn before sermon, and hymn during the offertory. A surpliced choir of twenty-four voices. 'Church Hymns' used. Singing congregational, very hearty and well attuned. Out voluntary, 'Let their celestial concerts all unite'.[70]

Holy Trinity, Minories, used *Hymns Ancient and Modern*, and St Alban, Wood Street, with St Olave used *Hymnal Companion*.[71] At St Bartholomew, Moor Lane, Cripplegate, on 11 June 1882, Box recorded the following:

Revival of Anglican Choral Worship 1839–62, Aldershot: Ashgate, 1997. See also Trevor Beeson, *In Tuneful Accord: The Church Musicians*, London: SCM Press, 2009. For the founding of choir schools at this period, see Alan Mould, *The English Chorister: A History*, London: Continuum Press, 2007, p. 194.

69 See Susan Drain, *The Anglican Church in Nineteenth-Century Britain: Hymns Ancient and Modern (1860–1875)*, Lewiston: Edwin Mellen, 1989, pp. 101–2, 105. Trevor Beeson, *The Church's Folk Songs from Hymns Ancient and Modern to Common Praise 1861–2011*, Norwich: Canterbury Press, 2011.

70 Charles Box, *Church Music in the Metropolis*, London: William Reeves, 1884, p. 129.

71 Box, *Church Music*, pp. 128, 129.

Prayers intoned. A surpliced choir of sixteen voices. Venite, Te Deum, and Jubilate chanted. Psalms chanted in choral unison, but the Glorias according to score. Hymn at the end of the third Collect. No Litany. Musical responses to the Decalogue. Nicene Creed, (Goss). Musical accompaniments to the celebration of the Eucharist. Hymn at the close. 'Church Hymnal' used.[72]

Of course, this was London, but the musical changes could be replicated in many other urban churches and not a few rural churches by 1882. The story of the choral revival that stemmed from Tractarianism and the Ecclesiologists has been recounted by Bernare Rainbow.[73] No clerk and gallery singers with flute, but organ with surpliced choir became the Anglican norm.

Reactions in Church and State

J. M. Neale, in his *Essays on Liturgiology and Church History*, published in 1863, had argued that the Prayer Book was too narrow and lacked beauty, and needed supplementing from ancient liturgies. As second-generation Tractarianism developed into Anglo-Catholicism, the Prayer Book rites were found inadequate and were supplemented or even replaced with liturgy from Catholic sources. Notable among these were Peter Medd's *The Priest to the Altar* (1861), Frederick George Lee's *The Altar Book* (1867), Orby Shipley's *The Ritual of the Altar* (1870) and A. H. Stanton's *Catholic Prayers for Church of England People* (1880).[74] Evangelicals and Broad Churchmen responded. As early as 1842, Thomas Spencer had published *The Reformed Prayer Book*, which removed from the Prayer Book those things to which the Tractarians appealed, and the things that Evangelicals found objectionable. In 1859 Lord Ebury founded an association for reforming the Prayer Book, later to become the Prayer Book Revision Society. In 1873, Ebury and his associates published *The Book of Common Prayer Revised*, carried out in such a manner as to exclude any Tractarian or Anglo-Catholic interpretations.[75] Evangelical clergy who seceded from

---

72 Box, *Church Music*, p. 133.

73 Bernare Rainbow, *The Choral Revival in the Anglican Church (1839–1872)*, New York: Oxford University Press, 1970.

74 Mark Dalby, *Anglican Missals and their Canons: 1549, Interim Rite and Roman*, Alcuin/GROW Joint Liturgical Study 41, Cambridge: Grove Books, 1998.

75 A. Elliott Peaston, *The Prayer Book Revisions of the Victorian Evangelicals*, Dublin: APCK, 1963.

the Church of England and formed what later became the Free Church of England, adopted a reformed Prayer Book on the lines of Ebury's.[76] Another move was to purchase advowsons to insure a continued Low Church succession, or reverse a ritualist tradition.[77]

At an official level, 1854 saw the appointment of a committee to take stock and action in the light of the 1851 census. An official change occurred in the Prayer Book – the removal of the commemoration of the death of Charles I on 30 January; the birth and restoration of Charles II on 29 May; and the Gunpowder Plot on 5 November. They had been added to the 1662 Book of Common Prayer on the authority of Convocation and the Crown, and were continued by Royal mandate. They were removed by Royal Warrant on 17 January 1857. Technically they were never part of the liturgy as authorized by Parliament, but, arguably, the commemorations had marked the extremes between which the 1662 liturgy was intended to be the mean. Though certainly not the intention, their removal was symbolic of the fact that the 1662 mean was no longer an acceptable mean. Notable ritualist court cases were Westerton v. Liddell (1855–57), Martin v. Mackonochie (1867–68), Sumner v. Wix (1870) and Hebbert v. Puchas (1870–71), with inconsistent conclusions. Gary Graber lists 11 proposed but failed attempts at Parliamentary ritual legislation between 1860 and 1873, such was the concern to bring order out of increasing chaos.[78] After much debate in Parliament, 1867 saw the appointment of the Royal Commission on Ritual. It resulted in four reports. The first dealt with vesture; the second with candles and incense; the third considered Prayer Book revision, and recommended the shortening of lessons, and the provision of proper lessons and alternative lessons. The fourth report dealt with services, and among its recommendations suggested that Morning Prayer, Litany and Holy Communion might be used together (as was the custom) or as separate services at the discretion of the minister. The Act of Uniformity Amendment Act was passed in 1872, which in addition to allowing the shortening of Morning and Evening Prayer on

76 A. E. Peaston, *The Prayer Book Tradition in the Free Churches*, London: James Clarke, 1964, pp. 70–87; John Fenwick, *The Free Church of England*, London: T&T Clark, 2004, pp. 225–43.

77 An example of the latter is St Michael's Church, Braintree, Essex. It was still an Anglo-Catholic church under J. W. Kenworthy in the early twentieth century. The vestments were destroyed under Peter James in the late 1950s, and the remaining candlesticks 'disappeared'.

78 Gary Graber, *Ritual Legislation in the Victorian Church of England: Antecedents and Passage of the Public Worship Regulation Act, 1974*, Lewiston: Edwin Mellen, 1993, p. 42.

weekdays, and the three Sunday morning services to be used separately, sanctioned a 'Third Service' on Sundays as a supplement to the statutory services of Morning and Evening Prayer provided in the Prayer Book.[79] The materials of the latter were to come from the Prayer Book, but Evangelicals had already established mission-type services that used hymns and extempore prayer, and saw this as sanctioning their own extra-liturgical practice. The Royal Commission also gave birth to the 1874 Public Worship Regulation Act that resulted in the Ridsdale case, and the imprisonment of some Anglo-Catholic clergy, notably Arthur Tooth of St James, Hatcham, R. W. Enraght of Birmingham and S. H. Green of St John's, Miles Platting, Manchester. This in turn brought the Act into disrepute, and bishops refused to use it.[80] The fourth report also resulted in discussion of a revised Prayer Book, known as the Convocation Prayer Book, 1880. Ronald Jasper noted of that book, 'Few of these proposals would have enriched the services of the Prayer Book. Liturgical precedents were frequently ignored, and with the exception of controversial points, such as the Athanasian Creed and the Ornaments Rubric, the changes were trifling.'[81] It was probably just as well that these proposals came to nothing.

The next official move of importance came in 1904, when the Royal Commission on Ecclesiastical Discipline was appointed to inquire into alleged breaches of the law. The evidence taken by the Commission was extremely wide, and included breaches such as the omission of the Creed in Westminster Abbey. Typical of Anglo-Catholic services was that of Verwood, Dorset. Morning Prayer was abbreviated by omissions. The visitor reported on numerous illegalities, and observed of the many children present at the Communion, 'the English Prayer Book they do not know'.[82] At St Saviour's, Hitchin, it was reported concerning the 10 a.m. service:

> The clergyman wore an alb, green chasuble, girdle, maniple, and stole, and was attended by two servers. There were two lighted candles on

79 Bryan D. Spinks, 'Not so Common Prayer: The Third Service', in Michael Perham (ed.), *The Renewal of Common Prayer: Unity and Diversity in Church of England Worship*, London: SPCK, 1993, pp. 55–67.

80 Graber, *Ritual Legislation*, pp. 123–30; James Bentley, *Ritualism and Politics in Victorian Britain*, Oxford: Oxford University Press, 1978.

81 R. C. D. Jasper, *Prayer Book Revision in England 1800–1900*, London: SPCK, 1954, p. 126.

82 *Minutes of Evidence*, p. 251, http://www.hath/trust.org/access_use#pd-us-google (accessed 20 January 2012).

the Holy Table, and two large brass standards lighted in the chancel ... A wafer was used instead of ordinary bread. Both during and after consecration the clergyman elevated the paten and chalice.[83]

It was clear that the rite was augmented with material from elsewhere. In reply, the vicar, George Gainsford, noted that he had been in the parish 40 years, and had always used vestments in accordance with the Ornaments Rubric. As for interpolations, the use of any hymn was interpolation and he denied many of the claims of the 'nameless spy'.[84]

Thus it was that the Report in 1906 came to make reference to the Prayer Book as being too narrow for the religious life of this present generation. It was not the liturgy that had changed, but English culture.[85] The impact of the Romantic Movement as well as continued industrialization and nineteenth-century technology meant that Queen Victoria had been born in one world and died in another. Some Evangelicals and Broad Churchmen, as well as Anglo-Catholics, omitted things from the Prayer Book, or substituted unauthorized material in worship; 1906 was a world apart from when John Skinner had 'read prayers as usual'. Although no revised liturgy was authorized in the nineteenth century, the flood of liturgical revision that came in the late twentieth century was set in motion by the Victorian assaults on the Prayer Book, both its textual limitations and on its ritual and musical performance. What could be deemed an 'Excellent Liturgy' in Van Mildert's day had, by the end of the nineteenth century, become 'too narrow for the religious life' and the liturgical appetite of a good many in the Church of England.[86]

---

83 *Minutes of Evidence*, p. 261.

84 *Minutes of Evidence*, p. 262.

85 For the discussion of Tractarianism and the Ecclesiologists in a broader cultural context, see Michael Hall, 'What Do Victorian Churches Mean? Symbolism and Sacramentalism in Anglican Church Architecture 1850–1870', *Journal of the Society of Architectural Historians* 59, no. 1 (2000), pp. 78–95. See also Dominic Janes, *Victorian Reformation*.

86 It is interesting that Walter Frere's correspondence from 1906 to 1907 changes from concern for rubrical change to the need for proper liturgical revision. *Walter Howard Frere: His Correspondence on Liturgical Revision and Construction*, ed. R. C. D. Jasper, London: SPCK, 1954, pp. 5–25.

8

Liturgical Development

From Common Prayer to Uncommon Worship

PAUL BRADSHAW

The intention expressed in the first English Prayer Book of 1549 that 'all the whole realm shall have but one use' may never have been fully realized, but in the twentieth century it was for the first time formally abandoned. Laxity in obedience to the rubrics, differences in their interpretation, and above all the additions, deviations and omissions made by the Ritualists in the late nineteenth century had rendered the ideal unfulfilled in earlier times. Yet if not in detail, at least in broad substance it had been true for over 350 years that the same services had been celebrated from the one Book in parish churches and cathedrals throughout the country. But all that was now to change in the twentieth century.

The first official movement away from the ideal came with the revision process leading up to the ill-fated 1927/1928 proposed book. In response to the recommendation of the Royal Commission on Ecclesiastical Discipline in 1906, Letters of Business were to be issued to the Convocations of Canterbury and York,

> to frame, with a view to their enactment by Parliament, such modifications in the existing law relating to the conduct of Divine Service and to the ornaments and fittings of churches as may tend to secure the greater elasticity which a reasonable recognition of the comprehensiveness of the Church of England and of its present needs seems to demand.

Thus began a process that was to last 21 years, including the period of the First World War, when representatives of the Church of England continued solemnly to debate matters of rubric and text while European civilization was collapsing all around them.

At first, the scope of the proposed changes was quite limited, but in July 1910 a report from the Lower House of the Canterbury Convocation proposed that an alternative form of Holy Communion 'along the lines of the Scottish Communion Office be provided',[1] and the following year the House debated a proposal to appoint a Joint Committee of both Houses to consider the advisability of providing an alternative rite of Holy Communion. Although the proposal was defeated, the vote was not overwhelming, 32 votes in favour and 47 against.[2] The writing was on the wall with regard to having more than one legal form of service in the Church of England.

In 1914, the Lower House considered a proposal for a specific form of alternative eucharistic prayer, one based on a suggestion that had been made in 1898 in a pamphlet by the scholar T. A. Lacey.[3] It involved minimal changes to the 1662 text, with simply a rearrangement of the order of various elements in the service, so that the Sursum Corda, Preface and Sanctus would be followed immediately by the Prayer of Consecration (without being interrupted any longer by the Prayer of Humble Access), and the Prayer of Consecration by the Prayer of Oblation – the order that the two had had in the 1549 Prayer Book. This proposal of Lacey's had received reluctant support from Charles Gore, at the time Bishop of Birmingham, who would really have liked to see something that went further than that, and more whole-hearted approval subsequently from a whole variety of other leading churchmen and scholars. It was thus overwhelmingly endorsed by the Lower House, but not by the bishops in the Upper House. In a lengthy debate, concern was expressed that a double use would create two sets of churches, and the Bishop of London, Arthur Winnington-Ingram, insisted that 'nothing was more hotly opposed by the whole Evangelical party' and that 'it would not satisfy the Catholic party'.[4] Not only were the Evangelicals staunchly opposed to the revision of the Prayer Book in general, as necessarily constituting a step away from the solidly Protestant position that they believed the 1662 version embodied, but they regarded the offering of 'ourselves, our souls and bodies' in the Prayer of Oblation before communion as much too Pelagian in char-

1 Canterbury Convocation, *Report of a Committee of the Lower House on the Royal Letters of Business*, no. 447 (1910), Resolution 54a.

2 *Chronicle of Convocation* (1911), pp. 343–67.

3 T. A. Lacey, *Liturgical Interpolations*, Alcuin Club Tracts 3, London: Longmans, 1898.

4 For details, see R. C. D. Jasper, *The Development of the Anglican Liturgy 1662–1980*, London: SPCK, 1989, pp. 84–5, 99; G. J. Cuming, *A History of Anglican Liturgy*, 2nd edn, London: Macmillan, 1982, pp. 166–8.

acter and as reversing the order of the gift of God's grace: only when worshippers had received God's grace in communion were they in a position to offer God anything.

However, the Lower House stood their ground, and eventually in 1918, after the Bishop of London had said that the Catholic party 'had pointed out that he was quite wrong in what he had said last time', the bishops agreed to the proposal, subject to the insertion, as a link between the two prayers, of an anamnesis section largely taken from the 1549 version of the prayer:

> Wherefore, O Father, we thy humble servants, having in remembrance before thee the precious death of thy dear Son, his mighty resurrection and glorious ascension, looking also for his coming again, do render unto thee most hearty thanks for the innumerable benefits which he hath procured unto us. [5]

Things were different in the Convocation of the Province of York. While the Lower House had approved the same proposal as Canterbury – although, significantly, adding an invocation of the Holy Spirit – the Upper House, where Evangelicals were strongly represented, remained intransigent in their opposition.[6] At the request of the Convocations, therefore, the Archbishop of Canterbury summoned a special conference of some 50 clergy of different schools of thought in May 1919 to try to resolve the matter. Under the leadership of the Anglo-Catholic liturgical scholar Walter Frere together with the Evangelical Bishop of Ripon, Thomas Drury, a large majority supported the proposal to leave the Prayer of Oblation where it was after Communion and instead to insert at the end of the Prayer of Consecration the anamnesis section proposed earlier, followed by:

> And we pray thee of thine almighty goodness to send upon us and upon these thy gifts thy holy and blessed Spirit, who is the Sanctifier and Giver of life, to whom with thee and thy Son Jesus Christ be ascribed by every creature in earth and heaven all blessing, honour, glory and power, now, henceforth and for evermore. Amen.[7]

---

5 *Chronicle of Convocation* (1918), pp. 86, 137–67.

6 York Convocation, *Report 277* (1912), p. xxiv; *Journal of Convocation* (1912), p. 112; (1915), p. 316.

7 Jasper, *Development*, pp. 100–1; *Chronicle of Convocation* (1920), pp. 66–9; Canterbury Convocation, *Report 529*, pp. 2–4.

Although this was much less than Frere would ideally have liked, it did introduce an explicit invocation of the Holy Spirit on the people and on the bread and wine, something characteristic of ancient Eastern Eucharistic Prayers, the absence of which from the Western tradition was regretted by liturgical scholars. But while leaving the Prayer of Oblation where it was may have brought some comfort to Evangelicals, the location of this epiclesis posed a problem for many Anglo-Catholics wedded to the Western theory of eucharistic consecration. Ever since the idea was first articulated by Ambrose of Milan in the late fourth century,[8] it had become accepted doctrine in the West that the bread and wine became the body and blood of Christ through the recitation of his words, 'This is my body', 'This is my blood', in the narrative of institution in the Eucharistic Prayer. To locate an invocation of the Holy Spirit in the latter part of the prayer, after those words had already been spoken, implied that this was not so and the consecration still needed to be effected through the action of the Holy Spirit, according to the understanding of the Eastern Church. This made it unacceptable to Anglo-Catholics, even though such an arrangement of the Eucharistic Prayer had already been adopted by the Episcopal Church in Scotland in the eighteenth century and from there had found its way into the Prayer Book of the Episcopal Church in the USA.

The proposed form was submitted to all four Houses of Convocation in 1920. It passed in three of them but ran into trouble once again in the Upper House of York, where amendments to delete the invocation of the Spirit altogether and to make changes to the doxology were at first carried, but in a final vote the northern bishops decided against making any change to the Prayer Book form.[9] The Eucharistic Prayer was not the only point of serious contention in the process of revision, however. The question of the possible continuous reservation of the consecrated bread and wine also raised very strong feelings on both sides. At first, it seemed possible to secure agreement that reservation for a limited time might be permitted solely for the purpose of the communion of the sick, but when it became clear that Anglo-Catholics intended to extend its use to permanent reservation for devotional purposes, including its solemn exposition and Benediction, Evangelical opposition to any form of reservation hardened, lest it seemed to open the door to legitimating practices of which they strongly disapproved.[10] These two unresolved

---

8 Ambrose of Milan, *De sacramentis* 4.14.

9 *Chronicle of Convocation* (1920), pp. 66–83, 151–62; *Journal of Convocation* (1920), pp. 56–7, 213–16.

10 See further Jasper, *Development*, pp. 101–5.

matters would continue to dominate the proceedings throughout further years of debate, for the 1919 Enabling Act had brought into being the National Assembly of the Church of England with a House of Laity as well as the Upper and Lower Houses of Convocation, and before any proposals for revision could go to Parliament, they would have to go through further scrutiny and approval in this body.

What had been firmly established by this stage, however, was that all the proposals that had been made, and not just a Eucharistic Prayer, would constitute alternatives to the provisions of the 1662 Book and not replacements for any existing services. Indeed, in 1922 the National Assembly accepted the principle that they should be in a separate volume and sanctioned for optional use for a specific period of time,[11] and it was only action by the House of Laity in 1925 that secured their inclusion within the Prayer Book itself.[12] Even so, the Church of England would effectively have two Prayer Books, although bound up within a single set of covers. The ideal of uniformity was being abandoned – and not just in England, as Resolution 36 of the Lambeth Conference, which met in 1920, declared:

> While maintaining the authority of the Book of Common Prayer as the Anglican standard of doctrine and practice, we consider that liturgical uniformity should not be regarded as a necessity throughout the Churches of the Anglican Communion. The conditions of the Church in many parts of the mission field render inapplicable the retention of that Book as the one fixed liturgical model.

Space does not permit me to trace in any detail the years of tedious debate leading up to the defeat of the proposed book in Parliament in 1927 and again in 1928. Suffice it to say that, not surprisingly, it was the deep divisions over the shape of the alternative Eucharistic Prayer and over provision for the reservation of the consecrated elements that played the principal part in stoking the opposition to the book's passage through the legislative process.[13] Perhaps, however, a few points from along the way are worth noting.

First, as early as 1912 Frere had put forward the view that what was ideally needed was a long period of authorized liturgical experi-

---

11 National Assembly, *Proceedings*, vol. 3, no. 2, p. 66.

12 Church Assembly, *Report* 169 (1925), pp. 5–6.

13 For further details, see Donald Gray, *The 1927–28 Prayer Book Crisis*, Alcuin Club/GROW Joint Liturgical Studies 60 and 61, Norwich: Canterbury Press, 2005 and 2006.

mentation and study. He thought that this would both meet the 'desire for enrichment and greater convenience in the traditional methods of service', and at the same time make 'provision for the general Church public of suitable opportunities for arriving at instructed judgment in these matters'.[14] Although surprisingly prescient of the later course of liturgical revision, this was an idea too much before its time to be taken up then, at least in England. As Frere pointed out, other parts of the Anglican Communion were already doing precisely that, but when the House of Laity did propose a period of experimentation in 1923, it was rejected.[15]

Second, as part of continuing attempts to secure common ground over the question of the Eucharistic Prayer, an unofficial conference sponsored by the House of Clergy and held in the Jerusalem Chamber of Westminster Abbey in November 1923 proposed the inclusion of two alternative forms of Eucharistic Prayer within the Alternative Order of Holy Communion. This, however, was unacceptable to the House of Laity, who wanted only one Eucharistic Prayer in this Alternative Order, a view shared by many clergy and certainly by the House of Bishops;[16] but once again it was a harbinger of what was to come many years later.

Third, there were others who still did not want the Church of England to adopt alternative forms of service at all, and these were not only those who wanted to retain the 1662 Book unrevised. Bishop A. C. Headlam of Gloucester expressed his regrets that the 1928 Book contained two forms of baptism, confirmation and Holy Communion: he thought the new forms were better than the old and the aim should be to make their use universal.[17]

After the proposed book had been defeated in Parliament, in theory that was the end of the matter and the 1662 Book remained the only legally authorized form of worship. But that was not in reality the end of the matter, for it had two consequences that were to exercise a profound influence on the Church of England for the rest of the century. The first was a widespread tendency to imagine that liturgical deviation did not require any official sanction; and the second was that any future attempts at revision would need to take a quite different course. The bishops themselves were partially responsible for encouraging the first

---

14 W. H. Frere, 'The Reconstruction of Worship', *Church Quarterly Review* 74 (1912), pp. 139–60, especially pp. 140, 146–7.

15 Jasper, *Development*, p. 129.

16 Gray, *1927–28 Prayer Book Crisis* 2, pp. 13–14, 17.

17 A. C. Headlam, *The New Prayer Book*, London: J. Murray, 1927, p. 95.

of these when in 1929 they put out the statement that 'during the present emergency and until further order be taken', they would not 'regard as inconsistent with loyalty to the principles of the Church of England the use of such additions or deviations' as fell within the limits of the 1928 proposals.[18] It is true that they did not intend a liturgical free-for-all but stated that decisions would be made by the diocesan bishop and would be conditional upon the goodwill of the people affected by the changes being made. But in practice that was not what happened, and the Church of England became accustomed to a greater degree of lawlessness with regard to forms of worship than it had suffered during the Ritualist controversies in the nineteenth century that had led to the process of official liturgical revision in the first place.

As Ronald Jasper observed, what the Church got quite unintentionally was a period of liturgical experimentation lasting for a number of years.[19] With or without the goodwill of the people, and certainly without reference to the diocesan bishop, Anglo-Catholics continued to use either the *English Missal* or some version of what was called the Interim Rite, transposing elements of the 1662 Communion service along the lines originally suggested by T. A. Lacey; Evangelicals took liberties with Morning and Evening Prayer while remaining more scrupulous in their adherence to the 1662 service of Holy Communion; and those in the middle felt free to adopt whatever features of the 1928 Book they happened to like. All this made unlikely a return to obedience to officially prescribed forms in the future, however much continuing efforts in official circles to define the meaning of the expression 'lawful authority' might suggest otherwise.[20]

The second consequence of the 1928 debacle was the lesson learned that a different method of doing liturgical revision needed to be adopted. When the Moberly Commission on Church–State relations reported in 1952, therefore, it proposed a period of experimental use for new forms of service of seven or ten years, with the option of renewal for a further period, before authorization was sought, so that the Church might arrive at a common mind.[21] These proposals were substantially embodied in the Prayer Book (Alternative and Other Services) Measure approved in 1965. This permitted the use of services alternative to those in the Book of Common Prayer for a period of seven years, with

18 Jasper, *Development*, pp. 147–8.
19 Jasper, *Development*, p. 149.
20 For these, see Jasper, *Development*, pp. 150–6.
21 Report CA 1023, *Church and State* (1952), pp. 30–2.

the possibility of extension to fourteen, provided that they had the approval of at least a two-thirds majority in each of the Houses.[22]

Under the category of Series 1 services authorized in this way in 1966 were nearly all those of the 1928 Book that had come into common use in the subsequent years, in order that they could now be made legal. Among the exceptions was the Confirmation Service, which was rejected by Evangelical votes in the House of Laity because of its doctrine that a special gift of the Holy Spirit was bestowed through the laying on of hands, forcing the bishops to return to using 1662 until an alternative form could be produced. Because of its controversial nature, no attempt was made to reintroduce the Eucharistic Prayer from 1928. Instead, three options were provided: the 1662 prayer unchanged; the form in the Interim Rite; and another form produced by the Church of England Liturgical Commission, which had come into being some years earlier. This consisted of the 1662 prayer plus the 1928 anamnesis and just the first half of the Prayer of Oblation, thereby avoiding any reference to the contentious issue of offering.[23]

This multiplication of options marks another major change in official liturgical texts in the Church of England. The services in the 1662 Book allowed hardly any alternatives. They were meant to begin at the beginning and proceed to the end without the minister having to make any decision about which prayer or other formulary was to be used. It is true that there were a few exceptions to this principle of uniformity, among them psalm alternatives to the canticles in Morning and Evening Prayer, inserted in 1552 because extreme Protestants had objected to the use of the latter, and the choice between the Prayer of Oblation or the Prayer of Thanksgiving after communion in the eucharistic rite. But in general the services were meant to be the same wherever they were celebrated. Series 1, however, not only allowed alternative forms of service to those in the Prayer Book, but more variations within the services, especially the Eucharist. The Gloria in excelsis, the sermon, the Offertory, the Prayer of Humble Access, and the Lord's Prayer all had alternative positions within the rite, and in addition to three possible Eucharistic Prayers, there were four options for post-communion prayers. Series 1 in one church, therefore, could be quite different in form from Series 1 in another.

Some options were also included in the Series 2 services drawn up by the Liturgical Commission at the same time, which were new compositions shaped to a large extent by what was then the state of knowledge

22 See Cuming, *History*, pp. 328–9.
23 Cuming, *History*, pp. 206–7.

of the liturgical practices of early Christianity, but there was only one form of Eucharistic Prayer, which had been hard fought over by Evangelicals and Anglo-Catholics pulling in opposite directions.[24] The same was largely true of the modern language Series 3 services produced in the 1970s – a number of alternative forms, a great many elements made optional ('the following may be said'), but only one Eucharistic Prayer.

Meanwhile, major liturgical reforms had been taking place in the Roman Catholic Church as a consequence of the Second Vatican Council and its Constitution on the Sacred Liturgy of 1963. The new eucharistic rite, promulgated in 1969, was not only in the vernacular in a contemporary style of English but had other features that were in time to influence the form that revised rites in the Church of England were to take. Chief among these were the permission given for the eucharistic president to use his own words at various points in the rite rather than simply reading official texts, and the inclusion of a choice of no less than four Eucharistic Prayers. The decision to abandon more than a thousand years of tradition of having just one Eucharistic Prayer in the Roman rite was taken not for the reason it had emerged in Anglican thinking – to attempt to reconcile seemingly contradictory doctrinal positions – but chiefly because liturgical scholarship at the time regarded the absence of reference to the Holy Spirit in the traditional prayer as a theological weakness and believed, erroneously as it now appears, that the prayer in the ancient church order known as the *Apostolic Tradition of Hippolytus*, which did include just such an invocation of the Spirit, had been the even older form of the prayer used at Rome. There could be no question of abandoning the established Roman prayer in favour of this recent discovery, and so it was kept alongside both a prayer developed out of that in the so-called *Apostolic Tradition* and two others as well, one employing material from ancient non-Roman practices in the West and the other based on the Eastern Prayer of St Basil.

When work began in the Church of England on the process leading up to *The Alternative Service Book 1980*, similar innovations found their way into the texts. At various points in the services the minister was now allowed to use 'these or other appropriate words' or 'these or other suitable words', and the modern-language Eucharist now offered a choice of four prayers, though obviously not the same ones as in the Roman Catholic Mass.[25] In the long term, however, even these and

---

24 See Jasper, *Development*, pp. 250–60.

25 For more detail, see Paul F. Bradshaw and Ronald C. D. Jasper, *A Companion to the Alternative Service Book*, London: SPCK, 1986, pp. 229–31.

other freedoms permitted within the book did not satisfy everyone in the Church of England. Not only did many Anglo-Catholics still import material from the Roman Catholic Church, but the growing Charismatic Movement demonstrated an increasing tendency not merely to supplement the provisions of the book with other songs and prayers but to abandon many of the official forms altogether; while those in the middle often felt no obligation to adhere strictly to the few mandatory rubrics and texts that there were but freely adopted alternatives that they preferred from a variety of sources.

The widespread extent of such tendencies is clearly demonstrated by the 'Service of the Word' legislation that was incorporated in the further round of liturgical revision undertaken at the end of the twentieth century under the rather optimistic title, *Common Worship*. This particular provision was clearly intended to bestow legality on the very wide variety of non-sacramental acts of worship that were already occurring in churches up and down the land. It lays down only very minimal requirements for a service to be counted as a legitimate Anglican Service of the Word. All that is mandatory is a greeting, a biblical reading, a scriptural song, a sermon, a Creed or Affirmation of Faith, and prayers. Of these elements only the affirmation of Faith, Prayers of Penitence and a Collect have to come from authorized Anglican sources, and if it is not the principal service on a Sunday or principal holy day, all these except the Collect can be omitted.[26] Thus, under these provisions, an Anglican service need have hardly anything in it that resembles the traditional forms of worship in the Church of England, or even what is being used in other congregations in the Church. Although the freedom given in the other services in the *Common Worship* family, especially baptism and the Eucharist, is by no means as extensive as this, they do offer a wide variety of alternative texts and opportunities for creative additions to the official forms that mean that there can be enormous differences between one celebration and another.

But in the end does this matter? Does it matter if Anglican churches have little similarity in the ways that they worship and in the words that they use? I believe that it does. The most important thing that the Book of Common Prayer did for the Church of England was to provide a bond between Christians of different theological persuasions. It enabled them to recognize one another as members of the same Church. This is not an argument for a return to a rigid uniformity of practice, but it is to recognize the great importance of some sort of

---

26 See *Common Worship: Services and Prayers for the Church of England*, London: Church House Publishing, 2000, pp. 21–7.

liturgical bond to a Church, and especially to an Anglican Church with all its other varieties, something that has been rather overlooked in a generation when individuality, freedom and creativity have become the watchwords. Moreover, if we only ever express in worship those things that we already believe, how will we ever be led to those things that we do not yet believe? No, there is much more to be said for a shared liturgical experience than is often heard nowadays, when the greater elasticity envisaged by the Letters of Business in 1906 seems to have been stretched to breaking point.

9

The Book of Common Prayer and Anglicanism

Worship and Belief

PAUL AVIS

Why is it that, amid all its diversity and in the face of its current tensions, it still makes sense to speak of the Anglican Communion as one thing? The Anglican Communion is not a theological fiction nor is it a figment of the Archbishop of Canterbury's imagination. The Anglican Communion exists; it is real in the lives of many Anglicans throughout the world. It is not, as some loose journalistic talk has it, a single global Church, but precisely a *communion of churches*. It is made up of self-governing churches that stand in a relationship of communion to each other: they share a common faith, order and sacramental life and have an interchangeable ministry and membership. That is the ecclesiological form that the Anglican Communion takes and that is also, in my opinion, the beauty of it. But what holds this communion of churches together?

First, we might mention the formal structures that exist – just a few – the 'Instruments of Communion': the Lambeth Conference, the Anglican Consultative Council, the Primates' Meeting and the ministry of the Archbishop of Canterbury. None of these so-called instruments has any juridical authority over the member churches of the Communion; their authority is moral and pastoral and works by persuasion, teaching and example. Then there are a number of more informal links and ligatures that help to bind Anglicans together around the world. These are the various networks: networks for relating to other faiths, for carrying out relief and development work, for the study of liturgy and promoting theological education – and not to be underestimated, the Mothers' Union. But I think that, to put our finger on the secret of Anglican identity – and on the root of its fragility – we need to look deeper still, to the profound historical, cultural, linguistic and literary sources of our common Anglican identity. These sources may seem rather diffuse, elusive and nebulous, but there is one contributor to Anglican coherence and identity that is very concrete and specific, and that is the Book of Common Prayer (BCP).

The formative significance of the BCP for Anglicanism

It is not easy for us, in our rather fragmented postmodern Western culture, with its penchant for mere tracks and traces, echoes and intimations, rather than real cultural presences, to grasp the kind of unity that has characterized the Anglican Communion until the present day. It is the unity of a reality that is diverse and diffuse, an organism that extends over centuries, is spread throughout the world, speaks many languages, inhabits various life-worlds, has no book of rules and lacks a centre of power. But as we engage at first hand with Anglicans and their churches around the world, a sense of 'oneness' can steal over us. There is a reality of *lived Anglicanism* and that is in no small measure due to the pervasive presence of the BCP in the formative period of the Communion. I was struck by Alec Ryrie's comment, in reviewing *The Oxford Guide to the Book of Common Prayer*, that by 'tell[ing] Anglicanism's story in a reasonably coherent way ... it almost makes me suspect, against my better judgement, that there is such a thing as "Anglicanism" after all'.[1] The Archbishop of Canterbury has made a similar comment in his Foreword to the *Oxford Guide*, where he notes that the BCP is 'unique among the worship books of Christendom in having become the touchstone for the ethos and even, for hundreds of years, the unity' of Anglicanism.[2]

A printed book is a solid object and a human artefact. It has stability and endures through time. It can travel – both geographically, from one nation to another around the world, and linguistically, through the language barriers of many peoples. When the book in question is a text that requires to be *performed*, rather than simply read over, and when we regularly use that text in our own language, we internalize its meaning through repetition. When that text is enacted, married to outward actions, it partakes of the sublime and the beautiful and its power over

1 Alec Ryrie, review of Charles Hefling and Cynthia Shattuck (eds), *The Oxford Guide to the Book of Common Prayer: A Worldwide Survey*, Oxford: Oxford University Press, 2006, in *Reformation* 15 (2010), pp. 223–4 at p. 224.

2 Rowan Williams in Hefling and Shattuck (eds), *Oxford Guide*, Foreword.

us is magnified. As a work of art, involving narrative, poetry, prayer, instruction and frequently music, form and content are fused together in a determinative way. As a *rite* it ceases to be an external object; it draws the whole person into its meaning and shapes who we are.

Worship is the unique activity of the religious person. In worship we invest and express the highest worth that we can conceive in a Being who is beyond words, both transcendent and at the same time the deepest reality of our own existence, the very ground of our being. There are analogies to worship in human relationships and in our response to things of beauty – loved ones, nature, music, literature and pictorial art (the words of Walter Savage Landor's epitaph come to mind: 'Nature I loved and, next to Nature, Art').[3] But the worship of God is unparalleled because God is the incomparable one.

Liturgy is by definition the work (*leiturgia*) of the Church and of the faithful individually. Worship, as the Second Vatican Council put it in its Constitution on the Sacred Liturgy *Sacrosanctum concilium*, is the supreme event of the Church's existence, the source and summit of the Christian life (*LG* 11; *SC* 7, 10), the fountain from whence the life of the baptized flows and the highest point that it can ever attain.[4] The liturgy, said the Council, builds the faithful into the temple of the Lord and strengthens them to proclaim Christ to the world. It constitutes the Church as a sign raised over the nations (Isa. 11.12) and beneath this sign the scattered children of God are being gathered together, assembled for worship (John 11.52). In worship Jesus Christ is carrying out his priestly office with and through his people: worship is enacted by Head and members together. Worship is part of the Church's participation in the trinitarian life of God, offered to the Father, through the mediation of the Son and in the power and under the inspiration of the Spirit.[5]

For Anglicans, it is the BCP that has facilitated that exalted activity. It has been for many millions of people and for five and a half centuries

---

3 Walter Savage Landor, 'I strove with none': Francis T. Palgrave, *The Golden Treasury*, 3rd edn with a 5th book, ed. Laurence Binyon, London: Macmillan, 1926, p. 469.

4 It is worth noting, though it is not in any way surprising, that a section report for Lambeth 1930 stated: 'the Church claims that the Eucharist is the climax of Christian Worship': *The Lambeth Conferences (1867–1930)*, London: SPCK, 1948, p. 194 (Committee Report on 'The Christian Doctrine of God', *ad fin.*).

5 *Vatican Council II: Vol. 1: The Conciliar and Post-Conciliar Documents*, ed. Austin Flannery, OP, rev. edn, Northport, NY: Costello, and Dublin: Dominican Publications, 1992, pp. 1–6.

the vehicle for the highest duty and greatest privilege of the human person. But in Anglicanism the liturgy – which for most of our history in most places and for most people means the BCP – also has a critical role as a key marker of identity of faith and community. Anglicans have no Pope to hold things together; they do not look to an extraordinary figure as their founder, as Lutherans look to Martin Luther, Reformed to John Calvin and Methodists to John Wesley. They do not have elaborate doctrinal codes as the Roman Catholics have Denzinger and the Lutherans have the *Book of Concord*. What Anglicans have – or should I say 'had'? – is a Prayer Book. As Louis Weil has said, 'In no other Christian tradition does the authorized liturgy take on so great a significance.'[6]

The facts and figures speak for themselves: more than 5,000 editions or impressions of the BCP (including the American versions) have been published; it has been translated into 200 languages, beginning with Latin in 1551, French two years later, Welsh in 1567, Greek two years after that, but not into Irish until 1608 (though the English edition for Ireland in 1551 was the first Irish printed book). It is particularly gratifying to learn that there are no less than three versions of the BCP in Inuit![7] I have not seen any estimate of the total number of copies that have been printed, but I suppose that it must be second only to the number of Bibles that have been produced since the advent of printing.

The concept of common prayer

'In the mid-sixteenth century a Book of Common Prayer was a wholly new concept', observes David Griffiths, the bibliographer of the BCP.[8] This is true if we are thinking of England, rather than of the Reformation

---

6 Louis Weil, 'The Gospel in Anglicanism', in Stephen Sykes, John Booty and Jonathan Knight (eds), *The Study of Anglicanism*, 2nd edn, London: SPCK; Minneapolis, MN: Fortress Press, 1998, p. 59. In the same volume, Marion J. Hatchett says, 'more than anything else, it is the Book of Common Prayer which is a principal bond among Anglicans throughout the world' ('Prayer Books'), p. 131.

7 J. Robert Wright, 'Early Translations', in Hefling and Shattuck (eds), *Oxford Guide*, pp. 56–60. David Griffiths, *Bibliography of the Book of Common Prayer 1549–1999*, London: British Library, 2000, p. 17. An earlier survey is William Moss-Arnolt, *The Book of Common Prayer among the Nations of the World: A History of Translations of the Prayer Book of the Church of England and of the Protestant Episcopal Church of the USA*, London and New York: SPCK, 1914.

8 Griffiths, *Bibliography of the BCP*, p. 5.

generally. What was new in England was the bringing together of services for various occasions and for the use of different persons (bishop, priest, lay person) that had previously been distributed between Mass books, breviaries, pontificals and so on, into one volume and setting it all within the frame of prayer undertaken in common. Although there were no doubt ideological reasons for this, in the interests of effective control and national cohesion, the invention of a single book of common prayer was in itself a remarkable act of integration and coherence and is not the least of Thomas Cranmer's innovations.

A single book of common prayer in the sixteenth century had several characteristics. First, it was *corporate*, it belonged to the whole body for the use and benefit of the whole body; it helped to bind the Christian commonwealth together as one; as the Act of Uniformity put it: 'now from henceforth all the whole realm shall have but one use'. In the draft canon law that Cranmer presided over, the abortive *Reformatio Legum Ecclesiasticarum*, Cranmer's second Prayer Book (1552), recently completed, is described as 'the proper and perfect judge and master of all divine worship' (*proprium et perfectum omnis divini cultus iudicem et magistrum*) – in other words, it was set forth as a juridical paradigm for the whole kingdom.[9] Second, it was *public* and therefore had something of a confessional and proclamatory character; it marked the commonwealth as a Christian nation. Third, it was *scripted*: it was a text in the hand and in the heart. Through its many layers of textual history, going back to the beginnings of Christian worship, it united those who used it with the whole Church in time and space, in a way that the extempore prayer favoured by some Puritans of the late sixteenth and the seventeenth centuries could not do. Fourth, it was in the *vernacular*, so that the unlearned could participate with understanding; and this too helped to embed the liturgy in everyday life. Cranmer the humanist, the scholar of the new learning, was not only devoted to the literature of antiquity, but also dedicated to the flourishing of vernacular literature, in Prayer Book and Bible.[10] Fifth, it was *mandatory*, imposed by law through the Act of Uniformity (which applied to all editions of the BCP except that of 1604): a uniform pattern of wor-

---

9 Gerald Bray (ed.), *Tudor Church Reform: The Henrician Canons of 1535 and the* Reformatio Legum Ecclesiasticarum, Woodbridge: Boydell Press and Church of England Record Society, 2000, pp. 344–5, and introductory matter, pp. 41ff.

10 Cf. Maria Dowling, 'Cranmer as Humanist Reformer', in Paul Ayris and David Selwyn (eds), *Thomas Cranmer: Churchman and Scholar*, Woodbridge: Boydell Press, 1989, pp. 89–114.

ship was imposed in place of the various late medieval 'uses'; common prayer meant a *common liturgical identity* for the realm.[11]

What all this adds up to is a programme of deeper Christianization of the population, whereby the medieval divisions between clergy, religious and laity, demolished by Martin Luther in his *Address to the Christian Nobility of the German Nation* in 1520, is replaced by a new understanding of the *corpus christianum* in which clergy and lay persons serve God with equal worth according to their vocation (the religious vocation having been abolished). In intention, the Reformers aspired to raise the laity to the level of spiritual proficiency that is expected of the clergy.[12] The BCP reflects and embodies a social ideal, the 'moral economy' of 'an organic – albeit hierarchical – society'.[13]

Undoubtedly, part of Cranmer's intention was to unify the kingdom under reformed, evangelical Christianity. Liturgy is a powerful instrument for uniting hearts and minds in a common cause. To worship with others, using the same words and actions, is one of the most powerful of social bonds. Samuel Taylor Coleridge writes in his notebook: 'for ever be this my motto "When I worship, let me unify"'.[14] When in the early 1990s the General Synod was debating the eight multi-choice versions of the Prayer of Thanksgiving in the draft eucharistic rites of *Common Worship*, I quoted these words of Coleridge in a Synod speech: 'when I worship let me unify'. It was probably the first and last time that that great Anglican lay theologian was quoted in the Synod. I favoured a

---

11 The Second Vatican Council strongly affirmed the meaningful participation of the laity in the celebration of the liturgy, by means of acclamation, responses, psalmody, antiphons, songs and silence, as well as by actions, gestures and general deportment. They are to participate 'knowingly, actively and fruitfully'; theirs is to be a 'full, conscious and active participation': SC 30, 10, 14 (Flannery (ed.), *Vatican Council II*, pp. 148, 143, 144). Provision is made for vernacular liturgy at the discretion of the ordinary: SC 36–37 (Flannery (ed.), pp. 150–1).

12 See Scott H. Hendrix, *Recultivating the Vineyard: The Reformation Agendas of Christianization*, Louisville, KY, and London: Westminster John Knox Press, 2004; Anna M. Johnson and John A. Maxfield, *The Reformation as Christianization: Essays on Scott Hendrix's Christianization Thesis*, Tübingen: Mohr Siebeck, 2012. See also, for the relation of law to social institutions in Germany, John Witte Jr, *Law and Protestantism: The Legal Teachings of the Lutheran Reformation*, Cambridge: Cambridge University Press, 2002.

13 Jeremy Gregory, 'The Prayer Book and the Parish Church: From The Restoration to the Oxford Movement', in Hefling and Shattuck (eds), *Oxford Guide*, pp. 103–4.

14 Samuel Taylor Coleridge, *The Notebooks of Samuel Taylor Coleridge*, Volume 3, *1808–1819*, ed. Kathleen Coburn, London: Routledge and Kegan Paul, 1973, no. 4058.

single Eucharistic Prayer, seasonally varied (as provided in the British Methodist Church)[15] and a shorter one, with a simpler structure, for use when children are taking part. But I did not convince the Synod. However, I still stand with Cranmer and Coleridge on this matter, and what better company could there be?

A liturgy catholic and reformed

Cranmer compiled the BCP from many sources: patristic, medieval, Eastern Orthodox and Protestant; and when he did not find to hand what he needed he wrote his own, which was in no way inferior to what he inherited. Cranmer was the consummate collator, adapter and improver. His method was one of revision not revolution, adaptation rather than innovation. His temperament led that way, but it was more than temperament; it was a method of safe progression towards the truth, as well as a politic regard for the unity of the realm and a pastoral concern for the spiritual unity of the Church.[16] The tension between continuity and reform gives the BCP its unique character and helps to account for its formative role in the identity of Anglicanism, which is both catholic and reformed. Here I take the influence of monastic patterns of prayer to stand for catholic continuity and the centrality of the Scriptures to stand for evangelical reform.

Cranmer's use of monastic models

It has often been observed that the BCP owes much to the Benedictine tradition. David Stancliffe is one who notes the affinity of the BCP with Benedictine spirituality, which combines ordered worship, ser-

---

15 *The Methodist Worship Book*, Peterborough: Methodist Publishing House, 1999.

16 Cf. Roger Beckwith in Cheslyn Jones, Geoffrey Wainwright, Edward Yarnold SJ and Paul Bradshaw (eds), *The Study of Liturgy*, 2nd edn, London: SPCK, and New York: Oxford University Press, 1992, p. 102: 'Cranmer was not only a cautious man, but a peaceable man. Faced with the necessity of making great changes, he followed Luther in not making greater ones than he could help; moreover, he made them by stages, not all at once.' See the whole passage. Bryan D. Spinks, 'Treasures Old and New: A Look at Some of Thomas Cranmer's Methods of Liturgical Composition', in Ayris and Selwyn (eds), *Cranmer*, pp. 175–88. Geoffrey J. Cuming, 'Thomas Cranmer: Translator and Creative Writer', in David Jasper and R. C. D. Jasper (eds), *Language and the Worship of the Church*, London: Macmillan, 1990, pp. 110–19.

ious study and the common life.[17] John-Bede Pauley makes a similar point: Cranmer's daily offices, drawn from the monastic hours, reflect the temper of Benedictine spirituality. The Rule of St Benedict, Pauley suggests, 'breathes an air of balance, moderation and discretion'.[18]

These are of course qualities that have often been claimed for the Anglican spirit. To take just one example: in his introduction to the well-known 1935 anthology of seventeenth-century Anglican writings, Paul Elmer More suggests that the 'love of balance, restraint, moderation, measure' characterize the temper of Anglicanism.[19] Needless to say, such claims are ripe for ideological deconstruction, and plenty of counter-examples can be produced where Anglicans have been neither moderate nor restrained. But I think that it cannot easily be denied that Cranmer's liturgy fosters a reflective spirit and a disposition to spiritual recollection. Many would say that this quality of modulated spirituality is clearest in Evening Prayer and is brought home to us most effectively in Choral Evensong. Pauley remarks that the BCP 'preserves the "monastic" quality of the hours'. Cranmer and the Caroline divines, he observes, 'expected the people to be "monastic" in their liturgical outlook'.

St Benedict lays down in his Rule that, to be reverent, common prayer should be 'short and pure'.[20] It is striking that the Second Vatican Council's Constitution on the Sacred Liturgy (SC 34) requires that liturgical forms should be marked by a 'noble simplicity', 'short, clear, and free from useless repetitions'.[21]

Before his change of heart in the 1840s, Newman defended the catholicity of the Prayer Book and its 'strong, plain, edifying language'. The BCP, he wrote in *The Prophetical Office of the Church* (1837),

17 David Stancliffe, 'Is there an "Anglican" liturgical style?', in Kenneth Stevenson and Bryan Spinks (eds), *The Identity of Anglican Worship*, London: Mowbray; Harrisburg, PA: Morehouse, 1991, p. 133. Cf. Keith Pecklers, in Paul D. Murray (ed.), *Receptive Ecumenism and the Call to Catholic Learning*, Oxford: Oxford University Press, 2008, p. 114.

18 John-Bede Pauley OSB, 'The Monastic Quality of Anglicanism: Implications for Understanding the Anglican Patrimony', in Stephen Cavanaugh (ed.), *Anglicans and the Roman Catholic Church: Reflections on Recent Developments*, San Francisco: Ignatius Press, 2011, p. 171.

19 Paul Elmer More and Frank Leslie Cross (eds), *Anglicanism: The Thought and Practice of the Church of England, Illustrated from the Religious Literature of the Seventeenth Century*, London: SPCK, 1935, p. xxii.

20 Timothy Fry OSB, *The Rule of St Benedict, in Latin and English with Notes*, Collegeville, MN: The Liturgical Press, 1981, ch. 20. See also James G. Clark, *The Benedictines in the Middle Ages*, Woodbridge: Boydell Press, 2012.

21 Flannery (ed.), *Vatican Council II*, p. 12.

transmits the ancient Catholic Faith simply and intelligibly ... Its words are not the accidental outpouring of this or that age or country, but the joint and accordant testimony of the innumerable company of Saints ... They are the accents of the Church Catholic and Apostolic as it manifests itself in England.[22]

The centrality of Scripture

The Reformers made a twofold appeal: to Scripture and the primitive Church. For the English Reformers, as for the Lutherans, the Bible was given to show the way of salvation and how Christians should live. It was not part of the Bible's purpose, as the Reformers and the Puritans tended to suppose, to dictate every aspect of worship or church government. For that God had given the pattern of the primitive Church and our capacity to reason, guided by the magistrate, the temporal ruler.[23]

Cranmer saturated the liturgy with Scripture; it is a tissue of biblical quotations and allusions. It is said that 80 per cent of its text is taken from Scripture. Cranmer's 'basic operating principle', says John Booty, was to restore the word of God to its central position in the common worship of the Church. He did this by increasing both the quantity and the prominence of Scripture in the liturgy and by setting word and sacrament side by side in his 1550 Ordinal as the content, as it were, of ordained ministry.[24]

22 John Henry Newman, *Lectures on the Prophetical Office of the Church*, London: Rivingtons, 1937, pp. 313–14. Cf. Sheridan Gilley, 'Prayer Book Catholicism', in Margot Johnson (ed.), *Thomas Cranmer: Essays in Commemoration of the 500th Anniversary of his Birth*, Durham: Turnstone Ventures, 1990, ch. 10.

23 Cf. Thirty-Nine Articles, VI (*Of the Sufficiency of the holy Scriptures for salvation*), XX (*Of the Authority of the Church*) and XXXIV (*Of the Traditions of the Church*). Richard Hooker: 'The word of God leaveth the Church free to make choice of her own ordinances', provided that these are 'not contrary to the word of God'. The governors of the Church would be guided by reason and by a sense of what was convenient and fitting, 'by the judgement of antiquity, and by the long-continued practice of the whole Church': *Of the Laws of Ecclesiastical Polity*, V, x, 1; vi, 1; vii, 1; *Works*, ed. John Keble, Oxford: Oxford University Press, 1845, vol. II, pp. 41, 28, 30.

24 John E. Booty (ed.), *The Book of Common Prayer 1559: The Elizabethan Prayer Book*, Charlottesville, VA: Virginia University Press/Folger Shakespeare Library, 1976, p. 360. See also Cranmer's 'Preface' in the Prayer Books of 1549, 1552 and 1559 (in 1662 this was retitled 'Concerning the Service of the Church' and a new Preface was provided): Brian Cummings, *The Book of Common Prayer: The Texts of 1549, 1559, and 1662*, Oxford: Oxford University Press, 2011, p. 5.

Cranmer's own valuation of the Bible can be seen in his homily 'A Fruitful Exhortation to the Reading and Knowledge of Holy Scripture'[25] and in his Preface to Tyndale and Coverdale's Great Bible (2nd edn).[26] The Collect that Cranmer composed for the Second Sunday of Advent, where we pray that we may 'in suche wise heare them, read, marke, learne, and inwardly digeste them; that by pacience, and coumfort of thy holy woorde, we may embrace, and euer holde fast the blessed hope of euerlasting life ...' breathes the spirit of *lectio divina*.[27]

The emphasis in Cranmer and his fellow Reformers was on edification, the teaching and formational function of the Scriptures. This approach laid the Prayer Book open to attack by Thomas Cartwright and other Puritans, at the time of the Admonition controversy, who questioned whether the way that the Scriptures were deployed *was* actually edifying. 'Cranmer's contention that the public reading of Scripture is *edifying*, was thrown back in the Church's teeth: how could then people be edified, it was asked, by vast chunks of uninterpreted Scripture read in liturgical tones?'[28] Richard Hooker's reply was that the reading of Scripture was not only a witness and testimony to God's saving acts, but also an intrinsic part of the Church's worship, 'a special portion of the service which we do to God'; it was offered to God as well as directed to the people. Hooker adumbrated a liturgical, almost a kerygmatic (proclamatory) understanding of the place of Scripture in common prayer.[29]

It was central to the rhetoric of the English, as of the Continental Reformation that the Church was being reshaped on the model of the primitive Church. The appeal to the primitive Church is pervasive in the writings of the Reformers. It is the corollary of the polemic that the Church of Rome had corrupted the ancient faith by many superstitions and abuses. To take just one example: the Act of Uniformity that imposed the 1549 BCP claimed that 'the most learned and discreet bishops and other learned men of this realm' had aimed to draw up an order for common prayer that reflected 'the most sincere and pure Christian religion taught by the Scripture as to the usages in the

25 http://www.archive.org/details/fruitfulexhortato7slsn.

26 Cranmer, Preface to the Great Bible, 2nd edn: http://www.bible-researcher.com/cranmer.html.

27 The 1549 version: *The First and Second Prayer-Books of King Edward the Sixth*, London: Dent, 1910, p. 34.

28 Doctrine Commission of the Church of England, *Believing in the Church*, London: SPCK, 1981, p. 97 (John Halliburton).

29 Richard Hooker, *Ecclesiastical Polity*, V, xix, i, v; *Works*, vol. II, pp. 64, 69.

primitive Church'.[30] The second Act of Uniformity (1552), made the same claim when it looked back to the 1549 Book, namely that it was 'agreeable to the word of God and the primitive Church'.[31] To be conformed to Scripture and primitive Christianity was the litmus test of evangelical authenticity for the Reformers. In the making of his prayer book, Cranmer regarded both the drawing on wholesome ancient precedents and the centrality of Scripture in the worship of the Church as aspects of faithfulness to early Christianity.

Lex orandi, lex credendi

For Anglicans, more than for any other kind of Christian, the liturgy in the broadest sense has a doctrinal function: it is where, more than anywhere else, Anglican beliefs are articulated. The principle *lex orandi, lex credendi* (the rule of prayer is the rule of belief) is an ancient one and is not confined to Anglicans, for all Christians pray as they believe and believe as they pray.[32] But, as the Church of England's Doctrine Commission once put it: 'if the *lex orandi* is important in other parts of the Christian Church, it is crucial in Anglicanism, which ... accords a rather lower place than many other communions to explicit definitions of doctrine ...'.[33] By this formula, as Geoffrey Wainwright points out in his notable work *Doxology*, a doctrinal appeal is made not only to the words that make up prayers, but also to 'a complex ritual act ... the liturgy which may serve as a doctrinal locus is the liturgy understood as a total ritual event, not simply a liturgy reduced to its verbal components'.[34]

The fact that Anglicans do not have an official systematic theology does not of course mean – *per impossibile* – that there is no Anglican

---

30 'An Act for the uniformity of service and administration of the sacraments throughout the realm' (First Act of Uniformity 1549: 2 & 3 Edward VI, c. 1), G. R. Elton (ed.), *The Tudor Constitution: Documents and Commentary*, Cambridge: Cambridge University Press, 1972, p. 393.

31 Elton (ed.), *Tudor Constitution*, p. 396 (5 & 6 Edward VI, c. 1).

32 *Lex orandi legem statuat credendi*: the rule of prayer establishes the rule of faith. Alternative version: *legem credendi lex statuat supplicandi*: let the law of prayer establish the law of belief. The formula derives from Prosper of Aquitaine, c. 435–42.

33 *Believing in the Church*, p. 81.

34 Geoffrey Wainwright, *Doxology: The Praise of God in Worship, Doctrine and Life; A Systematic Theology*, London: Epworth Press, 1980, p. 227. See his extensive discussion of the origins and various applications of the term in chapters VII and VIII.

doctrine, nor does it follow that there are no doctrines that are distinctively Anglican: there are, otherwise we would not know what it meant to be Anglican.[35] But Anglican churches are churches that conceive their relation to Christian doctrine liturgically.[36] They state their doctrines in the liturgical mode. To understand Anglican teaching we need to turn to liturgy. The Anglican instantiation of *lex orandi, lex credendi* is a further aspect of Cranmer's genius and, some would say, his chief legacy.[37] The BCP has therefore been described as the 'hermeneutical key' to the understanding of historic Anglicanism: 'we interpret and understand the Bible and the doctrinal and moral tradition of the Church through the way we worship and pray together as a community of the baptised.'[38] The contemporary liturgies of the Communion serve a similar function and so inevitably point to a wider range of Anglican belief, yet with a common core.

To some traditions this liturgical dependency of doctrine may seem an impoverished or even reductionist approach to doctrine. Not a bit of it: in fact it has the great merit and virtue of making doctrine inseparable from worship and worship the corollary of doctrine. This is another marker of the affinity that has often been observed between Anglicanism and the Eastern Orthodox tradition. Theology and spirituality, doctrine and devotion, are inseparable, two sides of the coin. As we internalize the liturgy through regular participation and repeated performance, we imbibe the faith and make it our own, so that it becomes second nature. The Collects of the BCP have a special role in this process of formation in Christian belief. Collects have a fascination for Anglicans; they are either deeply satisfying to our faith or they leave us feeling short-changed and affronted. *Common Worship* has taken a while to get its Collects right and I am not sure that it has fully succeeded. The salience of the Collects in Anglican spirituality highlights the fact that we do our theology in a doxological way and we pray with theological integrity.[39]

---

35 See the discussion of the 'no special doctrines' thesis in Paul Avis, *The Identity of Anglicanism: Essentials of Anglican Ecclesiology*, London and New York: T&T Clark, 2008, ch. 3; Stephen W. Sykes, *Unashamed Anglicanism*, London: Darton, Longman and Todd, 1995, ch. 6.

36 Oliver O'Donovan, *On the Thirty-Nine Articles: Conversations with Tudor Christianity*, 2nd edn, London: SCM Press, 2011, p. viii.

37 O'Donovan, *On the Thirty-Nine Articles*, p. viii.

38 James E. Griffiss, *The Anglican Vision*, Cambridge, MA: Cowley Publications, 1997, p. 109.

39 Cf. Martin Dudley, *The Collect in Anglican Liturgy: Texts and Sources*

Of course, the BCP is not the only source of Anglican doctrine. It is not the case that Anglicans have no doctrinal standards apart from the BCP or other prayer books. For the Church of England, the Articles of Religion and the 1662 Ordinal stand alongside the BCP as 'historic formularies' that clergy and other office-holders acknowledge in the Declaration of Assent (Canon C 15) as part of the Church's 'inheritance of faith', intended to provide 'inspiration and guidance under God' in their ministry. None of these texts is regarded as the last word and none is beyond criticism. The Articles have remained unchanged in the Church of England since the sixteenth century, though modified in the Episcopal Church and elsewhere. But *Common Worship* is the default liturgy for the Church of England now and the *Common Worship* Ordinal is a marked improvement on Cranmer's Ordinal of 1550, revised in 1662. The formularies are not holy writ, but neither are they museum exhibits: their function is to guide and inspire. They provide essential ballast to hold us steady, a rule of thumb for theological discernment and a benchmark of doctrinal orthodoxy.

A lightning conductor for intra-Anglican conflict

The BCP has sometimes been romanticized as an ideal and timeless form of prayer. Our love of Choral Evensong and the way it lulls us into a state of spiritual tranquillity plays into this illusion. In reality the BCP is a political, even ideological text and it has had a polemical function at various junctures in the history of the English Church since the mid-sixteenth century. It is a work of its time, or rather, in its various recensions, of its times.[40] As a mandatory text, imposed with legal sanctions, the BCP was an instrument of social control and conformity. The Collects for the sovereign, standing between the Commandments and the Creed in the Communion service, remind the congregation 'whose authority he [or she] hath'. And there was nothing that the magistrate desired more for his or her people than that, as dutiful subjects, they 'should pass their time in rest and quietness', as the second Collect at Evening Prayer puts it.

By virtue of its political complexion, the BCP has served as a lightning conductor for intra-Anglican conflict. It has been a hostage to battles about the identity of English Christianity. The struggle took

1549–1989, Alcuin Club Collection No. 72, Collegeville, MN: The Liturgical Press, 1994, p. 43.

40 So Rowan Williams, in Stevenson and Spinks (eds), *Identity*, p. 6.

place within the mind, heart and life of Thomas Cranmer himself and still continues. After Cranmer we might mention, simply as the major eruptions within ongoing seismic activity, the attacks by Elizabethan Puritans, particularly the 'Admonition to Parliament' (1572), which famously accused the 1559 edition of the BCP – the Prayer Book of Elizabeth I, William Shakespeare, Francis Bacon, Ben Jonson, Richard Hooker and Lancelot Andrewes – of being 'an unperfecte booke, culled & picked out of that popishe dunghil, the Masse booke full of all abhominations. For some, & many of the contents therin, be suche as are againste the woord of God ...'.[41] But we would surely want to set alongside that Richard Hooker's steadfast resolve to resist the Puritan onslaught, together with his sense of foreboding that he might not succeed and that the Church of England as he knew it might 'pass away as in a dream'.[42]

Then we should recall the Hampton Court Conference on the accession of James I and VI and 40 years later the abolition of the Prayer Book, along with episcopacy, cathedral foundations, the Christian year with its feasts and fasts (the former being the more missed) and the commemoration of the saints, by the Long Parliament in 1643 and the substitution of the Westminster Assembly's *Directory of Worship* (which did not catch on).[43] As Patrick Collinson observed, the Civil War was, in part, 'a war fought for and against the Prayer Book, for

---

41 Walter Howard Frere and Charles Edward Douglas (eds), *Puritan Manifestos*, London: SPCK, and New York: E. S. Gorham, 1907, p. 21, http://www.archive.org/details/puritanmanifestooofreruoft.

42 Hooker, *Ecclesiastical Polity*, Preface; *Works*, I, p. 125: 'Though for no other cause, yet for this; that posterity may know we have not loosely through silence permitted things to pass away as in a dream, there shall be for men's information extant thus much concerning the present state of the Church of God established amongst us, and their careful endeavour which would have upheld the same' (note 'would have').

43 See Judith Maltby, 'The Prayer Book and the Parish Church: From the Elizabethan Settlement to the Restoration', in Hefling and Shattuck (eds), *Oxford Guide*, pp. 90–1, and her *Prayer Book and People in Elizabethan and Early Stuart England*, Cambridge: Cambridge University Press, 1998. For the *Directory*, see E. C. Ratcliffe, 'Puritan Alternatives to the Prayer Book: The "Directory" and Richard Baxter's "Reformed Liturgy"', *Liturgical Studies*, ed. A. H. Couratin and D. H. Tripp, London: SPCK, 1976, pp. 222–43 (first published in A. M. Ramsey, et al., *The English Prayer Book, 1549–1662*, London: SPCK for the Alcuin Club, 1963, pp. 56–81). Documentation on these episodes is found in Edward Cardwell, *A History of Conferences and Other Proceedings connected with the Revision of the Book of Common Prayer; From the Year 1558 to the Year 1690*, 2nd edn, Oxford: Oxford University Press, 1841.

and against Archbishop Cranmer's [posthumous] continuing hand on the tiller of a national religious consciousness and sensibility'.[44] Battle resumed with the Savoy Conference on the Restoration of Charles II and there was further agitation in 1689. Although the text of the BCP remained stable (apart from various state prayers that were decreed occasionally) until revision in the 1920s, controversy over its use broke out from time to time. The Tractarians were dismayed when it was proposed to make the so-called Athanasian Creed (the *Quicunque vult*) optional and John Keble spoke of relinquishing the exercise of his orders and moving into lay communion. Controversies over ritualism and lawlessness in the second half of the nineteenth century led eventually to battles in Church and State over Prayer Book Revision in the 1920s.[45] Precisely the same issues of what it means to be a church that is catholic and reformed were fought out in the process of liturgical revision that led through the experimental services of the 1970s through the unlamented *Alternative Service Book 1980* to *Common Worship* in 2000, where a unifying formula is at work, made up of compromise, reticence, inclusiveness and choice. But the broad acceptability of *Common Worship* in the Church is also due to its secret weapon, which is to bombard us with a plethora of biblical images with which it is difficult to disagree.[46]

Abiding characteristics of Anglican liturgy

Are there any abiding principles of Anglican worship? Is there a liturgical identity that is recognizably Anglican, even if only what Wittgenstein described as a 'family resemblance'?[47] Four factors make this question particularly problematic: first, the effect of the liturgical movement of

44 Patrick Collinson, 'Thomas Cranmer', in Geoffrey Rowell (ed.), *The English Religious Tradition and the Genius of Anglicanism*, Wantage: Ikon, 1993, p. 99.

45 See Paul Bradshaw's chapter in this volume. From the ample literature on these controversies, see particularly Nigel Yates, *Anglican Ritualism in Victorian Britain 1830–1910*, Oxford: Oxford University Press, 1999; Martin Wellings, *Evangelicals Embattled: Responses of Evangelicals in the Church of England to Ritualism, Darwinism and Theological Liberalism 1890–1930*, Milton Keynes: Paternoster, 2003.

46 For the legacy of Puritan liturgical concerns in modern Anglican Evangelicalism see Christopher J. Cocksworth, *Evangelical Eucharistic Thought in the Church of England*, Cambridge: Cambridge University Press, 1993.

47 Ludwig Wittgenstein, *Philosophical Investigations*, trans. G. E. M. Anscombe, Oxford: Blackwell, 1958, p. 32 (no. 67).

the twentieth century in encouraging convergence in the liturgies of all churches towards primitive models; second, the phenomenon of liturgical creativity and diversity across the Anglican Communion, as contemporary liturgies have replaced various versions of the BCP; third the evolving character and comparative lack of stability of the Church of England's own liturgy and the number of multiple-choice options that are available; fourth, the extent of non-liturgical worship, especially among Evangelicals, some of which is permitted, provided essential principles are followed, but much of which is sheer lawlessness, like the uncanonical abandonment of robes in many Evangelical parishes. Even allowing for those countervailing factors, I think some kind of case can be made for an enduring character in Anglican worship and has to do with integration, balance and a sense of wholeness.

David Stancliffe made a brave attempt to claim such an identity 20 years ago, after liturgical experimentation but before *Common Worship*. There is, he wrote, 'an integrated feel about Anglican liturgy which has its origin in the union of heart and mind, of word and sacrament, of text and ceremonial'. It is, Stancliffe continued, 'earthed in a theology which is incarnational, and a sacramentality which is organic and affirmative'. Our liturgy is 'ordered, not regimented, and it is related to how we think and how we live'. For all the revision and diversity of liturgy across the Anglican Communion, we can (Stancliffe claims) still discern a family likeness. There is an elusive but distinctive Anglican style of worship that is due to liturgical hospitality, the folding of various layers upon one another, Eastern and Western, ancient and modern.[48]

Paul Gibson has singled out, with tantalizing brevity, the qualities of reverence, predictability, a coherent use of Scripture, and a balance of contemplation and doxology.[49] I would add that, alongside what is duly offered to God in the liturgy, there is a continuing sensitivity to how the rite is received by and provides for the spiritual needs of the worshipper, especially in Holy Communion. This is a pastoral dimension of liturgy which possibly we owe to Luther and his sense of the intimate relation between Christ and the Christian, an influence mediated through the Lutheran service books that Cranmer knew well.[50]

---

48 Stancliffe, 'Is there an "Anglican" liturgical style?', pp. 132–3.

49 Paul Gibson, 'Report on Liturgy', in James M. Rosenthal and Nicola Currie (eds), *Being Anglican in the Third Millennium: The Official Report of the 10th Meeting of the Anglican Consultative Council* (Panama City, 1996), Harrisburg, PA: Morehouse Publishing, 1997, p. 116.

50 Cf. Booty, *BCP 1559*, p. 361. Cranmer's knowledge of and debt to vari-

However, I doubt whether it is plausible to claim that there is a *unique* Anglican liturgical identity, given the way that the liturgies of various Christian traditions have converged on primitive models and learned and borrowed from one another and from the commonwealth of ecumenical study. For example, I think it is a moot point whether the eucharistic liturgy, daily offices and other rites of the Church with which the Church of England is in a Covenant relationship, the Methodist Church of Great Britain, could not be substituted for those of *Common Worship* without much loss and with some enrichment.[51]

The unique contribution of Archbishop Thomas Cranmer

Thomas Cranmer shaped the Church of England by his life, his death and his writing. Not only his liturgical work, but Cranmer's personal witness and martyrdom have left a profound impress on the Anglican consciousness. No one who has read or heard of how Cranmer, at the stake, put his right hand in the flames saying that the hand that had offended, signing retractions that he did not in his heart believe, should be the first to suffer, can ever forget it.[52]

There is little doubt that the Prayer Books are Cranmer's personal legacy to the Church. Though he did not act alone, the final form of the text comes from his own hand.[53] As Bridget Nichols points out, this is particularly evident in relation to the Collects of the BCP, which are marked by a recognizable consistency of style and an economy of expression. In those Collects that are translations or adaptations from Latin originals, we are impressed by their 'skilful negotiation between two languages, and their deft adjustments of content to conform to Reformation doctrinal precepts'.[54] Cranmer is the 'begetter', though not the 'only begetter', of the BCP.

---

ous Lutheran orders is brought out in E. C. Ratcliffe, 'The Liturgical Work of Archbishop Cranmer', *Liturgical Studies*, pp. 184–202 (first published in *Journal of Ecclesiastical History* 7.2 (1956), pp. 189–203).

51 *The Methodist Worship Book.*

52 Diarmaid MacCulloch, *Thomas Cranmer: A Life*, New Haven and London: Yale University Press, 1996, p. 603.

53 MacCulloch, *Cranmer*, p. 414; Gordon Jeanes, *Signs of God's Promise: Thomas Cranmer's Sacramental Theology and the Book of Common Prayer*, London and New York: T&T Clark, 2008, p. 11; Ratcliffe, 'Liturgical Work of Cranmer', p. 186: 'If he allowed others to supply him with forms of prayers, he so revised them as to stamp them with his own style. All trace of compositeness of authorship, if such indeed there were, had disappeared.'

54 Bridget Nichols, 'The Collect in English: Vernacular Beginnings', in Nichols

Cranmer's unique contribution to Anglican identity through his Prayer Books is theological, liturgical and poetical. To conclude, I offer a very brief comment on each.

Theological

Clearly, Cranmer was no mean theologian. The fact that he did his theology in a liturgical mode should not disguise that truth from us. Together with Jewel and Hooker, Cranmer must rank as one of the formative theologians of the reformed English Church. Gregory Dix, a notoriously unreliable guide to Cranmer's eucharistic theology, described the 1552 Prayer Book as 'the only effective attempt ever made to give liturgical expression to the doctrine of "justification by faith alone"'.[55] (Were Martin Luther's liturgies not effective in that sense?) But there is more to Cranmer's theological work than justification by faith, pivotal though that is. Gordon Jeanes puts it more generously: Cranmer, he writes, is 'able to speak of the grace of God with a clarity and immediacy lacking in many other theologians of his time'.[56]

Liturgical

Cranmer was not a stylist. He was not interested in language for its own sake. He was not a devotee of the aesthetic! As C. S. Lewis commented, Cranmer and his helpers wanted the Prayer Book to be admired 'not for original genius but for catholicity and antiquity, and it is in fact the ripe fruit of centuries of worship'.[57] In Cranmer's mind, language and meaning, liturgy and theology were fused. As E. C. Ratcliffe remarks, 'Cranmer was the master, or rather the creator, of English liturgical

---

(ed.), *The Collect in the Churches of the Reformation*, London: SCM Press, 2010, p. 10. Of 84 Collects for Sundays or holy days in the 1549 Prayer Book, only 7 have an earlier English form; of the remaining 77, 24 are new, the remainder adaptations (p. 17). See also Francis Proctor and Walter Howard Frere, *A New History of the Book of Common Prayer*, London: Macmillan, 1905, pp. 522–55. There were precedents in Primers and books of hours: cf. Eamon Duffy, *Marking the Hours: English People and the Prayers 1240–1570*, New Haven and London: Yale University Press, 2006.

55 Gregory Dix, *The Shape of the Liturgy*, 2nd edn, Westminster: Dacre Press, 1945, p. 672. For a brief discussion, see Avis, *Identity of Anglicanism*, pp. 87–94.

56 Jeanes, *Signs*, pp. 290–1.

57 C. S. Lewis, *English Literature in the Sixteenth Century, Excluding Drama*, Oxford: Clarendon Press, 1954, p. 215.

style, because he had apprehended the nature of worship.'[58] Cranmer's liturgical achievement rested on a solid theological foundation. I wonder whether that can be said equally of all modern liturgical revision.

Poetical

Christianity is at its most persuasive in the poetical mode. I have shown elsewhere why I agree with St Augustine that God is a poet and with William Blake that Jesus and the apostles were all artists, and why I see the Christian gospel as a work of art.[59] The power of poetry over our hearts and minds is unrivalled, except by music. The poetical mood of the Prayer Book is one of tempered fervour; its language carries us heavenward, as well as driving us to our knees; but it rarely pushes us further than we are able to go. As C. S. Lewis says, the Prayer Book 'dreads excess'; it is emotionally restrained like the Gospels.[60] In her study of the language of the BCP, Stella Brook singles out its 'sinewy immediacy' and a directness that belongs to the spoken word. She finds it better adapted than the King James Bible to 'the suppleness of native idiom'. She believes that the Prayer Book benefited from being written before the divorce between written and spoken English.[61] Of all the various epithets that might be and probably have been applied to the language of the BCP, I want to highlight its attributes of *integrity*, *resonance* and *pithiness* – altogether, what I can only call its honest-to-goodness quality. The mixture of 'down-to-earthness' and uplifting transcendence is truly a marriage of earth and heaven.

Finally

I am wary of slipping into the anachronistic use of the term 'Anglicanism', which is out of place when talking about the sixteenth-century Reformers. We get a glimpse of a recognizable, nascent Anglicanism at the end of the sixteenth century in Elizabeth I, Richard Hooker and Lancelot Andrewes – but little more than that until we get to the Caroline divines and George Herbert in the mid-seventeenth century.

---

58 Ratcliffe, 'Liturgical Work of Cranmer', p. 199.

59 Paul Avis, *God and the Creative Imagination: Metaphor, Symbol and Myth in Religion and Theology*, London: Routledge, 1999; Paul Avis, 'The Gospel as a Work of Art', *Theology* 104 (2001), pp. 94–101.

60 Lewis, *English Literature*, pp. 220–1.

61 Stella Brook, *The Language of the Book of Common Prayer*, London: André Deutsch, 1965, pp. 219, 119–20.

But if we are taking the long view, trying to assess Cranmer's place in the evolving tradition of the Church of England and of the Communion to which it belongs, I think it is permissible to locate him on an Anglican trajectory. If we do that, it is difficult to disagree with Gordon Jeanes' judgement that Cranmer is probably 'the most important individual in the formation of Anglicanism'[62] or to demur from Patrick Collinson's thought-provoking comment that Thomas Cranmer was 'the founder of the Church of England and of Anglicanism as we have known it'.[63]

---

62 Jeanes, *Signs*, p. 1.
63 Collinson, in Rowell (ed.), *English Religious Tradition*, p. 84.

Epilogue

A place for the 1662
Book of Common Prayer in the
twenty-first-century Church?

CHRISTOPHER WOODS

If the question 'Why do we celebrate the history of the Book of Common Prayer of 1662?' was in our minds at the beginning of this volume of essays, it is worth returning to it now. It is clear that the contributors to this collection are passionate about the detailed and complex history and legacy of the Book of Common Prayer of 1662, which arrived at its definitive state only after more than a century of liturgical, cultural, political and theological *hiatus*. It most certainly did not remain unaltered from Archbishop Thomas Cranmer's bureau; less so did it simply emerge as a fait accompli. Brian Cummings in Chapter 5 leaves us in no doubt about the complex political process that gave rise to the final version of Cranmer's original work of 1549. The Savoy Conference, which ended in 1661, was the purveyor of the same Prayer Book that is still used every week in many parishes, chapels and cathedrals today. Surely this must be the primary reason to celebrate the Book of Common Prayer.

The question in our minds may now be, 'Why is the Book of Common Prayer of 1662 still used in public worship?' In fact such a question is very pertinent, given the liturgical and cultural fluidity of the twenty-first century. Why should prescribed and rubricized liturgical worship remain as crucial a framework of prayer and devotion today as it was intended to be by the Reformers of the sixteenth and seventeenth centuries? As an attempt to respond to these questions, some of the points raised by a few of the contributors to this volume can be teased out further, before focusing on areas of liturgical language and forms of worship.

Both Stephen Platten and Bryan Spinks, in their respective chapters, rightly point us to the spirit of the Preface to the 1662 Book of Common Prayer and how the liturgical diet contained in it was intended to be 'the mean'[1] between the two extremes of 'too much stiffness in refusing, and of too much easiness in admitting any variation'.[2] This was as much, Platten argues, a 'political settlement'[3] as it was an attempt to appease differing theological standpoints, though of course one cannot completely divorce politics and religion. In *On Christian Theology*, Rowan Williams sardonically points out that 'the 1662 Book of Common Prayer is a document very heavily charged with polemic, and with many apparently innocent phrases that in fact are carefully designed to say or not say certain things'.[4] But it is partly due to the 'success' of this nuanced religio-political settlement that the 1662 Prayer Book continued with only relatively minor scuffles and tensions until the Victorian era dawned. Cleugh and Jacob chart the Prayer Book zeitgeist of the seventeenth and eighteenth centuries, with Spinks in Chapter 7 uncovering an increasing disgruntlement of some nineteenth-century church people towards the Prayer Book, partly it seems because the liturgical provision was considered to be theologically deficient in the minds of several factions. Paul Bradshaw in Chapter 8 moves us into the twentieth-century process of vast liturgical revision and sharply describes the series of moves away from a liturgy where 'all the whole realm shall have but one use'[5]. Strenuous challenges to the 1662 Prayer Book came from the debates of 1927/28 and subsequent liturgical revision in the twentieth century. Yet the integrity with which the Prayer Book has held together successive generations of Anglicans both in England and elsewhere in the Anglican Communion is remarkable. Paul Avis, in Chapter 9, reminds us of how the Book of Common Prayer played 'for most of our history in most places and for most people ... a critical role as a key marker of identity of faith and community'.[6]

Clearly, then, one of the major reasons why the Book of Common Prayer of 1662 remains in use for public worship relates to its integrity

---

1 Bryan Spinks, p. 118, 'the commemorations had marked the extremes between which the 1662 liturgy was intended to be the mean'.
2 Preface, Book of Common Prayer, 1662.
3 Stephen Platten, p. 7.
4 Rowan Williams, *On Christian Theology*, Oxford: Blackwell, 2000, p. 211.
5 Paul Bradshaw, p. 121.
6 Paul Avis, p. 135; also readers are referred to Christopher Irvine (ed.), *Anglican Liturgical Identity*, Joint Liturgical Study 65, Norwich: Canterbury Press, 2008.

in holding together conflicting voices of religious zeal through what Bradshaw calls a 'common bond' of prayer and devotion.

However, as MacCullough, Platten and Jeanes remind us, the importance of the Book of Common Prayer lies in no small part in its transformative power, not least in its huge influence on wider literature and culture throughout succeeding generations. Many turns of phrase in common parlance come directly from the language of the first English Prayer Book of 1549 (rather than, in fact, the Authorized Version of the Bible), such as 'read, mark, learn, and inwardly digest',[7] 'The world, the flesh, the devil',[8] and 'earth to earth, ashes to ashes, dust to dust'.[9] Even those with little to no contact with the Christian faith today will have heard of one or more of these phrases. When something has influenced the language of a culture so deeply, it is inconceivable that it should disappear from use. Here stands the Book of Common Prayer.

It is, of course, precisely language that has been the cause of the greatest tension in debates as to whether or not forms of public service should be revised or left untouched. Pastoral theology and doctrine have been important in such debates – not to mention ceremonial – especially in the planned revision of 1927/28. However, in the Anglican tradition the language of prayer *is* the language of faith, and the questions of religious language coinciding or conflicting with cultural language were increasingly at the forefront of the minds of many at the time. There was a realization, it is probably fair to say, that the Church had to converse consistently with English society, which, it seemed, was not altogether in unison with the position of the Church on several matters.[10]

However, this view was not so overwhelming as to triumph in the short term. In 1927, because it was not clear that the majority of the Church of England wished for a completely revised Book of Common Prayer, Parliament took fright and did not assent to any revision. This was a wake-up call. At that point the Book of Common Prayer was left unrevised; it remained as it had been since 1662 and to this day is the official liturgy of the Established Church.

---

7 From the Collect for the Second Sunday in Advent.
8 From the Litany.
9 From the Order for the Burial of the Dead.
10 For a fuller treatment on this issue, see Christopher Irvine, *Worship, Church and Society: An Exposition of the Work of Arthur Gabriel Hebert*, Norwich: Canterbury Press, 1993.

It is the quintessential nuance of the Church of England that prayer, Scripture and worship inform doctrine with that semi-permeable membrane of language in between. So far we have reflected largely on the spoken word, but it would be an oversight not to mention, at least briefly, the influence that English choral music has had on the *lex orandi, lex credendi* model of faith.

One of the most famous and well-loved rubrics of the Prayer Book is 'in quires and places where they sing ...',[11] a statement that places significant stress on the need for the language of prayer to come to life through the beauty of human song. When the Book of Common Prayer is coupled to music in the same phrase, Choral Evensong will swiftly come to mind and the names of Herbert Howells, Hubert Parry, Charles Villiers Stanford, Charles Wood, Ralph Vaughan-Williams and David Willcocks appear on the horizon. It was, ironically, in the early to mid-twentieth century, despite all of the political and liturgical unrest, that the English choral tradition reached a new zenith, intensifying the fusion of language and belief significantly. Among others, it is most likely through the dedicated work and technical, spiritual and musical vision of David Willcocks while at King's College in Cambridge that Prayer Book language *sung*, rather than *spoken*, now inhabits a trustworthy place in the devotional life of many people in the Church of England and beyond. Liturgical music is as ancient as liturgy itself and it was clear in Cranmer's mind that the musical tradition of the Sarum Rite was to be carried forward into the Book of Common Prayer. So important was it that in 1550 a theologian and musician by the name of John Merbecke published his *Booke of Common Praier Noted*. Merbecke's musical setting of the Holy Communion is probably one of his most well-known compositions and it is still used reasonably regularly in the Church of England. Notwithstanding this treasury, there was still, in the middle of the twentieth century, underlying pressure that a method to explore more progressive liturgical language be uncovered.

Rowan Williams writes:

The language of worship ascribes supreme value, supreme resource or power, to something other than the worshipper, so that liturgy attempts to be a 'giving over' of our words to God (as opposed to speaking in a way that seeks to retain distance or control over what's being spoken of: it is in this sense that good liturgy does what good

---

11 From the Order for Morning and Evening Prayer in the Book of Common Prayer.

poetry does). This is not to say that the language of worship itself cannot be starkly and effectively ideological; but where we find a developing and imaginative liturgical idiom operating in a community that is itself constantly re-imagining itself and its past, we may recognize that worship is at some level doing its job.[12]

The new route was the adoption of a 're-imagined' public liturgy, parallel to but not a replacement for the Book of Common Prayer. The 1950s and 1960s saw the beginning of one of the greatest 'reformations' of authorized liturgy since the publication of the Book of Common Prayer itself not more than 300 years previously. Change was palpable and it was not only felt within the Church of England. Most of Western Christendom was poised to renew its public worship. For the Roman Catholic Church this happened very rapidly as a result of the Constitution on the Sacred Liturgy, *Sacrosanctum Concilium*. For the Church of England, the process of revision was less swift, in that there were three successive 'experimental' rites culminating in the Alternative Service Book of 1980. By the time of the printing of the Alternative Service Book it seemed that liturgical revision had reached a plateau. Those who had longed for public worship to be expressed in a contemporary idiom were, for the time being at least, satisfied. Two books in which everything for 'church' was contained proved attractive and it meant that there was a short period of stability. All of this happened without any need for Parliament's involvement and so the political element that had been so prevalent in the provision of the 1662 Book of Common Prayer and in the debate of 1927/28 was bypassed.

It was never the intention that the Alternative Service Book of 1980 should remain permanently alongside the Book of Common Prayer. It was seen as an interim provision, and further revision was always likely. This, together with grass-roots-level 'developing and imaginative liturgical idiom'[13] (especially but not exclusively in the realm of innovative, informal services for families with young children),[14] meant that it was not long before a more mature and yet broader liturgical provision was unveiled. *Common Worship: Services and Prayers for the Church of England* deliberately uses the word 'common' to re-inject in the psyche

---

12 Williams, *On Christian Theology*, p. 7.

13 Williams, *On Christian Theology*, p. 7.

14 It is without doubt that the seminal Church of England report, *Faith in the City: A Call to Action by Church and Nation* (1985), had a large part to play in the desire for yet further 'progressive' liturgical provision.

of worshipping communities the centrality of the 'common bond' of prayer and devotion, which was in the minds of the revisers of the 1662 liturgies. *Common Worship* attempts to recover the connectedness – through the language of prayer – of vastly different worshipping communities. Still 'parallel' to the Book of Common Prayer, yet not explicitly 'alternative', the new model of liturgy is more radical than ever before in a number of different senses.

First, *Common Worship* seeks to allow as diverse, flexible and as locally nuanced a liturgical diet as possible, while still, theoretically, promoting liturgical unity. It does this by providing a 'structural' model, with key defining points along the way, so as to encourage the flow of liturgical 'meta-grammar' (sometimes called the 'deep structure'). In this sense, then, we are transported back to the Preface of the 1662 Prayer Book where 'too much stiffness in refusing, and of too much easiness in admitting any variation' are the extremes to be avoided. *Common Worship* rediscovers this intermediacy, but the danger is that the Church has allowed the extremes to be stretched further apart. The consequence of this is that the authorized liturgy has a much more difficult role to play than even the Prayer Book of 1662 did when it first appeared.

Second, *Common Worship* returns to a *pre*-Prayer Book model of public worship; to an almost Sarum-like ideal of English liturgy (even the rubrics in the *Common Worship* printed texts are 'Sarum red').[15] Instead of a single book, we have a library of service books for Sundays, weekdays, festivals and seasons, together with sacramental and pastoral office books and lectionaries. Such a radical shift requires patience in learning the first principles of liturgical grammar. The Church now looks to liturgists and liturgiologists for formation and encouragement, and indeed continued liturgical education throughout ministry is not an optional extra. It is with this approach in mind that a distinctive Anglican liturgical stability and integrity might be maintained rather than lost. But it is precisely from the Book of Common Prayer that we can learn afresh about formation. While the didactic model is no longer the ideal, the Book of Common Prayer nevertheless did educate and form the people of God. It became a teaching document as well as a manual for prayer, spiritual edification and comfort. Exhortations, homilies, the Articles and the Catechism all inform the nature of what is being prayed, why it is being prayed and how it is applicable to the lives of individual Christians.

---

15 See 'An account of the making of Common Worship: Services and Prayers for the Church of England', John Morgan, *Typography Paper* 5, 2003, pp. 33–64.

Third, *Common Worship* has deliberately cast the net far and wide. It does not try to serve a 'niche' market, yet neither can it be all things to all people, if for no other reason than ecclesial integrity, the boundaries of which have been pushed extensively to accommodate a broad spectrum of tradition. There is, however, a point at which the choice of a rite in a local context finally and publicly determines one's ecclesiology. If that rite is so far removed from the generous boundaries of what is authorized, then communion and fellowship with other Anglicans is brought sharply into question and the liturgically catholic spirit of the Church of England is ruptured. This is precisely the tension that the Book of Common Prayer initially tried to bring into balance.

Common Worship has deliberately reintroduced the best of patristic tradition and prayer, setting this alongside the most powerful texts of the medieval era and bravely fusing these with new and contemporary rites from both Roman Catholic and Eastern Orthodox traditions. All this stands alongside portions of the Book of Common Prayer 1662 and some of those proposed in 1928. If there is a word to describe *Common Worship*, it is 'integrated'. If it has failed, or needs to change and develop, the Church of England's synodical process allows for further piecemeal changes to be made to meet the needs of different worshipping styles and traditions of the Church.

How, then, in a Church that continually calls for its worship to be voiced in 'accessible language', can we envisage a sustained place for the Book of Common Prayer? The answers lie fundamentally in not looking to the most obvious or popular zeitgeist. Rather, we need to look at both the course of history but also at the kind of 'book' it is. Our contributors have demonstrated that the 1662 Book of Common Prayer emerged from a process of cultural, religious and political bargaining. At times it may even have appeared to be a manifesto of one political or religious view over another. However, in its original form and by virtue of its primary purpose and continued use, all of this political and religious bartering becomes less important. The Prayer Book is not a book about us (it is not a cultural history book). It is not only a book about the nature of God (it is not a fully systematized work of theology because it contains prayers; and prayers will always in the words of Williams attempt to be 'a giving over of our words to God)'.[16] The Prayer Book is about an articulated relationship between mortals and the immortal God. Even when words fail us, we can bring, through a beautifully crafted ancient prayer, something new to our relationship

---

16 Williams, *On Christian Theology*, p. 7.

to God. In that same prayer by means of his grace, God can always show something of that 'peace which the world cannot give'.[17] In this sense there is continued conversation, and where even the most remote appetite for prayer and conversation remains alive, then the Book of Common Prayer will always be there.

---

17 From the Collect for Peace at Evening Prayer.

Index

Lightning Source UK Ltd.
Milton Keynes UK
UKOW051651301012

201435UK00003B/35/P